domiKNITrix

WHIP YOUR KNITTING INTO SHAPE

jennifer stafford

NORTH LIGHT BOOKS
CINCINNATI, OHIO
www.artistsnetwork.com

11 10 09 08 07   5 4 3 2 1

Distributed in Canada by Fraser Direct
100 Armstrong Avenue
Georgetown, ON, Canada L7G 5S4
Tel: (905) 877-4411

Distributed in the U.K. and Europe by David & Charles
Brunel House, Newton Abbot, Devon, TQ12 4PU, England
Tel: (+44) 1626 323200, Fax: (+44) 1626 323319
Email: postmaster@davidandcharles.co.uk

Distributed in Australia by Capricorn Link
P.O. Box 704, S. Windsor, NSW 2756 Australia
Tel: (02) 4577-3555

Library of Congress Cataloging-in-Publication Data

Stafford, Jennifer.
Domiknitrix / Jennifer Stafford.
p. cm.
ISBN-13: 978-1-58180-853-7 (alk. paper)
ISBN-10: 1-58180-853-4
1. Knitting--Patterns. I. Title.
TT825.S7165 2006
746.43'2--dc22
2006020117

EDITOR: **JESSICA GORDON**
ART DIRECTOR/DESIGNER: **KARLA BAKER**
PHOTOGRAPHERS: **BRIAN STEEGE, TIM GRONDIN, CHRISTINE POLOMSKY**
ILLUSTRATIONS: **RACHELL SUMPTER**
WARDROBE STYLIST: **MONICA SKRZELOWSKI**
HAIR AND MAKEUP: **CASS SMITH, GINA WEATHERSBY**
PRODUCTION COORDINATOR: **GREG NOCK**

fw
F+W PUBLICATIONS, INC.

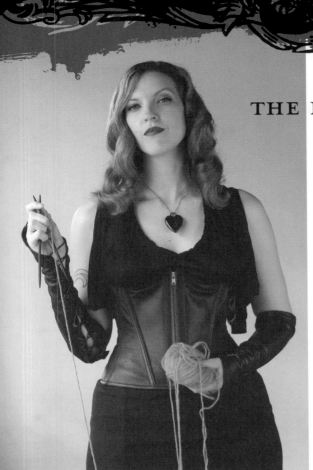

THE DomiKNITrix

Jennifer Stafford has been sewing since she was a wee kid, and she's been knitting since 1979. She has borne the DomiKNITrix mantle since February 2004 when she launched a Web site of the same name loaded with knitting techniques, unique projects, inspiration and attitude. She founded the DomiKNITrix company in 2005, dreaming of showing knitters how to take their knitting to the next level and of sharing her original knitwear designs with the world. The site has grown from a few users each day to 45,000 a month as of this writing. Jennifer lives in San Francisco where she has managed to hold tight to her position at a different kind of Internet media company for more than nine years.

dedication

This book is dedicated to the two most important men in my life: my father, John Stafford, and my husband, Ethan O'Brien.

Dad raised me single-handedly from the age of five and spoon-fed me a steady diet of female role models: bionic and wonderful, gun-slinging and sword-wielding. He told me many times that I was lucky to be born a woman because I can become anything I want to be.

In 1993, Ethan traveled halfway around the world to meet me: the girl next door. Without Ethan's support, this book would have been only a glimmer. Ethan designed the DomiKNITrix logo—the heart of the site and the perfect representation of myself. Only the love of my life could have created something so perfect.

whip your knitting into shape

badass knitting for
badass knitters

I AM THE DomiKNITrix

I discipline my yarn. I force it into the form I want it to take. I am persistent, firm and commanding. I am the DomiKNITrix.

If the yarn is wayward and the pattern not quite right, I rip out and reknit until I get what I want. It's classic, really. Pain begets pleasure—They're really not so very far apart.

As you might imagine, I would rather lead than follow. I don't like to let pattern writers tell me what to do. I am in charge, and the yarn is at my beck and call. I'm adventurous, and I like to design clothes that are a little different, or a lot. Who says a sweater has to be knit from bottom to top? Why not do it sideways or on the diagonal?

Well, the road less traveled is often more punishing, but then again, maybe that's why I like it. In taking those rough paths, I've managed to maverick my way through ideas that I've never seen tried before. I'm not going to tell you this is an efficient approach to designing knitwear—far from it—but maybe I can save you some time by sharing the patterns and methods that tease out the best possible results, sometimes in the most unusual ways.

A DomiKNITrix IS BORN

Of course, I haven't always been a badass knitter. I started out as just a plain bad crafter. In kindergarten I made macramé plant hangers and woven place mats. From there, I graduated to cutting up old satin sheets and lace curtains and sewing them into ill-fitting princess dresses. At age ten, I entered the year of the half-afghans. (They remained forever unfinished because I always got bored.) I sewed my own clothes for years, and not always well.

Many of these sad handmade pieces ended up in the trash or at the local thrift store (although I sincerely hope no unsuspecting children or awkward teens were forced to wear them).

Then I discovered knitting. At last, the perfect outlet for my brand of hard-knock discipline. Materials could be recovered from even the most disastrous project. No mistake had to be permanent because I could rip out the yarn and force it to see things my way. From that point on, there has been no turning back. I am bound to knitting for life.

I definitely learned knitting the hard way. I quit working from patterns long ago (the year was 1980, and the pattern was for a sweater), but that doesn't mean my first efforts were successful. My entree into designing was arduous and painful. An early project was a midriff-baring pullover with overlong sleeves I made for my best friend in high school. It wasn't exactly flattering. Although I meant it to come out that way, the proportion was all wrong for her petite frame.

MAKE IT HURT SO GOOD

After lots of ripping out and starting over—ah, the delicious pain of seeing those wrong stitches unravel—I was eventually turning out items I wasn't embarrassed to wear or give away.

Being a DomiKNITrix is all about bringing discipline and diligence to knitting, and above all using that discipline to create cool clothes and accessories you'll want to wear, use and give away with pride. I want you to experience the supreme satisfaction of creating a knitted piece that is well crafted and unhurried. A true DomiKNITrix has no room for shoddy workmanship or uneven stitches.

If you're looking for easy, mindless knitting, you're not made in the mold of a DomiKNITrix. That title is reserved for a knitter who craves challenge and who will take the time and effort necessary to turn out an astonishing knitted piece.

A DomiKNITrix will not be ruled by unwieldy yarn or needles. The stitches and the tools used to create those stitches are slave to the knitter, not the other way 'round. The

knitter is the mistress or master who whips the stitches into shape.

If you wish to become a true DomiKNITrix, the first lesson to learn is that you are in charge. Yarn does not respond to soft and limp hands. Hold your needles firmly, wield them like whips and direct the stitches to do your bidding.

WHY YOU NEED THE DOMIKNITRIX

Are you sick of wishy-washy knitting books with vague patterns and a total of three pages covering techniques? Did you learn to knit from a friend or a relative who showed you knit and purl (at most, and perhaps the wrong way) and then shoved you out into the world with no further instruction? Did you turn to the Web in desperation, only to find the blind leading the naked? And as for finishing...ha! A mere afterthought, I'm sure, if you learned how to do it at all.

No wonder you're shy about wearing your hand-knits out of the house. That seemingly simple pattern turned out looking sloppy and ill-made. Hours of work went into that ugly sweater, and now it will sit in the closet for a year or three before you can bear to give up and give it away, toss it, or tear out the yarn if it's salvageable.

You have knitted your last bad piece. Let me take you under my wing and whip you into shape. Yes, it may be painful to take the time to knit a gauge swatch. It may hurt to tear out hard-won stitches. It may take discipline to count stitches and learn how to fix mistakes. Yes, you'll need to commit to finishing the job down to the last detail.

But think of the pleasures inherent in those seemingly painful steps. Think of the joy of a gorgeous, perfect sweater with no holes, no messy shoulder seams you hope are covered by your hair. Follow the DomiKNITrix and you will arrive at that deserved and delicious happiness.

I've learned at least one lesson from every crafty item I ever chucked in the trash bin or gave away to the Goodwill. I am passing those lessons along to you rather than letting you tough it out and get discouraged. Learn from me, and you'll become a DomiKNITrix in your own right, a mistress who answers to no one and who always gets what she wants.

DOMINATE YOUR STYLE

Just as you must dominate your knitting, you must bend that knitting to your fashion will. I've refused to let my style be cornered or labeled, and you may see it as punk, goth, alternative, vintage and even a bit country or classic. Under it all, of course, my style is a well-tailored garment, not just a gimmick. That's why you like it.

If you truly want to become a DomiKNITrix, you're sure to have a yen for putting a unique stamp on your hand-knits. I've provided ways to tweak the designs so you can put your personality into them, in order to achieve a "Where'd ya get that?!" result every time.

Although there are some challenging patterns in this book, there are also plenty of small or straightforward projects for the domina who wants to start out slowly. There is even a whole chapter filled with Tasty Morsels (page 98) for those who need

a knitting quickie. From there, a DomiKNITrix who is comfortable knitting in the missionary position can progress to the On the Level chapter (page 150), where the projects are knit in the usual way, from top to bottom or vice versa. The final chapter (page 208) is for the adventuresome DomiKNITrix who likes her knitting hard. These more challenging projects are knit from side to side or diagonally (on the bias). However, there are a few simpler projects in this chapter to help you get used to the idea of constructing a knitted garment in an unconventional way.

When all is said and done, you'll have the knitting discipline and confidence needed to turn out a project that passes for store-bought. Your knitting will showcase the fine details that come only from dedication, discipline and the knowledge that you alone are in charge.

the DOMIKNITRIX MANIFESTO:
TOE THE LINE

During my twenty-seven years of making clothes, I have learned most of my lessons the hard way: by trial and error—lots and lots of errors. My mother was watching when I sewed my first teddy bear T-shirt, and that's why I remember my first lesson so well. I laid my teddy down on top of the fabric and cut out the shape of a T-shirt around him. Then I sewed it together and was befuddled when it did not fit Teddy. Mom had seen me leave off the seam allowances, but she bit her tongue and let me make the mistake before she explained it to me, because she knew that way I would never forget it.

I have thrown out many handmade items over the years because they were rarely worn, and each time I asked myself why. Well, the answers revealed that some details are very useful in clothes, so I make every effort to include these details for the sake of wearability. Here is my manifesto: principles I live by when designing knits. They say there's no substitute for experience, but perhaps you can learn a little something from mine.

THE LINE, THE LINE, THE LINE!

When I look at a piece of clothing, I see at a glance whether it's attractive. The line should be lean and close to the body, flattering the wearer. Self-conscious people often drape their bodies in extra fabric to hide themselves, which simply leaves too much to the imagination. When we look at a container, we assume the contents are the same shape as the container. If you want a baggy sweater, you can find one in almost every other knitting book out there, but not in this one. Choose the size that will fit you best based on your measurements. My designs include minimal ease for a close fit.

MATERIAL, COLOR AND TEXTURE MUST FLATTER THE WEARER

Many of us have fallen in love with yarns and then found we could not knit an attractive garment from them. Some yarns are best reserved for socks and other small objects where the yarn can really shine. Often the color changes in variegated and self-striping yarns conspire to thicken the waist of the wearer. I call these "art yarns" and reserve them for non-wearable projects or very small pieces. Also, very bulky or heavily textured yarns can add an inch or more to the wearer's girth when used in a sweater, but they might be very cool as a scarf, bag or hat.

KEEP THE FOCUS

Use a single unique feature to make each design distinctive. Most walking fashion disasters just have too much going on: too much jewelry or too many accessories competing for attention. The stylish lady getting all the looks is usually keeping it simple and dramatic. Think of a sweater as a work of art. The person looking at the piece should see a crisp focus in the artist's vision rather than a mad scramble of doodles at the corner of the canvas. A single design feature keeps attention focused on the purity of the design.

CREATE SMOOTH LINES WITH SIMPLE TEXTURES

You'll notice I mostly design with classic Stockinette, garter stitch and ribbing. Cables, bobbles, lace and other textures make for fun knitting, but they must be employed carefully to enhance the wearer's attributes. Fancy stitchwork can draw the eye to all the wrong places if it overpowers the knitting and distracts from the overall look of the finished object.

The more you knit, the more points you may have to add to your own manifesto. Every knitter is different, and so is every body. Over time, of course, you will learn what does and doesn't work for yours, so file these notes for future reference. If your aim is to wear a sexy sweater, figure out your sexiest parts and find ways to highlight them. Got a great rack? Then perhaps something with a V-neck or a fur collar will spotlight it. Have a tiny waist? Use darts to highlight your curves. And remember, tight sweaters save yarn!

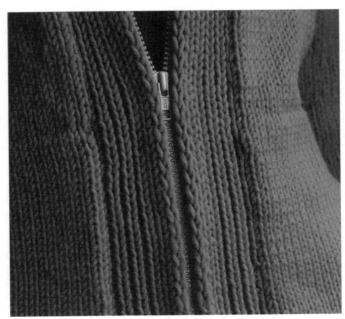

LET'S SKIP THE PLEASANTRIES

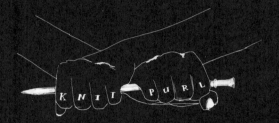

We'll get right to it. No need for small talk. This section gives you all the information you need to become a DomiKNITrix.

I've laid out some simple rules for you to knit by, as well as a primer of the equipment and materials you'll need and an in-depth instructional techniques section. Finally, I'll discuss the skills you must have to properly finish any project, because no self-respecting dom starts something without finishing it off.

Be a good girl and master these skills. If it helps your learning process, you can imagine me standing over you with a riding crop making sure you get things right.

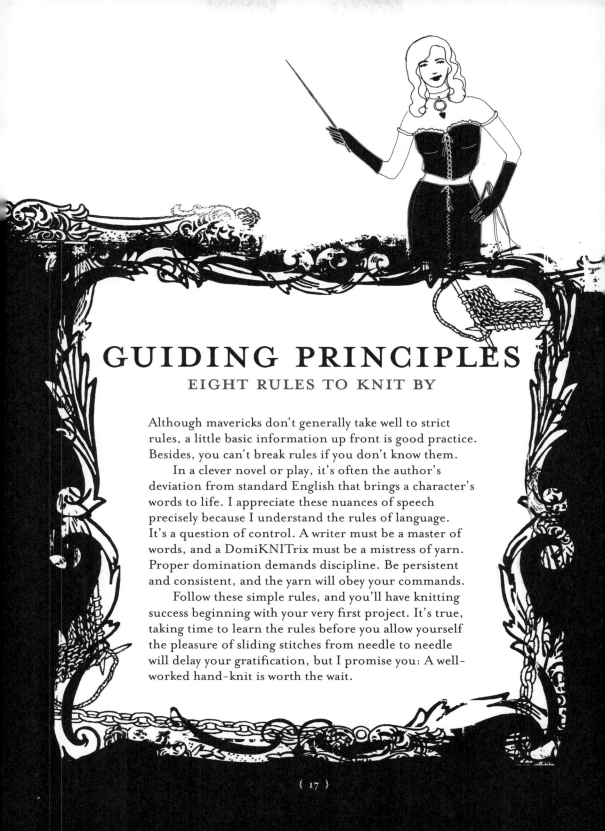

GUIDING PRINCIPLES

EIGHT RULES TO KNIT BY

Although mavericks don't generally take well to strict rules, a little basic information up front is good practice. Besides, you can't break rules if you don't know them.

In a clever novel or play, it's often the author's deviation from standard English that brings a character's words to life. I appreciate these nuances of speech precisely because I understand the rules of language. It's a question of control. A writer must be a master of words, and a DomiKNITrix must be a mistress of yarn. Proper domination demands discipline. Be persistent and consistent, and the yarn will obey your commands.

Follow these simple rules, and you'll have knitting success beginning with your very first project. It's true, taking time to learn the rules before you allow yourself the pleasure of sliding stitches from needle to needle will delay your gratification, but I promise you: A well-worked hand-knit is worth the wait.

a DOMIKNITRIX *is a mistress of time and space*

Time is a double-edged blade. It cuts both ways. We have the ability to reverse time by ripping out any knitted work with which we are dissatisfied for the small cost of making those stitches again the right way. Few other crafts allow you to "click undo" like this. When the yarn will not behave, simply punish it by ripping back to the point when it was last behaving. If the yarn is being very naughty, you can always wind it back into a ball and hide it in a dark place.

BE EVER VIGILANT

However, such severe punishment should be rare. Vigilance saves you the trouble of banishing yarn. Remember that old saying: A stitch in time saves nine. I am sure that was penned by a knitter who dropped a stitch while knitting by candlelight. If you keep a close eye on your work and your pattern, you will catch these little errors while they are still easily fixed.

SLEEP ON IT

Though ripping is a useful tool, it will take more time to do the knitting right, and some yarns will not knit up as nicely the second time. If you truly plan to rip, please sleep on it before you do. You might feel very differently in the morning, and allowing a little time to pass while you think about it could save a lot of time in the end. Sometimes there are ways to correct your mistake that don't require

the rip. I routinely perform minor surgery on my knits to save hours of re-knitting, and I've included many of those techniques here to save you stitches, too.

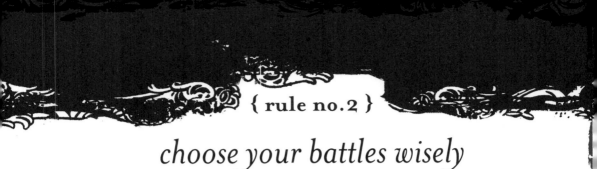

choose your battles wisely

The road to knitting hell is paved in good intentions and littered with tangled balls of bad yarn choices and half-finished projects forever suspended on needles in knitting purgatory. Do yourself a favor and pick the right yarn and the right pattern. Hastiness doesn't pay.

QUANTITY AND QUALITY

How many times have you fallen in love with yarn at the store, only to get it home and find you could not do a thing with it? Or perhaps what looked great wound in a ball is not attractive knitted up. If you aren't sure what you're going to do with a certain yarn, buy one ball and play around with it to be sure you still love it knitted up. You'll also see how much knitted fabric one ball makes so you can plan your project accordingly.

Once you choose your yarn, make sure to purchase plenty to avoid running out and having to switch to another dye lot.

CHOOSE YOUR PATTERNS CAREFULLY

Read through a pattern carefully before you commit to avoid finding out halfway through that you don't have the skills to knit it up or finish it. Or, if you choose to stick with a more difficult pattern, at least you'll know you have some things to learn as you go.

I'm definitely not here to tell you what's easy or difficult. I know one knitter who chose a long-sleeved cardigan with bobbles, cables and a button band as her first project and did a flawless job—she just needed a little help sewing it up. If you're excited about a project, go boldly forward and pay extra attention to Rule No. 5: You Must Knit a Gauge Swatch (page 22).

timing is everything

There is a time and place for mindless knitting and a time and place for knitting to learn.
Don't mix it up, princess. You'll be sorry
you did.

SOCIAL BUTTERFLY

The knitting group at the café or bar is not
the time for knitting a complicated project
where each stitch must be counted. Instead,
bring along a piece you've been knitting long
enough to have the feel of the pattern. I never
bring complicated projects for group knitting because I know I knit poorly while I'm
socializing. I keep an easy hat or scarf project
on the back burner that I can bring to social
occasions so I can be a social butterfly without
punishing the project.

BREAK OUT THE HARD STUFF

When you have a complicated bit of knitting to
do, cut out all distractions. If you're a movie-
or TV-watching knitter, tune into something
you've seen before, or that you don't have
to pay full attention to. Don't have a serious conversation with your significant other.
Don't talk on the phone. Give your knitting
your full attention. Have the pattern in front
of you and refer to it often.

TOO TIGHT
Tense knitters wrap the yarn so tightly that it
cuts off circulation on the tension fingers and
stitches have to be forced off the needles. Here,
notice how the knitted fabric itself is being
pulled, and the tendons of my wrists are tight.

JUST RIGHT
When you're relaxed, the stitches have more
room to breathe, and they slide easily off the
needles. The stitches rest a bit further from the
tips. Here, notice how the knitted fabric is not
being pulled at all, and my wrists are relaxed.

get a grip

You've got to be willing to abuse your knitting (not your hands) to get great results. You need self-control to master the correct handling of the needles.

MANHANDLING THE NEEDLES

While you're learning, holding the needles is foreign and a strain, so you may be a little tense. Don't work so close to the tips that you risk dropping stitches, but don't work so far from the tips that the work feels tight and uncomfortable. Once you are confidently forming stitches, you need to remind yourself to relax your grip any time your hands are tense.

You are striving to find that "just right" feeling where you can relax and knit in peace. At first even relaxing takes discipline, but soon it will become second nature.

you must knit a gauge swatch

I don't care if you don't want to knit a gauge swatch. I don't care if you hate it. If I could, I would stand over you with my whip and force you to knit it. Then wash it the same way you plan to wash the finished garment. Quit your sniveling. It isn't that bad.

NO PAIN, NO GAIN

It takes discipline to make this small investment in perfection. Think of it this way: A few minutes knitting this tiny little swatch up front assures that you don't waste time ripping and re-knitting your entire project later, or giving it away to a larger (or smaller) friend when you find it does not fit, or chucking it when you wash it and see that it shrinks or bleeds.

DIRTY LAUNDRY

Laundering your swatch before you knit your project allows you to adjust for gauge before you start. If you don't care for the quality of the laundered swatch, you can always just have the garment dry cleaned, presuming the yarn label indicates this is alright to do.

SIZE MATTERS

Make sure the swatch is large enough for you to assess whether you're really on gauge. A fraction of a stitch might not reveal itself if you're measuring only one inch, but over a four- or six-inch square, you might find you're getting one less stitch, which would result in a much baggier sweater than intended.

The knit stitch is your building block, and it's got to be the right size. When you are working to perfect a new technique, practice it thoroughly on your gauge swatch before introducing it into the larger project. Different stitches knit with the same yarn on the same needles often have different gauges. Make sure to knit your swatch in the stitch the majority of your garment uses.

EXTENDED SWATCH

Some balk at the thought of re-knitting a 4" (10cm) square repeatedly. But there's no need for that. Here's what I do: With the needle in a size recommended for the yarn, cast on enough stitches to make a 4" (10cm) square, plus a few extra stitches. For example, if the ball says 23 stitches over a 4" (10cm) square, cast on 29. Knit a couple of rows in garter so the swatch doesn't curl, then knit four rows in Stockinette, working the extra edge stitches in rib or garter. Distribute the yarn over the needles so it seems natural and relaxed, not all stretched out or scrunched up. Use a ruler to measure how many stitches it takes to make 4" (10cm). If that number is close to the gauge on the yarn band, knit a number of purl bumps equal to the needle size you are using. When you return to the swatch later, just count the purl bumps to remember what needle size you used.

The large gray swatch at far left is unwashed, and the large green swatch is felted. The white stitching on the two smaller swatches represents the 4" (10cm) area before the pieces were felted. Notice how the gauge changed after washing, and also how the light gray in the striped swatch darkened considerably when the dark green stripes bled in the wash.

GETTING GAUGE

Continue to knit another inch and measure the gauge again. Are you still getting the correct number of stitches to the inch? If not, change to smaller or larger needles, depending on if the gauge is too loose or too tight. When there are fewer stitches to the inch than recommended, your gauge is too loose. Switch to smaller needles. When there are more stitches to the inch than recommended, the gauge is too tight. Switch to larger needles.

When you switch needle sizes, knit a number of purl bumps on the first row that equals the needle size. I often knit up a long gauge swatch using a wide range of needle sizes so I can decide which fabric is the most desirable for the garment I have in mind, and which needle size best brings out the character of that particular yarn (see the swatches pictured at the bottom right of this page). Sometimes I love the way a bulky yarn works when it's knit on a tighter needle than recommended, like the City Coat (page 224). An extended swatch may prove useful if you decide to use the yarn on a project with a slightly different gauge.

Once you're in the swing of your project and have knit a few inches, I recommend taking the gauge again. It's not uncommon to loosen up once you get going, and it's good to double-check before you continue.

things I have learned from gauge swatches

✗ I like this yarn, but it would be better suited for a scarf than for a sweater.

✗ These colors bled when knit together and laundered, even in the gentlest way. I'm so glad I didn't ruin an entire sweater, but decided instead to knit two separate things from those yarns.

✗ This yarn changed so much after one wash that I knew the finished sweater wouldn't fit quite the way I had in mind without a lot of recalculating. I decided to make it into a bag instead, where it would matter less if the proportions changed after washing.

there are no mistakes in knitting, just techniques you haven't learned yet

Most knitting mistakes, when done consistently, create textural interest. They're only "mistakes" when they are not intentional.

AVOID CARELESS MISTAKES

A dropped stitch can be beautiful if it's part of the pattern. If it isn't, though, it's just an ugly hole. Take the time and care to fix a mistake when you catch it. Otherwise, your eye is guaranteed to go straight to the scar every time you look at your finished piece.

FIX YOUR MISTAKES

When you discover a major mistake, consider ripping back to just before you made it. Often knitters will notice problems but decide they are too much trouble to correct. So, they just ignore them and knit on. To me, this is like throwing good money after bad. If you find a major problem, be prepared to rip out your work, or find a way to fix it without ripping. To be sure you notice your flaws promptly, always knit in good light, and pay attention to your work, at least occasionally. If you can't decide whether to rip, show it to someone who doesn't knit and see if they can find the flaw. If they do and you still have doubts, consult an experienced knitter before you rip.

YOU MEANT TO DO THAT

With discipline, the same "mistakes" that create nasty holes and bumps can look absolutely gorgeous. The key to an attractive knitted piece is symmetry, proportion and consistency.

Any technique employed repeatedly and consistently becomes a pattern. That's right, you meant to do that! Look to the Tying Up section (page 74) to find specific methods you can use to correct your mistakes when they aren't part of your grand design.

turn mistakes into motifs

✗ One yarn over will make a hole in your knitting. But if you repeat that yarn over and add in one decrease to match each yarn over, suddenly you are knitting lace.

✗ A slipped stitch can cause one stitch to appear stretched out while the stitches beside it are very tight. However, slip every other stitch, and then knit the slipped stitches on alternate rows and vice versa: Now it's a textural fabric with greater strength that may be even more interesting worked in two colors.

✗ One dropped stitch makes a run or ladder we must tend to, but some texture patterns advise you to first increase one stitch, then several rows later to drop that stitch down to make a repeating pattern.

clothes should be fitted and wearable

I've been sewing my own clothes (or trying to) even longer than I've been knitting. As a result, my knitwear styles include many of the shaping and finishing details found in sewn clothing. With a hand-knitted garment, there is no reason to settle for anything less than what you really want. I've provided detailed explanations with loads of photos in Knitting Directions (page 42) and Tying Up (page 74) so you can master the techniques that let you customize any garment to your personal taste.

THINGS YOU WILL FIND IN MY PATTERNS

ZIPPERS: It's quickest to get in and out of a sweater with a zip, which is easier to install than buttons and holes. There is a lot of aversion to zippers in the knitting world, which I think gives short shrift to zippers. The real beef is with badly installed zippers. They curl up if not installed properly, and especially if installed before the sweater is blocked. See page 86 in Tying Up for more information on installing a zipper.

BUTTON BANDS: When knitting on a button band, add as many buttons as you like, even if you only want one. The band adds weight and structure to the design, and allows you to wear it closed, open or anywhere in between. A myriad of button choices also gives you many ways to own the look, even if you never button up. See page 90 in Tying Up for more information on adding button bands.

DARTS: Lining up your increases (or decreases) in a row creates the appearance of a sewn dart and highlights the style line. In sewing, a dart helps to fit the waist, bust and shoulders by stitching up extra fabric and hiding it inside. A knitted dart reduces the number of stitches in a given area to achieve the same effect.

POCKETS: Any garment is more useful with pockets. They provide a place to keep your stuff, or just to warm your hands. Knitting a pocket opening is easy to do, so long as you plan ahead, but it is still possible to add a pocket as an afterthought if you have a little more yarn. The pocket bag may be knitted, but should be sewn out of fabric instead if the yarn is very bulky. See page 88 in Tying Up for more information about adding pockets.

FACED HEMS AND COLLAR FACINGS: When you double the fabric at the edge of the garment, it adds amazing drape to the fabric. Your finished sweater will look like haute couture.

THINGS YOU WON'T FIND IN MY PATTERNS

CROCHET: I'm a knitter and prefer not to crochet. Some patterns make up for sloppy shaping by having you crochet a stable edge, but I think it's more helpful to show you how to incorporate the edging into the fabric from the start, or to knit on edgings after binding off for a more beautiful end product.

BLOCKING: I prefer to fit the garment precisely, so I do not have to block the piece. By tailoring a knitted piece, you create a finished product that holds its shape and needs to be reblocked only after washing. However, a shot of steam can conceal a wealth of sins.

MAKE ONE INCREASES (M1): Lifted (or raised) increases are clean, especially when lined up row after row, as ins the L'il Red Riding Hoodie (page 152). Although there is a symmetrical increase that can be paired with a make one increase to achieve a mirrored effect, I most often use paired lifted increases, which are much neater when aligned in the finished garment. Make one and its mirrored sister are recommended only when the increases won't show.

BLOUSON HEMS: Tight ribbing below a Stockinette stitch on larger needles makes most people look fat. If you are going to put the time and energy into knitting something, don't you want it to be flattering?

INCREASES OR DECREASES DISTRIBUTED EVENLY ACROSS THE ROW: Why distribute the increases evenly around? Instead, line them up to emphasize the shapeliness of the sweater.

WHIP-STITCHED SEAMS: I'd rather knit a seamless sweater than sew a single seam. And if I am forced to sew seams, I would definitely never choose this kind. The whip stitch is rarely as flexible as other seaming stitches and is more likely to be visible. Use mattress stitch (see page 78) for vertical seams and Kitchener stitch (see page 80) for horizontal seams.

THREE NEEDLE BIND-OFF: This bind-off creates a taut seam unless done very loosely. It is also very visible, but some prefer it for stability at shoulder seams. I prefer flexible Kitchener stitch instead.

a quest for perfection

The human spirit is always growing and reaching for more. We stretch to become more flexible, practice to jump over a higher bar, study to get a better grade, or work longer hours to earn more money. It is our very nature to want more, and to want to be more. Why should you approach your knitting any differently?

Although these designs may seem challenging on first inspection, you will find you learn a few new tricks in each pattern. I think of trying new things in knitting like walking a new path in the forest. The first time, perhaps there is no path, and I stumble along—maybe I even get lost. The second time, the way is more familiar. And after repeated walks down that same path, the way is worn and I can see where I need to go and barely need to think about it at all. It becomes natural and no longer scary. By the time you have knit several of these projects, I know you will be proudly calling yourself an accomplished knitter.

On my quest to perfect the designs showcased in this book, I spent a fair amount of time playing around and discovering the perfect stitch motif or method of increasing for each project. Pictured here are several of my yarn brainstorms. Clockwise from upper left: Mohawk, Diva, Homegrown and Elfin Goth.

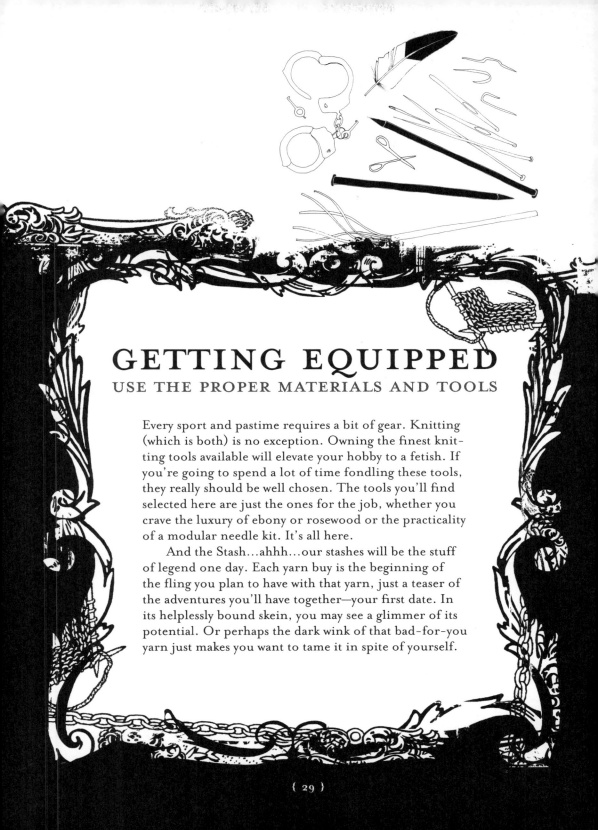

GETTING EQUIPPED
USE THE PROPER MATERIALS AND TOOLS

Every sport and pastime requires a bit of gear. Knitting
(which is both) is no exception. Owning the finest knitting tools available will elevate your hobby to a fetish. If
you're going to spend a lot of time fondling these tools,
they really should be well chosen. The tools you'll find
selected here are just the ones for the job, whether you
crave the luxury of ebony or rosewood or the practicality
of a modular needle kit. It's all here.

And the Stash…ahhh…our stashes will be the stuff
of legend one day. Each yarn buy is the beginning of
the fling you plan to have with that yarn, just a teaser of
the adventures you'll have together—your first date. In
its helplessly bound skein, you may see a glimmer of its
potential. Or perhaps the dark wink of that bad-for-you
yarn just makes you want to tame it in spite of yourself.

yarn selection
and project choices

The place we most need to be disciplined is the very place where we are sure to lose control: the local yarn store (LYS). Shopping at the LYS is like looking for a soul mate at a dance club. We're repeatedly drawn to the bad boys, the trouble makers. The losers all seem to gravitate toward us. Then we wonder why those relationships don't work out. As we wander the aisles at our favorite shop, pawing the soft and colorful balls of yarn, we are often smitten by something with eyelashes, or sequins, or a funky yarn in a plethora of colors. We take it home and play with it. If we're smart, we knit up a gauge swatch and discover it's not "the one" before we wreck a sweater with it. But often we're so in love, we've gone and rented an apartment with it before we discover we just can't stand it. Here are some tips for your mating game.

ANIMAL, VEGETABLE OR MINERAL?

Our senses draw us to animal fibers: They're soft and warm, they smell of lanolin and they keep us warm when we get wet. Those who are allergic run screaming for all the same reasons. Vegetable fibers are the bespectacled granola cousins of animal fibers: smart, vegetarian, but a little harder to get along with and not always as flexible as we'd like. The mineral yarns are the boys with asthma you meet in a chat room. They're all pretending to be something they're not, engineered to fool you into thinking they're wool, cotton or eyelashes. Oh, and they don't breathe very well.

ANIMAL

Wool fiber comes from sheep and goats typically bred to be shorn. Alpaca, llama, mohair and cashmere are also considered wool. Humans have developed a synergistic relationship with these animals over the years, which is why so many different quality wools are available today. Like human hair, wool has a core with a layer of cuticle on top. The quality of this cuticle influences how the wool feels. When the scales of the cuticles are roughed up and interlocked, they become fulled or felted and take on a very different quality. Wool usually takes the same name as the breed of sheep from whence it comes. (If it's just called "wool," you may conclude it's from a sheep. Baa.) Wools are differentiated by fiber length (staple), loft (fluffiness), lanolin content and animal of origin.

MERINO SHEEP

Merino wool comes from the world-class merino that have been bred for hundreds of years to provide finer-quality fiber and more of it. Merino wool has some special properties that other wool yarns lack. Merino fibers are finer than most wool, and the fabrics made from them do not shrink easily. Merino garments are popular with the ultra-light backpacking set because they are very light, yet surprisingly warm, even when wet.

LLAMA

Llama yarn has a long, smooth fiber more similar to human hair than wool. Usually it is blended with wool because, like mohair, llama cuticles are very smooth and do not interlock with each other as well as they do when some wool is added. Llama has a very nice drape in the finished fabric.

ALPACA

Alpaca has a soft drape and pleasant fuzz to it, yet it lacks the elasticity of most wools. Ribbing and edgings knitted with alpaca have a tendency to sag unless the alpaca has been blended with another more elastic fiber.

ANGORA

Mohair comes from angora goats and sometimes from angora rabbits, and is usually blended with other wool. The cuticle fibers are smoother than other wools, so it does not felt very well unless blended with other wool (but the blends are fabulous for felting!).

CASHMERE GOAT

Cashmere is incredibly precious, and because of this it is often mixed with other more affordable fibers to bring the luxury down to an earthly price. In the past, cashmere was harvested only in the disputed Kashmir region

kinky sheep grease

FIBER LENGTH (STAPLE): In general, longer individual fibers make finer yarn, and they need fewer other long fibers blended with them to make a nice yarn. For example, the wool of the Wensleydale sheep gives a very long fiber that may be spun into a very fine, smooth yarn with no additions, but the American bison (or buffalo) has a very short fluffy fiber that spins into a fluffy yarn and benefits from having a longer staple fiber blended with it. People who find woolens itchy are often bothered more by shorter staple fibers.

LOFT: The kinkier the individual fiber, the better it spins into yarn, since the kinks lock into each other in the spinning process and hold the yarn together. For example, merino is very kinky indeed. These kinks also make for a fluffier yarn with more loft, and the resulting air pockets create a warm fabric. Some fibers are hollow, like alpaca, which means a lighter fabric that provides more insulation. This isn't technically loft, but I file it here because this is a rare quality in fiber and it contributes to the warmth of the handknit.

LANOLIN CONTENT: The more lanolin or "sheep grease" left in the wool, the more virgin the wool. Like virgin olive oil, it is an acquired taste, and not for everyone. Some who find wool irritating are allergic or sensitive to lanolin. However, sheep grease makes wool more water resistant and drier than wool that has had the lanolin laundered out.

of Pakistan and India, by shepherds who followed the goats and removed cashmere fibers caught on bushes and shrubs. But now cashmere goats are herded in many other countries and the wool is sheared from their bodies, making this luxury fiber more available and less costly than in the past.

SILKWORMS

Silk has many of the properties of a vegetable yarn, but it is technically made by silkworms and therefore an animal product. Silk is incredibly strong and light and can be spun into a very fine fiber. Because of its high cost, it is often blended with other fibers.

VEGETABLE

I love vegetable fibers—they breathe well, allowing perspiration to evaporate rather than trapping it. Their breathable properties make them great for summer projects. Vegetable fibers take dyes very well, though they do fade over time. In general, vegetable fiber yarns are not very elastic relative to their animal and mineral cousins, and if they're stretched out, they usually do not bounce back. (Don't use vegetable fibers to knit garments that need to stand up well under stress, like dresses and skirts, unless you want a saggy rear.) Because they naturally biodegrade, some may have less life over time than yarns made from animal or mineral fiber. Vegetable fibers are also very likely to shrink or change gauge when laun-

did you know?

In British English, "wool" is nearly synonymous with yarn because it's almost the only fiber used in the chilly British Isles.

dered, so make sure to launder your gauge swatch accordingly (see page 22).

New vegetable fibers are appearing on the yarn market, including banana, soy silk and bamboo. This is exciting because these fibers are often taken from waste products from other manufacturing processes and are harvested with sustainable methods.

BAMBOO

Bamboo yarn is made from bamboo. It seems impossible, but a chemical process removes the fibers from this woody substance that grows like a weed. The fibers are then spun into yarn. Beware: Bamboo may shed its fibers and fuzz up. When I tried knitting with it, the piece looked ratty before I finished. As always, let your swatch be your guide.

COTTON

Cotton can be lovely to knit with, but it shows every inconsistency and flaw in your knitting, especially in finer gauges. Cotton blended with synthetic is more forgiving for a beginning knitter.

CANNABIS PLANT

Hemp is made from the same plant from whence rope is derived, which is still illegal to grow in the United States. Hemp fibers have a rough appearance similar to linen, and can have a rough feel while knitting and a more rustic appearance in the finished piece. However, the resulting knitted fabric is very hardy, just like rope. Hemp can easily be substituted for cotton, and it has a very nice drape.

FLAX PLANT

Linen is taken from the flax plant. This yarn can also feel rough, but it wears beautifully over time and has a lovely drape. Although woven linen fabrics have a tendency to crease, this is less of an issue with knits.

WOOD PULP

Lyocell (trade name Tencel) is made from cellulose fibers taken from trees grown for this purpose. It is a more recent addition to the yarn marketplace, and it is a very nice substitute for cotton and the other vegetable fibers listed here. It has a nice drape and is often found blended with other fibers.

MINERAL

Synthetic yarns are made from petroleum products that are heated and then sprayed into fibers that are then spun into yarn. Synthetics are more elastic than vegetable fibers, and because they are made chemically, you occasionally see 100 percent synthetic no dye lot yarns. Because the ingredients in no dye lot recipes are always the same, yarn colors are consistent, whereas in animal and vegetable fibers, the circumstances they were grown under influence the way they take dye. I find synthetics most desirable when blended with animal or vegetable fibers. They are also very affordable and machine-washable, making them a popular choice for afghans and baby clothes. Over the years, the synthetic yarn manufacturers have gotten in the habit of changing the names of their product whenever the current name gets a bad rap. Currently, the popular name is microfiber. Nylon and acetate fibers should be avoided because of their tendency to retain body odors.

care and feeding of wool garments

Finished woollen objects should always be gently hand-washed and dried flat. Avoid wringing and dramatic temperature changes to prevent felting. The one exception to this rule is superwash wool, which is treated so it can be laundered in your washing machine. One treatment uses an acid bath to eat away at some of the scaly cuticles that cause wool to felt. Another method is to coat the wool with a polymer bath to smooth over the scales, a bit like applying conditioner to your own hair, but more permanent. There are two important things to know about superwash wools: (1) Do not dry them in a dryer, but lay them flat to air dry; and (2) The treatment process takes a bit of the life out of superwash, so it cannot be ripped out and reknit indefinitely like untreated wool.

pick your poison

Since yarn is the main ingredient for any knitted project, you really must make a smart and studied decision when choosing your fiber. This is no time to be frivolous and pick a skein based solely on looks. Knitting a project is no one-night stand. You'll be logging some serious hours with whichever balls or skeins you decide to bring home with you. Before you enter the local yarn store (LYS), you need to have some particulars in your head. Know about how many yards you'll need for the project, know the gauge and the needle size called for in the pattern, and have a good idea of what kind of fiber you'll want to use. Following is a guide to help you with these all-important and potentially project-threatening decisions.

CHOOSING THE RIGHT YARN

So what is the best yarn for a project? How do you know if it's OK to substitute another yarn for the yarn listed? If you plan to make something like a scarf or a dishcloth, then it doesn't really matter all that much, since these don't need to fit the body. However, when making clothing, yarn choice is key to a well-fitted garment. The wrong yarn can lead to wasted efforts and unintended results. When considering a yarn, buy a single ball and swatch it. Trust me, you don't want to buy ten balls of the wrong yarn. You don't.

TAKE ADVANTAGE OF THE YARN

The piece of paper attached to each ball holds a wealth of information, so start there. Select a yarn with the same gauge as the recommended yarn for the pattern. The gauge is more important than the fiber content, the needle size or the color. Gauge rules the decision.

On some balls, there is a grid with a number on the vertical and horizontal edges and a pair of needles with a number next to them (see page 36). These drawings represent the stitch and row gauge and recommended needles. Some ball bands provide only the number of stitches over 4" (10cm) and a

recommended needle size, but leave out the row gauge. If the gauge is the same as is called for in the project, you should explore the yarn further. If it's not the same gauge, ask yourself: How much do you love the yarn, and are you willing to swatch it until you get the correct gauge and then keep looking if it doesn't work out? If you don't love it enough, move on.

YARN WEIGHT

Next you'll need to find out if the yarn falls into roughly the same weight category as the recommended yarn. Check out the chart on page 240 to find the established standards for yarn weights.

VERIFY YARN WEIGHT

If you have focused in on a yarn you love and want to verify the wisdom of your choice before buying it, see if you can measure the number of wraps per inch. Wraps per inch is the closest indicator of whether a yarn will substitute well, but this information is rarely found on the ball band. However, there is an affordable little tool you can carry with you to the yarn store (and they'll probably be happy to sell you one, too) to help. Simply wrap a bit of the yarn around a wraps per inch tool until you have reached the marker and count the number of wraps. If the recommended yarn is available (and it might not be), do the same with it. If the number of wraps per inch is the same, this is a very good sign that the yarn will work well.

COSMETICS

So you think it's going to work, huh? Now ask *one* more question before you buy: Does this yarn have a look and feel similar to what you see in the photos of the finished object? If you are a maverick like me, maybe you want to use a yarn that is radically different from the recommended yarn. But if you are bound and determined to get a result that matches that photo, look carefully to see if you have chosen a yarn that has a similar fluff, shine and texture. If you're happy, buy one ball and swatch.

MAKE UP YOUR MIND

Still haven't found the yarn of your dreams? If you've done your research and you still can't decide, ask the "big brain" by posting to an online forum about knitting, like the KnitList (www.knitlist.com) or Knitter's Review (www. knittersreview.com). Wiseneedle.com also has a guide to gauges of discontinued yarns. If you're using an older pattern that calls for a yarn you can't find, check there to compare your yarn's gauge.

It bears mentioning again: Whatever yarn you choose, take it out for a spin before you commit. The gauge swatch can be a fling, but you'll have to go steady with the sweater. The two swatches pictured at right are knit out of fuzzy, nubby yarns. After knitting the swatches, I realized I couldn't imagine committing to an entire sweater with either. So I used the yarn to knit a small collar instead.

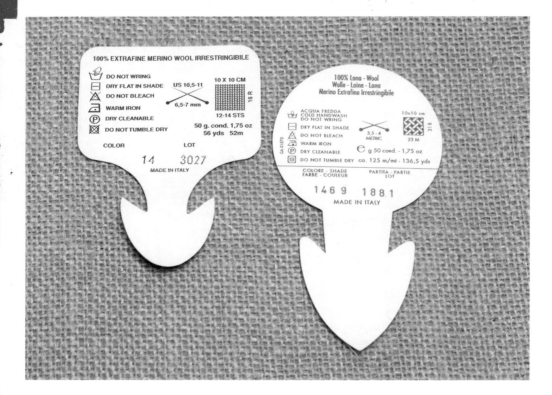

LOST IN TRANSLATION

To decode the needle size information on the ball band, first ask: Where did this yarn come from? Because U.S., U.K. and European needle sizes are differently numbered, and everyone but the United States uses the metric system, knowing the yarn's origin helps us understand the needle size. If the yarn is from Europe or the United Kingdom, check the chart on page 240 to translate the recommended needle size. Remember that you should choose the needle size that gets you to the gauge, not the other way around. Otherwise, you are setting yourself up for disaster. The needle size given on the ball band is just a guideline, not a rule. In some cases, the yarn I've used for a project has a gauge tighter than is recommended on the ball band. In those cases, if you choose to substitute yarn, you must select a yarn that knits to the same gauge as the recommended yarn, not the gauge you find in the pattern.

Now get down to business and knit a swatch until you get gauge. Once you achieve gauge, check to see if the swatch is tight and stiff or loose, limp and full of holes. The most important question is this: Once you achieve the intended gauge for your project, do you still love the way that fabric feels in your hand? Do you love the way it drapes? Is it beautiful? If the answer to any of these questions is no, keep looking.

PLIED YARN VS. SINGLES

By now I'm sure you have noticed that even within a fiber group, yarn textures can vary widely. This is often the result of the number of plies used in the yarn. Some yarns have actually been knitted themselves.

To make single-ply yarn, fiber is combed so the scales all go in the same direction, then it is spun counter-clockwise into a single ply, also called a Z-twist.

Several of these singles may be twisted together in the opposite direction from the original twist, clockwise or to the right, to create an S-twist. Twisting several plies together creates a plied yarn, which resembles rope in texture. This counter-twist has the added benefit of trapping more of the fiber's loose ends and securing them inside the twisted plies. It also results in stronger yarn.

It's also possible to twist together several plied yarns to make multi-ply yarn. The third twist is done Z-style to create what is called a cabled yarn. The third twist adds loft and texture, and further secures more fiber ends by twisting them inside.

CLIMATE CONTROL

Now that you are armed with all of this fiber information, how should you use it? When deciding on any project to knit, it's important to think about the recipient and what type of climate that person lives in year-round. I live on the West Coast, where the climate is warmer and vegetable fibers are welcome because they breathe. My friends in Los Angeles wouldn't dream of knitting with wool, because there are so few times of year when it can be worn comfortably. But I have friends on the East Coast who use wool exclusively. I once made a lovely wool cable sweater for my husband, and since he never wore it, I thought I would. That's when I discovered it was too warm to wear on all but the coldest day in San Francisco. Live and learn.

three things to know about yarn plies

✘ The S- and Z-twists can cause your knit stitches to appear asymmetrical, especially where decreases are worked. SSK decreases don't usually look as nice as the k2tog decrease because the S-twist causes the left-leaning SSK to appear to lean farther to the left while the k2tog leans to the right and counteracts the S-twist.

✘ The downside of a single ply is that the individual fibers are more likely to come loose and fuzz up since they are secured only when they pass inside the core of the twist. Singles are also the weakest kinds of yarn.

✘ When splicing yarn to add in a new ball, you will be told to first divide the plies in half. If using a single ply, you actually split the ply itself into two halves, each one comprised of many fibers.

TOYS AND EQUIPMENT

There are many tools available in the knitting and yarn world. The ones listed here I personally can't knit without, and I recommend them to anyone who wants to become a better and more powerful knitter. If you're a relatively new knitter, you might find yourself trying to get away with finishing projects on a wing and a prayer. You'll grudgingly buy a set of needles here and a darning needle there. But before you know it, you'll find you need a toy box for all your gear.

KNITTING NEEDLES

Knitting needles come in just about every size, shape, color and material imaginable. There are straights, circulars and double-points. Needles are fashioned in many different mediums, from everyday plastic to exotic rosewood or ebony. You will find needles in all widths and lengths—fat, skinny, long and short. There's something for every predilection and fetish.

NEEDLE MATERIALS

All you really need is two pointy sticks to start knitting. I even tried using dowels I sharpened in a pencil sharpener when I was a kid. Can you say "splinters and split yarn" ten times fast? I've seen knitters make do with pencils, chopsticks and stiff wire, or pay exorbitant fees for Pyrex, vintage tortoise shell or ivory needles. Any of these produce a knitted end product; each has its own particular benefit or charm.

PLASTIC needles are a bit more flexible than other materials, and some have more spring to them than others. They are smooth and warm to the touch.

CASEIN is a milk protein derived from milk processing. Needles made from this material are flexible and warm to the touch. One knitting pal prone to holding a double-pointed needle in her mouth says they are not very tasty, but they're lovely needles regardless.

WOOD needles made from bamboo, ebony rosewood or birch are flexible and warm to the touch, not to mention made of renewable resources. The points are blunt and well suited to yarns with fewer plies, and they are a good fit for loose knitters. The texture of the wood keeps the stitches on the needles nicely and is not at all prone to splintering. Years of use may blunt the tips. A little love from an emery board or fine-grit sandpaper will fix this easily. I also think it's rather sweet how bamboo takes on the color from a very rich red yarn, but doesn't give it up when you use the same needles to knit with white.

METAL needles are the workhorses of the needle world. I've never known anyone who's broken a metal needle, though they may bend. Modern metal needles are usually made of aluminum, the lightest of available metals, and they're usually color-coded by size. However, vintage needles sometimes turn up in steel. Just remember that vintage steel rusts, which could leave behind unpleasant marks on any light-colored knit.

STRAIGHT NEEDLES

When most of us begin to knit, we reach for straight needles, the iconic shape associated with knitting. Straight needles work very nicely for smaller projects, like dishrags or scarves.

However, there are some downsides to using straight needles, particularly for larger projects like sweaters or blankets. Straight needles are limited in their length, and thus in how many stitches they can hold. They are also pointy and unfriendly to fellow passengers on the bus or train, or to couch-mates, for that matter. Can you imagine knitting a blanket (or a City Coat, page 224) on them? Guest knitter Miriam Tegels knit the green Mod Coat (page 234) on straight needles, if you can believe it, but she said it took a lot of discipline to keep the stitches from jumping off the needles at the beginnings and ends of the rows. Bunching stitches on straight needles can hide mistakes or prevent you from noticing that your project is turning out two sizes larger than intended. Straight needles also put all the weight of the project on your left wrist and forearm at the beginning of each row, and transfer it slowly to the right wrist by the end of each row.

CIRCULAR NEEDLES

Once you move on to larger projects, I recommend you graduate to circular needles. Circulars support your ergonomic health by balancing the knitting load in your lap. I also like them because they make it easier to try on the work in progress. When you hold up that straight needle with your sweater hanging from it, you need a lot of imagination to see whether or not it's working out as you'd intended. Circular needles are particularly brilliant for working projects in the round (their main function). A sweater or a hat knit in the round requires almost no piecing together or sewing at the end. The longest circular needles can hold an almost unlimited number of stitches—even an entire queen-sized afghan! And just think of the possibilities when you use two pairs of circular needles together. Double the stitch count, double the fun!

INTERCHANGEABLE CIRCULAR KNITTING NEEDLE KITS

It can be quite an investment to purchase every single size of circular needle you'll need over a lifetime of knitting. However, you can amass them all at once by buying an interchangeable knitting needle kit (see image below). And it turns out to be quite a bargain in the long

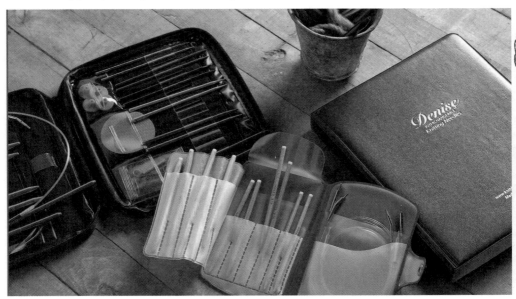

From left: Interchangeable aluminum circular needle kit color-coded by size; bamboo kit in a smaller, more portable case; plastic needle kit inside closed box.

run. As you've surely noticed, every project seems to require a different needle diameter, sometimes even different sizes for the ribbing and the body (two sets of needles). Or another set for the collar (three pair). Trouble matching the gauge? To the LYS to replace the original pairs with three more pairs in the right size (infinite sets of needles!). These differing lengths and diameters can add up to a lot of money spent on needles per project, and many trips to the yarn shop, where you're sure to be tempted to buy even more yarn.

The interchangeable kits supply a range of needle diameters and cable lengths that can be combined in a multitude of ways to work with almost every knitting project you can imagine. And the end caps allow you to move the project into resting status without risking a dropped stitch when passing all of those stitches onto a holder. So really, an investment in an interchangeable knitting needle kit will save not only money, but time and trouble as well. You'll never again settle for the wrong gauge because you lack the right needles.

Double-pointed needles made from casein (top) and bamboo (bottom).

DOUBLE−POINTED NEEDLES

These small sticks with points on both ends (see image at bottom left of this page) seem like Medieval torture devices to some knitters, and many are terrified to pick them up at all. Although there are other ways to knit circular projects, when the opening becomes very small, there are few choices but to switch to DPNs to close it up. You may cling to your circulars until the stitches are stretched so tightly that you cannot knit another stitch, but eventually you'll need to pick up those DPNs. You will need one of them to make an I-cord at a minimum. My double-pointed friends, though tiny, are mighty. What else can you use to knit a devil horn or a sphere with no sewing up?

CROCHET HOOKS

Although I don't do a lot of crochet these days, I still keep an assortment of crochet hooks for finishing up my knitted projects. Often you'll need a hook to weave in a yarn end that's too short to thread through a darning needle, or to fix a dropped stitch.

SWIFT AND BALL WINDER

When yarn is sold in hanks, you've got to wind it into a ball before you knit it up, or you are in for a world of tangle. An umbrella swift and ball winder make this easy, even fun to do, and you won't need to ask anyone to hold the yarn for you while you wind. The amount of twist in the yarn will be exactly the same before and after, though it would not be if you wound it by hand.

STITCH MARKERS

These vital tools are simple plastic or rubber rings, sometimes open rings, that are used to mark your place in the work. You can easily make your own markers from bits of scrap yarn. Some make their own stitch markers at bead shops for a fashionable look. I use markers to help me remember where I'm

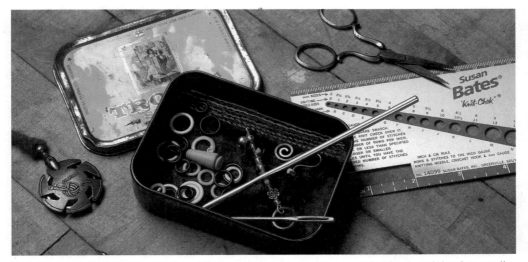

Tools from left: Notched yarn cutter; stitch markers, end protectors, crochet hook and darning needle (in tin); gauge tool and scissors.

placing my increases and decreases, since I always line them up one above the other. The open ring marker is an improvement on the basic marker, since it can be easily removed and repositioned.

NOTCHED YARN CUTTER

No knit kit is complete without a notched yarn cutter, a small circular metal tool that looks like a gentle version of a ninja's throwing weapon. Rounded arms cover a sharp blade, making the notch cutter completely safe in a knitting bag or yarn basket, yet always sharp enough to cut any yarn. Simply bring the yarn into a notch and slice it against the blade. Some knitters even thread a notch cutter onto a chain or a cord and wear it as a necklace. Scissors are fine if you can risk the sharp points in your bag, but I don't want to cut anything unintentionally, least of all myself!

MEASURING TOOLS

As a DomiKNITrix, you must take gauge seriously. And if you do take it seriously, you must always have accurate measuring tools on hand. Always have a retractable measuring tape that fits neatly into your bag. It's handy at the

hardware store too. Also keep a clear ruler for taking gauge with your knitting. Or you can use a gauge tool, a little square of plastic with ruled numbers on the sides and an L-shaped cutout along two ruled edges. Place the stitch gauge over your knitted swatch and count how many stitches and how many rows fit inside the cutout. Then divide the number of stitches by the number of inches (how long and wide the cutout is) and you've calculated your gauge.

SEWING MACHINE

Finish your knits faster with the aid of a sewing machine. You can knit your sweaters much faster as tubes if you are prepared to reinforce and then cut down the middle. This technique is called steeking, and I love it!

QUALITY LIGHTING

Watch what you're doing to keep ripping to a minimum. Whenever I end up with a dropped stitch or wrong dye lot, I always find I've been knitting with too little light. I recommend full-spectrum lighting, which is the closest thing you can get to the sun in a lamp.

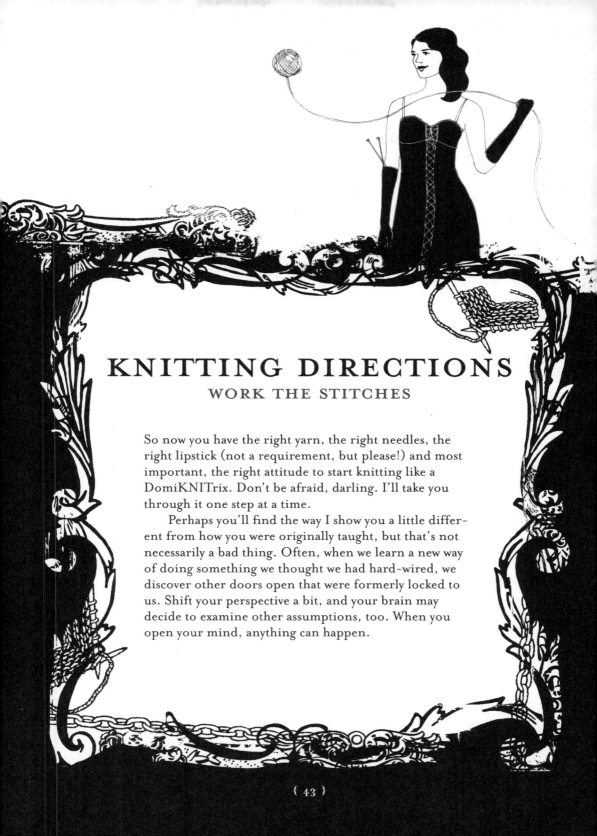

KNITTING DIRECTIONS
WORK THE STITCHES

So now you have the right yarn, the right needles, the right lipstick (not a requirement, but please!) and most important, the right attitude to start knitting like a DomiKNITrix. Don't be afraid, darling. I'll take you through it one step at a time.

Perhaps you'll find the way I show you a little different from how you were originally taught, but that's not necessarily a bad thing. Often, when we learn a new way of doing something we thought we had hard-wired, we discover other doors open that were formerly locked to us. Shift your perspective a bit, and your brain may decide to examine other assumptions, too. When you open your mind, anything can happen.

casting on

Even though this part of the knitting process truly is easy, don't be discouraged if you have to ask someone to help you with it the first few times. Practice it long enough, and you'll never forget how to do it. Just like riding a bike...and...eh-hem...other things. And don't be afraid to learn new methods. I know one lifelong knitter who only six months ago learned a second type of cast on. She never even knew there was a different option. Each different cast on produces a slightly different effect, and there are more methods than I have the space to cover here. The most important thing is to cast on loosely. Casting on too tightly is the easiest way to ruin your sweater from the very first step, or to create a sock that no foot will ever wear. One way to get a looser cast on is to use a needle one or two sizes larger than you'll use to knit the sweater. I recommend doing some swatching with these different cast ons so you can pick a favorite.

LOOP CAST ON

This is the simplest cast-on method to learn, but it does not provide the most stable edge. Beginners, please start here and tackle another method later. The cast-on number is the total number of stitches on your needle, including the slip knot in the count.

ONE MAKE LOOP

Make a slip knot and slide it onto a knitting needle. Snug the knot just enough so it is secure but can still slide back and forth easily. Hold the short tail along with the needle in your left hand. Loop the working yarn around your thumb and the needle.

TWO TIGHTEN LOOP

Tighten the loop around the needle, again snugging the yarn so it is secure but can still slide back and forth easily. Repeat steps 1 and 2 until the required number of cast-on stitches is on the needle. Remember to include the slip knot in your count.

LONG TAIL CAST ON

Long tail cast on is a favorite of mine, and I use it on most projects. It has a nice stable edge, and is pretty easy to learn. I use it only when I have no intention of removing the cast-on row later so I can pick up and knit from this edge. It *can* be removed later, but with more effort than the other techniques. When you use this cast on, you've effectively knitted the first row while casting on. If your piece will have a Stockinette edge, seriously consider learning the long tail cast on, which offers a more stable edge that is less likely to curl. When using the long tail cast on, it's best to purl the next row since this method is, effectively, producing a knit row.

ONE MAKE LOOP

Leaving a yarn tail that is four times the width of the edge to be cast on plus 6" (15cm), make a slip knot and slide it onto the needle. Pass the long tail around your left index finger as if to knit continental style (see page 48). Loop the working yarn around your thumb and the needle.

TWO PASS YARN OVER NEEDLE

Pass the left yarn over the needle, and then bring it around the needle from top to bottom.

THREE TIGHTEN LOOP

Lift your right thumb to the point of the needle and allow the loop to slip off over the needle. Pull gently to tighten the loop. Repeat steps 1 through 3 until the required number of cast-on stitches is on the needle. Remember to include the slip knot in your count.

PROVISIONAL CAST ON

Provisional cast on is the one to choose when you know you'll remove the cast-on row later, like for picking up stitches or for grafting. A provisional cast on is done with a scrap of waste yarn that will be removed later. When this crochet chain is made of the main yarn and left in place, it looks the same as "knitted cast on" or "knitting on," which is created with a knitting needle rather than with a crochet hook. It leaves a pretty chained edge that looks like a bind off and lacks elasticity like one, too.

ONE CROCHET CHAIN
Make a crochet chain with one more chain than the number of stitches you'll be casting on.

TWO FINISH CROCHET CHAIN
Cut the yarn and pull the end through the last loop to secure the crochet chain.

THREE SLIDE NEEDLE THROUGH BUMPS
Turn the crochet chain so the side with the bumps is facing up. Simply slide the knitting needle through each bump, inserting needle from front to back. Wrap the working yarn around the needle and pull it through the bump. Each loop picked up on the needle will become a stitch in your knitted project. Pick up the same number of bumps as the required number of cast-on stitches. When you're ready to remove the provisional cast on, simply tease out the yarn end you pulled through in step 2, then pull slowly while passing each loop to a waiting knitting needle. Now the loops are ready to be grafted, knit or whatever's next.

TUBULAR CAST ON

This cast on creates a very professional look, but it's tricky to do. It creates a beautiful edge for knit one, purl one ribbing since the cast on itself looks like a row of ribbing. You may also like it as a cast on for Stockinette pieces. For clarity, I've used two different colors of yarn to illustrate this kind of cast on, but it is generally done with just one color of yarn.

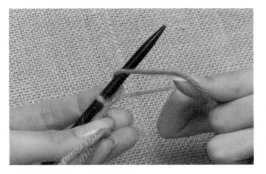

ONE CAST ON STITCH

Use a needle two times larger than gauge needle. As with long tail cast on, leave a tail four times the length of your cast-on edge. Tie a slip knot and place it on the needle. With one yarn end tensioned by your thumb and the other end tensioned by your forefinger, rotate your hand 360° so strand A (blue) catches strand B (purple), then form a stitch with B on needle.

TWO ROTATE NEEDLE, CAST ON STITCH

Now rotate 360° back in the opposite direction so strand B catches strand A. Form a new stitch on the needle with A.

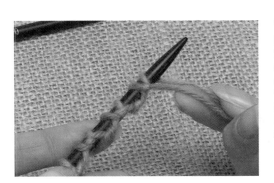

THREE CONTINUE CAST ON

Make sure each stitch goes all the way around the needle, and don't let go until you've cast on all the stitches. To finish, tie the loose ends in a knot. When you knit the first row, note that the stitches you have cast on alternate between knit and purl. On the first row, knit into the backs of the knit stitches and purl the purl stitches normally.

CONTINENTAL and ENGLISH

Even if you already know how to knit, I encourage you to read over this section. Most American knitting classes seem to prefer teaching the English technique, of which I am not fond myself since it takes more steps to accomplish the same stitch, and generally slows down the whole process.

Continental knitting originated in Austria and Germany. The women in my family have a history of meeting others who knit very fast, and then learning their speedy technique. One of the master knitters in my family, my Step-Grandma Darlene, learned the continental technique from a woman in her community who seemed to be knitting something different every time she saw her. One day Darlene approached her to ask how many works in progress she had at home. That was when she learned that the only kinds of knitted objects at her house were of the finished variety. She really could knit that fast.

If you are already set in your ways with the English style of knitting, you may still find there is something to learn here. If you currently knit English and experience wrist pain, maybe it's time to learn another technique you may find easier on your wrists. I can vouch that this technique is extremely fast, and many English knitters have marveled at my speed and the unusual way I knit. Unless you are an English-style knitter who uses a knitting pouch or belt, or otherwise anchors your right needle in your underarm, you probably can't knit as fast as a continental knitter.

This technique is often referred to as the left-handed technique, and I find that often the knitting teacher will show the left-handed person in the class how to do this and not the rest of the class. To her, I ask: Why? This technique is just as well suited to those who are right-handed, and it's faster and less straining for everyone.

KNITTING CONTINENTAL STYLE

When you knit in the continental style, each hand has a job, so the work is shared equally. The left hand throws the yarn and the right picks the stitch and works it. In the English style, you are actually picking the stitch with your left hand and throwing the yarn with your right.

ONE INSERT RIGHT NEEDLE INTO STITCH

With the yarn wrapped around or under your left index finger, insert the right needle into the first stitch on the left needle from front to back. The right-hand needle should cross behind the left-hand needle.

TWO WRAP YARN WITH LEFT HAND

Use your left hand to wrap the working yarn around the right-hand needle counter-clockwise.

THREE CREATE NEW STITCH

Pull the wrapped yarn through the stitch on the left needle, and bring the yarn up on the right needle to create a new stitch, allowing the old stitch to slide easily off of the left-hand needle. The new stitch remains on the right-hand needle.

PURLING CONTINENTAL STYLE

Before beginning a purl row, be sure the purl bumps are lined up in a straight line. If the first purl is pulling up away from the straight line, you may have an extra yarn wrap, creating an extra stitch. Begin with yarn in front of the needle for the purl row.

ONE INSERT RIGHT NEEDLE INTO STITCH

Insert the right needle into the first stitch on the left needle from back to front. The right-hand needle should cross in front of the left-hand needle.

TWO WRAP YARN WITH LEFT HAND

Use your left hand to wrap the working yarn around the right-hand needle counter-clockwise.

THREE CREATE NEW STITCH

Pull the wrapped yarn through the stitch on the left needle, and bring the yarn up on the right needle to create a new stitch, allowing the old stitch to slide easily off of the left-hand needle. The new stitch remains on the right-hand needle.

KNITTING ENGLISH STYLE

Despite my strong preference for continental-style knitting, the English approach is a handy thing to know if you are less than an expert yourself, and if you move between groups of continental- and English-style knitters seeking advice and support. They'll be much more able to help if you know how to knit with their technique.

ONE INSERT RIGHT NEEDLE INTO STITCH

With yarn wrapped around or under your right index finger, insert the right-hand needle into the first stitch on the left-hand needle from front to back. The right-hand needle should cross behind the left-hand needle.

TWO WRAP YARN WITH RIGHT HAND

Use your right hand to wrap the working yarn around the right-hand needle counter-clockwise.

THREE CREATE NEW STITCH

Pull the wrapped yarn through the stitch on the left-hand needle, and bring the yarn up on the right-hand needle to create a new stitch, allowing the old stitch to slide easily from the left-hand needle.

PURLING ENGLISH STYLE

When purling, remember that after inserting the needle into the stitch, the yarn is then passed over the working (right) needle to make each stitch. Passing the yarn under the needle is another way of knitting called "combined," which we haven't the space to discuss here.

ONE INSERT RIGHT NEEDLE INTO STITCH

With yarn wrapped around or under your right index finger, insert the right-hand needle into the first stitch on the left-hand needle from front to back. The right-hand needle should cross in front of the left-hand needle.

TWO WRAP YARN WITH RIGHT HAND

Use your right hand to wrap the working yarn over the right-hand needle counter-clockwise.

THREE CREATE NEW STITCH

Pull the wrapped yarn through the stitch on the left-hand needle, and bring the yarn up on the right-hand needle to create a new stitch. The old stitch will slide easily from the left-hand needle.

working with
CIRCULAR NEEDLES

JOINING STITCHES

When knitting in the round, instructions always caution you not to twist the cast-on row while joining. Why? Well, then you might find yourself knitting a Möbius strip rather than the intended sweater or hat! There is a time and a place for twisted knitting, but in this case you should really keep it straight. Circular knitting is a fantastic way to create effortless Stockinette stitch. Simply knit every row—no purling necessary. Circular knitting also saves finishing time. Hats, sweaters and other projects knit in the round are virtually seamless. Give this technique a whirl if you'd like a no-sew project.

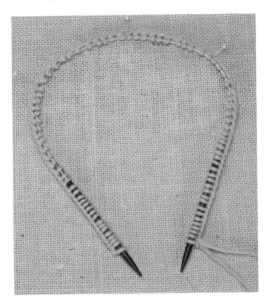

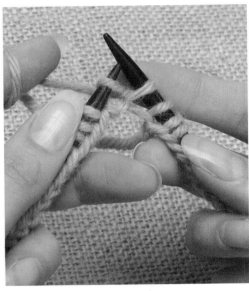

ONE CAST ON STITCHES

Cast on the required number of stitches and spread them out evenly across the length of the circular needles. Lay down the circular needle on a flat surface so the working yarn is on the right and the points are facing you. Straighten the cast-on row so the bottom of each cast-on stitch is on the outside of the circular needle. If you used the loop cast on, closely inspect the needle for any loops that have twisted around, creating what may look like a yarn over.

TWO JOIN STITCHES

To join the stitches, simply slip the right-hand needle into the first cast-on stitch on the left-hand needle from front to back. Pull working yarn through to make a new stitch, just as for knitting with straight needles. Remember, simply knitting every row produces Stockinette stitch. If you'd like to create garter stitch, purl every other row. If you'd like to create ribbing, simply alternate knit and purl stitches as desired, and knit the knits and purl the purls in remaining rows.

HIDE THE JOIN

Here's an extra tip: If you've done this before, you'll notice that the join always seems to show. When you're new at this, I think it's helpful to be able to see where the round begins, but once you're comfortable and would prefer to hide the join, try the easy technique illustrated below. It works equally well on circs or double-points.

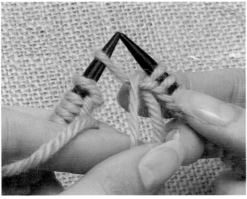

ONE TRANSFER EXTRA STITCH TO LEFT-HAND NEEDLE

After you've cast on all the required stitches, cast on one extra stitch, straighten the row, then transfer the extra stitch to the left-hand needle.

TWO KNIT FIRST TWO STITCHES TOGETHER

Slide the right-hand needle through the first two stitches on the left-hand needle and knit them together.

THREE BEGIN KNITTING IN THE ROUND

Voilá! The join is hidden. Begin knitting in the round.

double-pointed needles

Wielding DPNs is a true sign of knitting mastery. It takes a little discipline to get this technique right, but the payoff is incredible when you see the 3D sculptures you can create. DPNs are really not difficult to use, but those who are intimidated by them will be impressed to see you working with them comfortably. The start can be rough, but then it'll be smooth sailing.

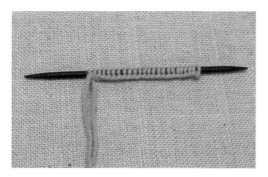

ONE CAST ON STITCHES ONTO ONE NEEDLE

Cast on all stitches onto one needle. If the number of stitches is too many to fit on one DPN, put an end cap on the starting end to hold them all. Don't use a straight needle since you'll need access to the first cast-on stitch when you join.

TWO DIVIDE STITCHES ONTO REMAINING DPNS

Divide the stitches evenly amongst the needles. If working with a set of four needles, distribute the stitches across three of them and knit with the fourth. If the set has five needles, divide stitches across four needles and knit with the fifth. As you divide stitches, pass them as if to purl; otherwise, your cast-on row will have twisted stitches. If casting on a small number of stitches, you may also choose to divide the stitches over three needles instead of over four. Lay the work on a table or another flat surface. Slide the needles around into the shape of a triangle (or square if using four needles) and line up the stitches so that the bumps from the cast on are inside the triangle (or square). Check that the cast-on row has not twisted between needles. The left needle will have the first stitches you cast on and the right needle will have the working yarn end.

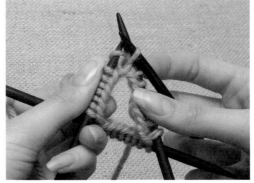

THREE **JOIN WORK**

Hold the needle with the working yarn in your right hand, and the needle with the first cast-on stitch in your left hand. Pick up a free needle with your right hand and slide the tip into the first cast-on stitch from front to back. Wrap the working yarn around the tip of the free needle and knit the first stitch.

FOUR **ROTATE NEEDLES**

Knit to the end of the first needle. Now rotate the work while you transfer the now empty needle back into your working hand and knit the stitches on the next needle. Repeat until you reach the yarn tail, and you've finished one round.

more to know

LONG TAIL CAST ON WORKS BEST: Loop cast on twists more easily than long-tail style, so I recommend long tail when working on DPNs. Casting on to multiple DPNs can be a real headache, but this approach keeps your cast-on row even and saves energy for what comes next.

STITCH MARKERS NEED NOT APPLY: Although I usually prefer to weave in yarns ends as I go, I do not do it on circular projects because the yarn end helps to mark the beginning of the round. If I were to use a stitch marker here, there would not be an adjacent stitch to hold it in place and it would fall off.

AVOID THE GOTCHAS: If you're new to DPNs, after a few rows you may notice what looks like a dropped stitch in between the DPNs. This can occur when you loosen up the tension of the yarn while rotating the work to the next needle, and it is easily resolved by pulling the first and last stitch on each needle extra snug before continuing. This will become second nature in no time and you'll be amazed at the cool shapes you are now armed to create.

DIVVY IT UP: Presuming you have a set of five needles (not always available at your LYS), you may choose whether to spread the stitches across three or four needles based on the number of stitches in the cast-on row and whether it divides evenly by three or four. Often this is dictated by the pattern.

increases

Increases are a very simple way to create a custom fit that puts va-va-voom into your sweaters. Even if you've got "more curves than San Francisco's Lombard Street," as one knitting friend used to say, you can knit a piece to show them off. Increases allow you to add a new stitch to the needle where there was none before. Here are several methods.

LIFTED { RAISED } INCREASES

Lifted increases offer the most defined line. When aligned vertically, they form a line that defines the style of the garment. Lifting the yarn from the row below makes it appear that the increase was made a row lower than it really was. Use a row counter to avoid any confusion.

RIGHT LIFTED INCREASE { RLI }

ONE INSERT NEEDLE INTO STITCH BELOW

With right needle, lift the right leg of the stitch below the next stitch to be worked and place it on left needle.

TWO CREATE NEW STITCH

Knit the new stitch as you would knit any other stitch.

LEFT LIFTED INCREASE { LLI }

ONE INSERT NEEDLE INTO STITCH BELOW

With left needle, lift the left leg below the stitch just knitted onto left needle.

TWO CREATE NEW STITCH

Knit the new stitch as you would knit any other stitch.

MAKE ONE INCREASES { MI }

Make one increases are commonly used in many patterns. If you plan to use this increase, you really should learn to use its twin sister, MIL. MIR slants to the right, and MIL slants to the left, so they can be used when you want a symmetrical effect. This increase is like casting on a single stitch loop style.

MAKE ONE RIGHT { MIR }

Twist a loop onto the right needle so the working yarn slants to the right.

MAKE ONE LEFT { MIL }

Twist a loop onto the right needle so the working yarn passes under the yarn on top of it, slanting to the left.

KNIT ONE FRONT AND BACK { KFB }

I like to increase by knitting into the front and back of a stitch (KFB), especially when I am working in garter, as in the Jughead Hat (page 210) and the City Coat (page 224). Increasing with this method creates a mark when used in the middle of a Stockinette fabric, but looks great on the edge of a garter fabric.

ONE KNIT INTO FRONT OF STITCH
Knit into the front of the stitch, but do not slip the old stitch from the needle.

TWO KNIT INTO BACK OF STITCH
Now knit into the back of the same stitch, and slip it from the needle.

THREE CREATE NEW STITCH
There is now a new stitch on your right-hand needle.

mirrored DECREASES

Decreases allow you to reduce the number of stitches on the needles and create a dart if you align them row after row. Mirrored decreases make the garment perfectly symmetrical because one leans to the left, the other to the right. I think it's equally important to be able to do these symmetrical decreases from the wrong side of the piece, and you will find p2tog and SSP commonly in my patterns. Often it is necessary to decrease more steeply than is possible to do if all of the decreases are on the right side rows.

RIGHT SIDE DECREASES

Most times, decreases are worked on the right side. The most often used right side decreases are knit two together and slip, slip knit. Used together on the right side, they create mirrored decreases.

KNIT TWO TOGETHER { K2TOG }

Knitting two stitches together is the simplest of decreases. Simply insert the working needle into two stitches at a time instead of just one, and knit the two stitches together.

To knit two stitches together, simply insert the right-hand needle through the next two stitches on the left-hand needle from front to back, with the right-hand needle crossing behind the left-hand needle. Knit as you would with one stitch.

SLIP, SLIP KNIT { SSK }

Often the beginner learns only how to knit two stitches together, and doing this on both sides causes one column of decreases to appear zig-zagged and sloppy. The SSK is the left-leaning symmetrical sister of k2tog that brings a perfect shapely symmetry to your knit piece.

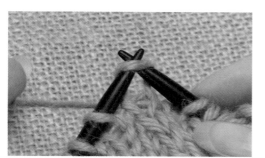

ONE SLIP FIRST STITCH

Insert the right needle into the first stitch as if to knit, and slip it onto the right needle.

TWO SLIP SECOND STITCH

Slip the second stitch knitwise in the same manner as in step 1. There are now two slipped stitches on the right needle.

THREE KNIT SLIPPED STITCHES TOGETHER

Insert the left needle into the fronts of both slipped stitches. Wrap the working yarn around the back needle (right-hand needle), and knit the two stitches together as one stitch.

FOUR FINISH SSK

When the two slipped stitches have been knitted together, you'll clearly see that the decrease leans to the left.

COMPLETE MIRRORED DECREASES

Here I've used SSK on the right side and k2tog on the left on every right side row to make mirrored decreases that lean in toward each other. Purl all wrong side rows.

WRONG SIDE DECREASES

Sometimes it's not possible to decrease as steeply as needed unless you are also working decreases on the wrong side row. This is why it's important to know how to create the same symmetry in decreases done from the wrong side of the piece, even if they are a little trickier to execute.

PURL TWO TOGETHER { P2TOG }

Purling two stitches together is the simplest of decreases. Simply insert the working needle into two stitches at a time instead of just one, and purl the two stitches together.

SLIP 2, KNIT 2 TOG TBL { SSP }

This decrease is the wrong side sister of the SSK decrease. It leans to the left when viewed from the right side, making it the perfect complement to p2tog.

To purl two stitches together, simply insert the right-hand needle through the next two stitches on the left-hand needle from back to front, with the right-hand needle crossing in front of the left-hand needle. Purl as you would with one stitch.

ONE SLIP TWO STITCHES

Slip the next stitch from the left-hand needle as if to knit. Slip a second stitch from the left-hand needle as if to knit. There are now two slipped stitches on your right-hand needle.

TWO SLIP STITCHES BACK TO LEFT-HAND NEEDLE

Slip both slipped stitches together back onto the left-hand needle as if to purl.

THREE PURL SLIPPED STITCHES TOGETHER

Insert right needle into both of these slipped stitches from behind and purl them together.

JOINING NEW YARN

My favorite way to add in a new ball of yarn is to splice it in by splitting the ends of the new and old yarn and twisting them together. The spliced portion is the same thickness as the rest of your item, with no telltale knot. Splicing works especially well with natural fibers that have fewer plies. Always weave in the short ends, or they'll poke out at inopportune places. Spit splicing is a technique I do not recommend. Who wants to drool on their knitting? And it leaves a crusty residue behind and fiber in your mouth. Yuck. (Smokers, beware: Nicotine stains on your fingers and lips will transfer to the knitting.)

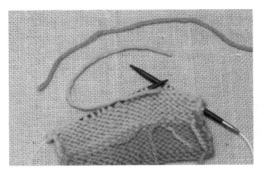

ONE POSITION NEW YARN

When you come to the last few inches of yarn in one skein, bring in a new skein and lay the tails so that the ends travel away from each other.

TWO UNTWIST TAILS

Untwist the plies in each yarn tail for 3" to 6" (8cm to 15cm).

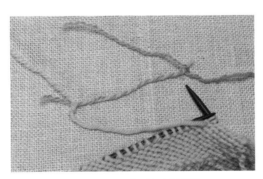

THREE TWIST TAILS TOGETHER

Take one ply from each strand and twist them around each other like plies of rope, leaving the remaining ply dangling. Use both hands. Tie the short ends of each remaining ply together loosely. Now the next ball is ready to be knitted invisibly into your work.

FOUR BEGIN KNITTING WITH NEW YARN

While you knit, weave in the remaining ends of the spliced yarn by twisting it around the working yarn loosely at the back of your work before knitting each stitch.

short rows

Short rows (often used in bust and shoulder shaping) are great for shaping knitted fabric, and there's a nifty trick to help you hide the wrap's bar and keep your knits looking smooth. When working a short row, you simply work part of the row, and then turn around and knit back to the beginning. If you don't wrap the stitch while doing this, you'll find a hole in your knitting when you knit past this point, so be sure to always wrap.

WRAP, TURN

"Wrap, turn" always appears at the turning edge of a short row and is an abbreviation for short row wrap. Do not knit the wrapped stitch until the next row. This wrap prevents a hole in the knitting and keeps the fabric firm. If you wish to hide it on the subsequent row, lift the bar from the wrap onto your needle and knit or purl it together with the stitch above. When working short row wraps, don't twist the stitch. Slip as if to purl.

ONE SLIP STITCH WITH YARN IN FRONT

Work a partial row and slip one stitch with yarn in front (wyif) as if to purl.

TWO TURN WORK, PASS SLIPPED STITCH BACK

Turn the work, and then pass the same stitch back wyif, as if to purl. Bring the yarn to the back to continue knitting.

THREE KNIT WRAP TOGETHER WITH STITCH

When you reach the wrap on the next row, lift it onto your needle and knit (or purl) it together with the stitch it wraps.

FOUR WRAPPED VERSUS UNWRAPPED

Note the difference in each green patch. The patch below was made leaving out the wrap. The patch above includes the wrap. See how nicely the wraps hide the short rows?

LACE-KNITTING BASICS

Knitted lace is one of the most beautiful things to have on the needles, but it can be intimidating the first time you try it. Lace is formed by working a balance of yarn overs and decreases to create regular holes. Several knitting operations are very common in lace knitting, and I like to play around with combining them in different ways. Other decrease methods covered on pages 58–60 are also commonly used in lace patterns. Knit up a little swatch and play around with these operations, remembering to always make one decrease for every increase.

YARN OVER { YO }

Loop the yarn over the needle without knitting a stitch. Knit the following stitch as usual. This creates a hole in the knitting.

YOYO

Most knitting books show this as *yo* repeat two times. I think it's much more fun to call it a yoyo. This creates a larger hole in the fabric than the simple yo. However, on the following row, you must remember to knit one of them and purl the other, or the fabric will not hold. The yoyo makes a great buttonhole.

SL2-K1-PSSO

ONE SLIP STITCHES
Slip two stitches together as if to knit.

TWO KNIT ONE
Knit the next stitch.

THREE PASS SLIPPED STITCHES OVER
Pass both slipped stitches over the knitted stitch to create a left-leaning double decrease.

PICKING UP STITCHES

Making new stitches at the finished edge of a piece is the perfect way to add button bands, sleeves, trims or edgings. Picking up a stitch means you are creating new knitted stitches attached to the edge of the piece. Many beginners think picking up a stitch is simply putting the needle through a stitch at the edge and knitting it on the next row. This would make the edge full of holes and stretched out. The number of stitches you pick up per row depends on your gauge. Follow this guide: Pick up one in the interlocking edge, one in the open bar, then alternate, skipping a row every three or four rows as needed. If the edge of your piece looks sloppy, pick up your stitches one row or one stitch in, but this may change the garment's size.

ONE INSERT NEEDLE INTO SIDE STITCH

Insert your needle into the first interlocking stitch at the edge of the knitting.

TWO CREATE NEW STITCH

Wrap the new yarn around the needle counterclockwise and pull the yarn through to create a new stitch.

THREE CONTINUE PICKING UP STITCHES

Insert your needle into every other stitch and pull up a new stitch each time. In this photo, I've picked up one stitch for every two rows.

FOUR CHECK STITCHES TO MAKE SURE SPACING IS EVEN

Here I've picked up one stitch for every row— too many stitches if I were to continue in Stockinette (it would create a ruffle), but just right for ribbing.

PICKING UP STITCHES ALONG A FINISHED EDGE

Have you ever knitted a sweater too short and wanted to lengthen it? Well, it's quite easy to remove your cast on and pick up the upside-down loops to lengthen it. Note: This approach is not effective with ribbing.

ONE UNDO CAST-ON TAIL

Begin by inserting your needle into the cast-on stitch near the yarn tail and gently pulling it loose.

TWO SLIP STITCH ONTO FREE NEEDLE

As the yarn tail slips through, have a knitting needle of the correct size waiting, and slip the "upside-down" stitch onto it with the right leg of the stitch in front of the needle.

THREE CONTINUE PLACING STITCHES ON NEEDLE

As you progress, the yarn tail will grow longer with each stitch. If you won't need the yarn tail for knitting, snip it off to speed up the process.

FOUR GET READY TO KNIT

Take another look and notice those upside-down stitches look (gasp!) just like normal stitches. Because the knit stitch is symmetrical, now you're ready to knit those stitches in any texture you like and make that sweater as long as you want it to be.

special effects

Once you know the basics, you can play around a little and create some interesting special effects on your knitted pieces. The rolled slip stitch edge and twisted knitting are two of my favorite easy ways to spice up your knitting. If you've been learning the techniques like a good knitter, you pretty much have all the knitting tools in the arsenal at your disposal. It's now just a matter of combining them in ways that give you what you want.

ROLLED SLIP STITCH EDGE

Slipping a stitch at the beginning and/or end of each right side row creates a beautiful chained edge. Slipping two stitches on each right side row creates the look of a sewed-on I-cord, but with much less effort. This edge can tighten up the edge of the piece, so it's important to try it first on a gauge swatch before starting the piece. On a garter piece, it's just fine. Since the gauge of this texture is already tighter, it matches well.

ONE SLIP FIRST STITCH(ES)
Slip the first one or two stitches as if to purl.
(Always slip stitches only on right side rows.)

TWO SLIP LAST STITCHES
Slip the last one or two stitches as if to purl.
(Again, always slip stitches only on right side rows.)

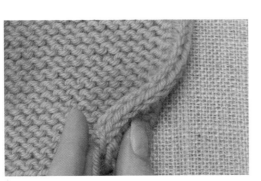

FINISHED ROLLED SLIP STITCH EDGE
Notice how the edges seems to roll without the entire piece curling. Check out the City Coat sleeve (page 224) to see this trick in action.

TWISTED KNITTING

By knitting and purling into the back loops (instead of the fronts) of stitches, you may create a tighter fabric that appears to be twisted and that is great for areas requiring enforcement, such as elbow patches (see L'il Red Riding Hoodie, page 152). Twisted knitting requires a bit of dexterity, especially on the purl rows, but the result is well worth it.

TWISTED KNITTING
On the right side (knit rows), insert the right needle into the back of the stitch and knit it.

TWISTED PURLING
On the wrong side (purl rows), insert the right needle into the back of the stitch and purl it.

SEVERAL ROWS OF TWISTED KNITTING
When you've knitted several rows of twisted stitches, you'll see the subtle difference. It takes a little extra work to make, but it wears like iron.

color work

When you wish to add a design in another color to your knitting, you may choose from several techniques. The trick is knowing which to use and when. For the charted knits in this book, I recommend using a combination of color-work methods for the best results.

INTARSIA

Intarsia is the simplest way to introduce another color into a design. For large areas of color, use bobbins to keep the yarns untangled. Twist the strands in back of the work at every change in color, as shown. This technique conserves yarn, since you aren't swagging any color, and has elastic results, since there are no swags to tighten up the fabric.

ONE SECURE OLD COLOR ON RIGHT SIDE

From the right side, turn the work so you can see the back. Bring the new color under the old color, then wrap the old color around the new color to prevent a hole.

TWO KNIT WITH NEW COLOR

From the wrong side, lift the new color from under the old color and wrap the old color around the new color. If the two colors fail to link or twist, a hole will result.

INTARSIA IN PROGRESS

Here's an example of what your intarsia should look like as you go along.

DUPLICATE STITCH

Duplicate stitch is a simple way to add color as part of the finishing work. If handling multiple strands of yarn simultaneously seems unmanageable, duplicate stitch is a good way to get a picture onto your knitting. To add color with duplicate stitch, thread a darning needle with yarn and stitch over the legs of each stitch in the pattern you wish to create. Be aware, however, that tiny bits of the background yarn will show through. If this doesn't bother you, duplicate stitch may be the easiest way to add a bit of color, or to personalize a piece as an afterthought. You can even use duplicate stitch to make a store-bought piece uniquely your own.

ONE BEGIN FIRST STITCH

Thread a darning needle with yarn and tie a knot in the end. Bring the needle up through the fabric at the base of a stitch. Slide the needle under both legs of the stitch.

TWO FINISH FIRST STITCH, BEGIN NEXT

Bring the needle back down through the base of the stitch at the point where you brought the yarn up. Slide the darning needle under both legs of the next stitch in the pattern.

THREE CONTINUE DUPLICATE STITCH

Continue stitching over the knitted stitches, mimicking the V of each stitch with your darning needle and thread.

FOUR FINISH STITCHING

Continue in duplicate stitch until your design is fully realized. Secure the yarn at the back of the work.

STRANDED KNITTING

Also known as Fair Isle, stranding yarn or yarns across the back of your knitting is another way to incorporate multiple colors into your knitting. Simply drop the main color and switch to the contrast color, and so on, in order to create the look you want. This color work technique is probably the most demanding: Two strands need to be handled throughout the row, and they tangle easily. If you consistently bring one color from below and the other color from above, the yarn will twist less.

I like to use the baggie trick: Before starting, put each ball of yarn into a sandwich-sized zipper-seal plastic bag. Cut one small corner of the bag and poke your yarn end through this hole. Zip the yarn inside and get knitting. The yarn may still tangle a bit, but at least the whole ball won't get into the fray. If there are lots of color changes, detangle once a row so the situation doesn't get out of control. If there are only a few colors, and if you are working flat instead of circular, rotate the piece clockwise when you turn the row; that way, at least some of the yarns will detangle themselves as you work back. Some knitters like to knit stranded by holding one yarn in each hand, knitting one color English-style and the other color continental-style. Fair Isle knitting uses more yarn than intarsia or duplicate stitch, since all those swags really suck it up, and they need to be done loosely to keep the project elastic. The looser the swags, the more yarn is consumed, but this is a good use of yarn, since a Fair Isle sweater stranded too tightly can be almost unwearable.

The Sweetheart (page 184) was knitted using intarsia (see page 68), but you could knit the sweater plain and add the bow afterward with duplicate stitch.

MOSAIC KNITTING

Also known as slip stitch color work, this nifty technique allows you to work with multiple colors without handling two different yarns in each row. Instead, alternate between two rows in each color. On rows one and two, slip any stitches where you want the color from the row below to show instead of the working color. On rows three and four, knit the stitches you slipped on previous rows, and slip the knitted stitches from previous rows. Slipped stitches do stretch out, so use this method for repeating patterns where half the stitches of each color are used on every row. It works great for vertical stripes, checkerboard, herringbone and houndstooth. The downside? You knit twice as many rows, since you knit only half of the stitches on each row.

ask yourself

So how do you know which color work technique to use? Just ask yourself a few questions to figure out the best choice.

Is it a big chunk of color with well-defined edges?
intarsia

Is it a small repeating pattern?
Fair Isle or mosaic

Is it just the tiniest smidge of color?
duplicate stitch (or intarsia, but only if you are a perfectionist)

Are you light on yarn?
intarsia or duplicate stitch

Do you have a lot more yarn than you need for the project?
Fair Isle or mosaic

Will you have to carry the yarn more than five stitches across the back?
intarsia

Does the project need to be very elastic?
intarsia

Knit a small swatch to test the effect of the technique you plan to use. The swatch may reveal it's a poor choice, or give you a chance to perfect your tension before embarking on the project. The swatch at the top of the page is argyle worked in a combination of intarsia and duplicate stitch. The images at bottom represent, clockwise from top left: Intarsia, Fair Isle, short rows with and without wraps, short rows, intarsia and Fair Isle combined. (See page 62 for more on short rows.)

DIMENSIONAL KNITTING

Knitting certainly does not limit itself to just the two-dimensional plane. You'll notice that many of my projects have a three-dimensional aspect, like the Devil and Snow Devil Hats (page 138) or the Strings of Purls (page 126). Sure, dimensional knitting sounds complicated and looks quite impressive, but it is actually quite easy. Don't believe me? Take a look.

I-CORD

Elizabeth Zimmermann, grand doyenne of knitting, coined the term Idiot cord, stating that even an idiot could make it. Over the years, this term has been politically corrected to "I-cord." This knitted cord is just about the easiest thing you can make with DPNs. It's fun to make, but it uses a lot of yarn and takes a surprisingly long time. Then again, once you've knitted a few rows of it, you could easily crank out a few feet while watching your favorite drama. See the rolled slip stitch edge (page 66) for a way to knit an I-cord edge right onto your item as you go.

ONE CAST ON STITCHES

Cast on the required number of stitches onto a DPN. Two to four stitches works best.

TWO PREPARE FOR FIRST STITCH

Slide the stitches down the DPN so the first cast-on stitch is at one end of the DPN. The working yarn should be farthest from the point.

THREE KNIT I-CORD

Pull the working yarn from the last stitch to the first stitch and knit. Continue knitting all stitches. Instead of turning the entire needle when you finish a row, simply slide all the stitches to the end of the needle again (without turning the needle at all). Keep pulling the working yarn to the first stitch in each row. Pretty soon you'll have a lovely tube—without having purled a stitch!

USING TWO CIRCULAR NEEDLES TO MAKE A TUBE

This technique is extremely fast, and it avoids the Stockinette curling problem by flattening itself out naturally. Because the tube is neatly closed up, any yarn ends simply hide inside, saving finishing time. However, be sure to get plenty of yarn for any tubular project, since you'll need twice as much to make a tube as a flat piece of the same dimensions. The fact that I've taken a lot of words to describe this process belies how incredibly simple it is. Once you have mastered it, you can knit a tube with such astonishing speed that you can crank out a sock in just a few hours.

ONE CAST ON STITCHES

Cast on an even number of stitches onto one needle (twice as many as you need to reach your desired width, since the tube will be folded in half vertically).

TWO FOLD IN HALF, SET UP NEEDLES

Fold the work in half, and slip half the stitches purlwise to a second circular needle of the same size but of a different color. Then slide the stitches to the opposite end of both circular needles so the working yarn is at the needle behind and the first stitch you'll knit to join the tube is in front.

THREE BEGIN KNITTING

Grab the needle end attached to the front needle. Join the two sides of the tube and knit with the front needle (Figure 1), using the working yarn from the back needle.

FOUR CONTINUE KNITTING

Knit half of row one on the front needle, then turn the work. After you turn, drop the needle end so you don't continue knitting the next side with the same needle (Figure 2).

try this: mixed-size setup

You can make this already quick technique even faster by substituting one circular needle with a slightly smaller gauge. Follow the steps to the left, but add these specific instructions:

{ 1 } *Set up two pairs of needles so the smallest available size is on the passive end and the size needed to get gauge is on the active end. This pairing enables higher speeds, as the stitches slip more easily off the passive end. Be sure to cast on with the gauge needle if using the mixed-size setup.*

{ 2 } *The front needle should be small, and the back needle should be the right size for gauge.*

{ 3 } *This needle should be the gauge needle.*

figure 1

figure 2

TYING UP
FINISH IT OFF

If you start something, you'd best be willing to finish it. And finish it right. Don't leave a project languishing on the needles for weeks or months or…gasp…years. Don't be a project tease.

Often we bind off the last of our stitches and raise a glass to our new finished object. But is it really finished? Do those little white lies go well with your white wine?

Now don't get me wrong. I like to keep a variety of projects in the rotation as much as the next knitter. But once the knitting is done, each day that I can't wear my unfinished garment is a day of torment. Sewing up, stitching zippers and weaving in loose ends will transform your piece from mediocre to sublime. Take some time and care to do these things well, and your finishing skills will be transformed, too. Be prepared to spend a fair amount of time on finishing. Because these details bring it all together, you'll want to give them some extra attention.

BINDING OFF

When you've finally finished knitting your masterpiece, you've got to secure all those stitches. Binding off does the job, and there's more than one way to get it done. Choose the method of binding off that works best for your project.

TRADITIONAL BIND OFF

This method of binding off produces a chained trim at the bound-off edge. However, it will lack elasticity unless it's done very loosely. If your bind off is usually too tight, try using a needle two sizes larger in your right hand.

ONE KNIT TWO STITCHES
Knit the first two stitches as you would for a normal knitting row.

TWO PASS FIRST STITCH OVER SECOND STITCH
Insert the left-hand needle into the first knitted stitch and pass that stitch over the second knitted stitch.

THREE FIRST STITCH BOUND OFF
There is now one less stitch on the needles.

FOUR CONTINUE TO BIND OFF
To bind off the next stitch, knit one more stitch, then pass the preceding stitch over that one. Continue to knit one stitch and then pass the preceding stitch over it until you have bound off all the stitches. Cut the yarn and pull the tail through the final stitch.

ELASTIC BIND OFF

This method of binding off produces an edge that looks just like a garter row and is more elastic than the traditional bind off.

ONE KNIT ONE AND PASS TO LEFT NEEDLE

Knit one stitch and pass it back to the left needle.

TWO KNIT TWO TOGETHER AND PASS STITCH

Knit two stitches together and pass the resulting stitch back to the left needle.

THREE FINISHED BOUND-OFF EDGE

Continue binding off stitches until they've all been bound off. Pull yarn tail through last stitch. Notice how nice and stretchy the edge is.

TUBULAR BIND OFF

Tubular bind off is another technique that will give your piece couture flair. This bind off looks especially grand in a large-gauge knit, as seen in the Swizzle Vest (page 200).

ONE INSERT NEEDLE INTO FIRST STITCH

Thread the yarn tail through the darning needle, and slide the needle through the first stitch.

TWO INSERT NEEDLE INTO BACK LOOPS

Insert the darning needle through two stitches through the back loops. Slip one stitch off the needle.

THREE SLIP STITCH OFF

To bind off the next stitch, roll the work forward and insert the darning needle through the front loops of the next two stitches. Slip one stitch off the needle. Continue alternating between the front and back loops, sliding one stitch off the needle each time.

Mattress Stitch

Mattress stitch is the perfect seam for sewing together two pieces of knitted Stockinette fabric at the selvages. I love its invisible quality. It joins two halves of the knit stitch in the middle so they look like any other stitch. Worked properly, this seam adds structure to your knits. Use a darning needle and the same yarn used to knit the project. If the yarn is very thick, use just one ply to create a less bulky seam, or use a finer yarn of the same color. Although the sewing yarn will be hidden by the seam, it can show when stretched, so a closely matching yarn is best. Some knitters prefer to use a different yarn so they can find it when it needs to be undone, which might be helpful if you're new at this and you're not satisifed with your first effort.

AT THE EDGE

Mattress stitch at the very edge of your piece leaves a minimal inner seam and saves yarn. Start by orienting both pieces in the same way, with cast on at the bottom and bind off at the top.

ONE ARRANGE PIECES, BEGIN SEAMING

Butt the two pieces of knitting up against each other as you intend to sew them. Thread a darning needle onto the tail of one of the pieces or onto a piece of scrap yarn. Pull the needle under the knotted yarns of the edge stitch and up again.

TWO CONTINUE SEAMING

Move the darning needle to the opposite piece and pull it under the knotted yarns of the edge stitch and up again.

THREE FINISH SEAMING

Continue threading the needle in and out of the knotted yarns of the stitches on each piece until you finish. Oops! Do you notice we have a few extra rows on the left? Next up: How to ease in extra rows.

EASING IN EXTRA ROWS

This technique allows you to adjust mismatched pieces without reknitting. You'll be stitching three rows in on the left for every two rows on the right, and no one will be the wiser but you!

ONE PULL OUT STITCH AND RE-SEAM

Gently pull out the mattress stitch for about half the seam. Insert the darning needle under the knotted yarns, then up again in the middle of the next knot (three rows higher). Continue to work in mattress stitch normally on the shorter piece (only two rows higher).

TWO EASE IN EXTRA ROWS

Insert the needle into the same hole it comes out of on the longer side, then bring it up three rows higher.

THREE FINISH RE-SEAMING

See how the pieces now appear to match, even though there are still more rows on the left piece.

SEAMING GARTER

When seaming garter stitch vertically, begin by noticing that the purl bumps present themselves as either smiles or frowns. The stitches at the edge of the piece are naturally a little tighter, but you can still see them smiling and frowning if you look closely.

ONE PULL YARN THROUGH

Thread a darning needle with the yarn tail, insert the needle into the first smile on the left-hand piece, and pull the yarn through loosely.

TWO COMPLETE FIRST STITCH

Then insert the needle into the adjacent frown on the right-hand piece. Draw the yarn snug (but not tight) here.

THREE FINISH SEAM

Repeat steps 1 and 2 until you complete the seam. If it weren't for the different colors here, you wouldn't even be able to see this seam.

GRafting
{ Kitchener Stitch }

Use Kitchener stitch any time you need to join two rows of knitted loops together, most commonly at shoulder and pocket seams. Kitchener stitch done correctly looks like just another row of knitting and is as perfectly elastic as your knitted fabric. I almost always try to use the end of the yarn that I used to knit the piece. However, if you used a novelty or bouclé yarn, sew up with a smoother yarn in a coordinating color. If you wish to graft with one continuous piece of yarn, allow a yarn end four times longer than the piece is wide. However, you may find it easier to work with a shorter piece to avoid tangles and to place less strain on your rotator cuff and shoulder.

GRAFTING STOCKINETTE

Check the sewing yarn to be sure it has the same amount of twist as the yarn still on the ball for the most invisible seam. If it is frayed, you may wish to twist it up a bit to match the yarn's natural twist. And remember, practice makes perfect. If you're about to seam an heirloom, practice the stitch on some swatches first. If you overwork the sewing yarn, the Kitchener row may lose its invisible quality, so a dry run is warranted. I work from left to right, but everyone has her own preference. You will be sewing with the yarn in an S, just as it was knitted.

ONE THREAD NEEDLE THROUGH FIRST LOOP

Line up both needles with active stitches in the same direction. Thread a darning needle onto the yarn tail from one of the two pieces. Thread the needle through the back leg of the first stitch on the bottom needle.

TWO SEAM FIRST STITCHES

Thread the needle through the first two stitches on the other knitted piece, then bring the needle back through the back leg of the first stitch on the top needle, then bring the needle back through the first piece between two legs of the next stitch.

THREE SLIP STITCH FROM KNITTING NEEDLE

Bring the darning needle back to the bottom piece and insert it under the next two legs. Then let the first leg slip from the knitting needle.

FOUR CONTINUE GRAFTING

Bring the darning needle back to the top piece and insert it behind two legs of the stitch. Let the first leg of the stitch slip from the knitting needle.

FIVE TIGHTEN UP GRAFTED STITCHES

After loosely grafting a few stitches, snug them up so they look to be the same size as the stitches above and below them.

SIX FINISH SEAM

Continue seaming until the pieces are grafted together. The fabric should look completely seamless when you finish.

GRAFTING GARTER

Doing the Kitchener stitch in garter is a little trickier. First things first: One side of the work needs to end with a knit row, and the other side needs to end with a purl row, or it will be impossible to conceal the grafted row.

OΠE POSITION KNITTED PIECES

Position the two pieces to be grafted together so the active stitches and the finished edges of the pieces are adjacent. Notice the top piece presents a purl row, and the bottom piece presents a knit row. For an inset piece like this one, begin with the active stitches (grafting) and finish with the finished edges (mattress stitch).

TWO BEGIN GRAFTING

Thread the darning needle onto a yarn tail and slide it through the first stitch from the back of the stitch through to the front of the stitch on the bottom piece.

THReE SLIDE DARNING NEEDLE THROUGH TWO STITCHES

Slide the darning needle through the first two stitches on the second knitted piece. Although these stitches were purled last, we're "knitting" them now with grafting. This step is the same as step 4 in grafting Stockinette on page 81.

FOUR SLIDE STITCH OFF NEEDLE

Slide the darning needle down through the first stitch on the bottom piece and up through the next stitch. Slide that stitch off of the needle. Repeat steps 3 and 4 until the entire piece is grafted.

FIVE FINISH GRAFTING

Continue until all of the active stitches are grafted together.

GRAFTING RIBBING

Grafting ribbing is a real challenge, enough so to warrant practicing on a swatch. For this technique, make sure both pieces have active stitches at their bottom edges. Because the Vs of the knit stitch are mixed in with purl stitches, grafting them together at the top creates a half-stitch jog. If you plan to graft ribbing, I recommend using provisional cast on at the start of one piece. You'll need this technique for The Slink (page 216). *Important note: Although the swatch shown has a variable number of knit stitches in the ribbing, this description is for k1, p1 ribbing.*

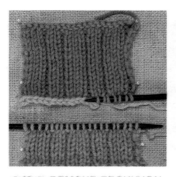

ONE REMOVE PROVISIONAL CAST ON

Begin by removing the provisional cast on at the bottom of one piece, and butt the two pieces together with all stitches lined up on the needles.

TWO THREAD YARN THROUGH FIRST TWO STITCHES

Working from left to right and starting with the bottom piece, insert the needle under the right leg of the knit stitch, then into the center of the purl stitch, and pull the yarn through loosely. Slip the knit stitch off the needle and leave the purl stitch on until you have grafted the other leg of the purl stitch.

THREE THREAD YARN THROUGH FIRST TWO STITCHES ON NEXT PIECE

Insert the needle into the purl loop on the top piece from back to front, then under the left leg of the next knit stitch, twisting the knit stitch a bit to the right. Pull the yarn through loosely. Slip the purl stitch off the needle and leave the knit stitch on until you have grafted the other leg of the knit stitch.

FOUR CONTINUE GRAFTING

Insert the needle into the center of the purl stitch on the bottom piece from back to front, and slip it off the needle. Then insert the needle behind the left leg of the next knit stitch, and pull the yarn through from back to front, leaving the knit stitch on the needle.

FIVE COMPLETE FINAL GRAFTING STEP

Insert the needle under the right leg of the knit stitch on the top piece from front to back, and slip it off the needle. Then insert the needle into the purl loop from front to back, leaving the stitch on the needle while pulling the yarn through. Repeat steps 2-5 to complete the graft.

GRAFTING FACINGS

A facing should mirror the piece it faces, but with fewer stitches so the outer fabric is slightly larger than the inner fabric. The difference in stitches causes the facing to naturally lay flat and mold to the body's contours. Most facings include a turning row or rows, which help the facing fold up naturally. This is especially important given Stockinette's inherent tendency to curl.

ONE FOLD OVER FACING, LINE UP STITCHES

Fold over the facing and line up the stitches evenly, with the needle point to the left.

TWO GRAFT FIRST STITCH

Count the number of rows in your facing and add one. This is how many rows you'll count up from the turning row to choose which row to sew through. Thread the darning needle with the yarn tail and pull it through the first stitch on the needle and the first stitch behind it on the fabric. Bring the needle down and graft the next stitch on the needle, as for grafting Stockinette (see page 80).

THREE CONTINUE GRAFTING

Insert the needle from bottom to top into the next stitch on the fabric, and gently pull the yarn through.

GRAFTING FROM WRONG SIDE

Here is the completed back of the facing.

GRAFTING FROM RIGHT SIDE

And here is the completed front!

the keys to success when grafting facings

WORK ON WRONG SIDE, BUT CHECK RIGHT SIDE FREQUENTLY: The stitches you're sewing down are on the wrong side of the piece, so you should be, too, so you can see what you're doing. Check the right side often to be sure you haven't made any glaring errors.

KEEP THE TENSION LOOSE AND TIGHTEN UP LATER: If you keep tension loose while sewing down your facing, it's easier to keep aligned. Tighten things up every few inches. Remember, you want the facing to be just as elastic as the front.

STAY ALIGNED: Be sure to always work in the same column of stitches. Count from the stitch on the needle down to the stitch on the fabric you'll sew it to. Once the facing is sewn partly shut, it becomes harder to see, and it's easy to creep over one stitch, causing your facing to lean. Also stay aligned within the row. Some knitters actually sew a marking into the row to make it easier to stay on track. Try this: When working on the back of a Stockinette piece, pick a row of smiles (or a row of frowns), and stay within that row for the whole seam. After sewing through each new stitch, find the smile next to it, and sew through it. If you are struggling, you may mark the stitches you'll be grafting every five stitches or so to keep you on track.

REMEMBER YOU ARE GRAFTING A NEW ROW: Don't forget that by grafting, you are adding one more row of knitting, so you may need to aim a little higher than you think when stitching it down to allow room for this new row.

crochet chain

Occasionally, you may need a bit of stabilization or reinforcement at the edge of the knitting, or at a pocket or collar edge. This can be done easily by crocheting a simple chain through the knitting to stabilize the fabric.

ONE CROCHET THROUGH FABRIC

Begin by inserting your crochet hook through the fabric in a stitch where you wish to add stabilization. Pull a loop of yarn through the fabric at that point, then insert the hook into the next stitch in the same column and pull another loop through the fabric and the first loop, maintaining only one stitch on the hook.

TWO FINISH CHAIN

Continue to chain stitches through the knitted fabric in a straight line to create a stabilizing reinforcement.

zip it good

I have noticed quite a few experienced knitters who shy away from designs with zippers because they are afraid they will install them badly. When installed properly, the zipper will lay flat without any ripples, but the first time you try it, I recommend practicing on a pair of swatches before installing a zipper on a sweater or coat. There are two major factors that cause even properly installed zippers to end up wavy. The first is that the sweater is too small for the person wearing it, so the stretchy knit gives way, but the zipper ripples because it cannot stretch. The second is that the sweater is laundered after the zipper is installed, and in the process the yarn shrinks or changes gauge, while the zipper does not.

INSTALLATION PREPARATION

CHOOSE THE ZIPPER

If your jacket or coat opens all the way up the front, you need to purchase a separating zipper.

COVER THE ZIPPER IF NECESSARY

If you aren't able to find a zipper in the same color as your finished item (a very common malady), buy a ribbon in a color that matches your finished item. The ribbon should be 4" (10cm) longer than the zipper. If the ribbon is made of a fabric that may shrink, buy a little extra.

BLOCK OR STEAM THE FINISHED OBJECT

If you plan to block or steam the finished object, do it before installing the zipper. When steaming knits, do not touch the iron to the fabric; hover near it so the steam can penetrate. Pressing the fabric compresses the texture and could destroy the piece.

STEAM OR IRON THE ZIPPER

If covering the zipper with ribbon, steam the ribbon at the same time. It is important to pre-shrink all of the materials to keep the zipper from becoming wavy later.

PIN ON THE ZIPPER

If you want to sew in the zipper only once, I strongly recommend you pin the zipper every 3" to 4" (8cm to 10cm) on each side. Then open up the zipper and carefully try on the sweater or coat. If the zipper doesn't hang smoothly—if it pulls at all, or has a ripple—you will have the same problem once it's sewn down. If the sweater fabric is looser than the zipper, pin it again until it lies flat. If the zipper is wavy behind the fabric, it is too loose and needs to be pinned more tightly. A little caution up front will save you the time and trouble of repeatedly sewing in this zipper.

INSTALL ZIPPER

Now that your zipper has been steamed, covered, pinned and fitted, you are ready to stitch it down. Use quality sewing thread in a color compatible with the zipper (or ribbon) and your knit fabric. Polyester thread works best.

Start sewing from the bottom up so you can try on the piece periodically to make sure the zipper is still lying flat. Do *not* allow the fabric to creep and stretch as you sew. If you let the fabric creep up even just a hair with each stitch, you will end up with exactly the wavy zipper you set out to avoid.

PRACTICE THE ZIP

Figures 1–3 below illustrate installing a zipper on practice swatches.

FIGURE 1: Tie a knot in your sewing thread, then thread the needle. Anchor the knot in the zipper tape, not in the knitting. The knot should be on the same side as the zipper pull so it will be concealed when finished.

FIGURE 2: Insert your needle straight through the knitting and zipper as you work, not at an angle. Work in a stabbing motion, pushing the needle through to the back side, pulling all the thread through, and then stabbing through from back to front. Use short stitches so your thread doesn't show in the knit, but do be sure to catch a few plies of the yarn with each stitch.

FIGURE 3: Notice the stich guide on the zipper tape. That raised line on the tape tells you not to sew between there and the zipper teeth, or you will increase the risk of the knit catching in the zip when you open and close it.

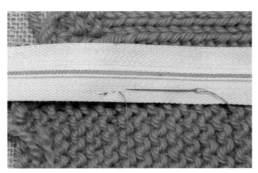

figure 1

figure 2

figure 3

POCKETS

A pocket is simply a gash in the knitting with a second piece applied to the back. Here is a guide to three different ways to add pockets to a garment that does not include them. You'll find the patch pocket in the L'il Red Riding Hoodie (page 152) and the planned welt pocket in the City Coat (page 224).

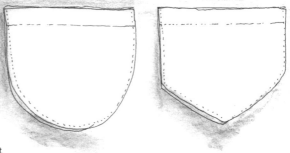

PATCH POCKET

A patch pocket is probably the easiest one to add, since you simply need to knit a square (or another pocket shape) and sew or graft it to the front of your sweater, leaving an opening at the top or side, as you wish. If the opening is at the side, be sure to sew it closed at the bottom so that your things don't fall out of the pocket. You may add your own unique touch by using contrast thread or embroidery floss to sew on the pocket, or by making the pocket out of another yarn entirely.

PLANNED WELT POCKET

This type of pocket opening is horizontal if knit on a top-down or bottom-up sweater, or vertical on a sideways knit. Plan to purchase extra yarn for the pockets if the pattern did not plan for them. Decide where on the knitted piece the pocket(s) will be placed. When you reach the bottom edge of a pocket opening, knit a few short rows in a flat texture, such as ribbing or garter, as wide as you want the opening to be. Then simply bind off. Cast on the same number of stitches and insert these stitches in the gap between the bound-off stitches. Move these stitches onto the same needle holding the rest of the waiting garment. Continue knitting the sweater, then sew a piece of fabric or another knitted square behind the pocket opening.

The above illustration shows two different common pocket shapes. Image at left is the patch pocket on the L'il Red Riding Hoodie (page 152). Image on opposite page shows the planned welt pockets featured in the City Coat (page 224).

STEEKED WELT POCKET

This pocket requires only a little bit more yarn, and may sometimes be what Elizabeth Zimmermann called an "afterthought pocket." Mark each pocket welt with pins; reinforce the edges with machine stitching or a crochet chain, and cut the gash. Pick up stitches for the pocket welt at the edge that will be in front of the hand. Knit a flat texture for the welt and sew its edges down. Sew a matching plain fabric pocket bag to the back to keep the look light. If the yarn is a finer gauge, you might knit the backing out of the same yarn, but I don't recommend this for heavier fabrics, because then you'll see the bulk under the finished pocket.

If machine stitching frightens you (and that's OK—it *is* scary to do!) consider using the crochet chain to reinforce your pocket before you cut. Leave at least four stitches in between the chain edges so the yarn ends aren't too short; otherwise, they might wriggle free when you cut.

BUTTON BANDS

As you may have noticed, I'm a huge fan of zippers. They are sexy and punk rock, and they add minimal bulk to a sweater. I'm a busty girl myself, so I stay as far away from buttoned sweaters as I can, since they seem to gap at the bosom, lose their buttons, or make me look like Mr. Rogers in drag. However, because I know others are built differently, I will illustrate here how to install a button band. Button bands are not difficult to add, even if they aren't written into the pattern.

BUTTONS DICTATE BAND WIDTH

A button large enough to close a sweater should be at least ¾" (2cm) in diameter, and the button band should be wider than the buttons. In fact, button bands should be wide enough to overlap without making the sweater any tighter, since you've knit the sweater to fit yourself perfectly, no? The wider the band, the less likely the sweater is to gap at the bustline. See L'il Red Riding Hoodie (page 152) for an example of a sweater pattern written for either a button band or a zipper. Notice that the button bands are 1½ times the width of the zipper bands to provide enough overlap to securely fasten the buttons.

CALCULATE

To calculate how many stitches to pick up for a top-down sweater, simply multiply the number of edge stitches by 1½ and knit that number of stitches on both sides of the front. Place the buttonholes every 2½" (6cm) apart or closer, on the left front for a woman, right front for a man. Any farther than 2½" (6cm) and you are likely to have a gap problem. Buttons on sweaters work best if the buttonholes are horizontal. A vertical buttonhole is likely to stretch into an oval shape and let go of its button. Remember to use ribbing, garter stitch or another flat texture with the same row gauge as the sweater. Otherwise your button band will not lie flat enough to button up. If the row gauge is not the same, your band will either ruffle or cause the edge to be too tight.

SMALL BUTTONHOLES

On the buttonhole row, work a decrease, then a yo or a yoyo. If you choose a yoyo for a bigger button, be sure to decrease again after the yoyo to keep your stitch count on track.

LARGE BUTTONHOLES

For larger buttonholes, bind off a few stitches. Place a button on the band and count how many stitches wide (=x) that button is, rounding down if there's a half-stitch in the count. Also note how many stitches are remaining on each side (=y). On the buttonhole row, knit y stitches, then bind off x stitches, then knit y stitches again. On the following row, when you reach the buttonhole gap, use the loop cast on or knitted cast on to make x new stitches to close up the hole.

fix your mistakes

When you finish your lovely garments, you want to burst out the door and show everyone, maybe even sashay down the aisle of the supermarket like it's a fashion runway. But that awful wire hanger that gets caught in a stitch before you even leave the house can leave you snagged and deflated like a soufflé. But don't worry, Sweetie—where there is a will there is a way!

Sometimes you'll catch a mistake while the piece is still on the needles. Other times, some trauma may befall your piece, calling for a little TLC to get it back into fashion circulation. Once you are armed with these finishing skills, you will have the ability to combine them in unusual ways so you can perform knitting surgeries without ripping out hard-won stitches.

SNAGS

Snags should, of course, be avoided, but they *can* be fixed. With your basic understanding of how knitted fabric is formed, you already know that every stitch is linked to those around it. Cutting any one stitch can cause a hole to grow and grow. So instead of cutting, tease the snag back into place. As long as the snag is small and the fabric sturdy, you can use the easy snag fix. But don't worry if it's not: I'll also show you ways to fix trickier snags and split snags.

EASY SNAG FIX

This trick works best with minor snags. First make sure the snag is not twisted or tangled; if it is, untwist or detangle. Gently stretch the fabric to the left and right of the snag. Repeat the gentle stretch from top and bottom. Now switch back to the side-to-side stretch, then the top-to-bottom one. Repeat until the snag is gone.

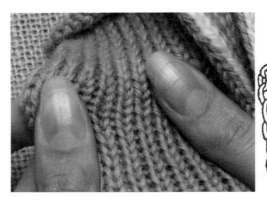

figure 1

TRICKY SNAG FIX

If the fabric is very fine or the snag is very large (or both), arm yourself with a tool such as a knitting needle or crochet hook. The finer the yarn, the finer the tool should be. I usually use a knitting needle of the same gauge I used to knit the sweater. A blunt tip is ideal. Untwist the snag if necessary, then insert the tool under the loop of yarn next to the snagged loop. Gently pull half of the snag into the adjacent loop (figure 1). Move the tool to the stitch on the opposite side of the snag and pull the remaining half of the snag through it. Pull the extra yarn through adjacent stitches in this manner until you have eased out the entire snag (figure 2).

figure 1

figure 2

SPLIT SNAG FIX

Choose a crochet hook that is the appropriate size for the yarn involved. Insert the hook from behind and pull the snag through to the back to hide it (figure 3).

figure 3

DROPPED STITCHES

If you've knit one or two rows since dropping the stitch, it's best to rip back to the point of the mistake. If you've knit several rows since the drop, that stitch's yarn is missing. If this happened in a spot that's hidden in the finished garment (i.e. underarm) you can steal the yarn from in between the stitches on either side of the dropped stitch, but this can really tighten up the surrounding stitches. If it's only a couple of rows, you can pick the stitch back up with a crochet hook, then distribute the tightness from that missing yarn to the surrounding stitches.

ONE HOOK STITCH

Work on the knit side whenever possible. Insert your crochet hook into the last knit stitch, then hook the next loop above it and pull it through.

TWO WORK BACK TO CURRENT ROW

Repeat step 1 until you've picked up the dropped stitch through all the rows.

THREE SLIDE STITCH BACK ON NEEDLE

Slide the picked-up stitch back onto the right-hand needle.

RIPPING

Also known on the Web as frogging...rip it, rip it...ripping is simply undoing stitches. If you've already knit a few rows or a few inches before you catch an error, all is not lost! This next part is a little scary, but also exciting, because it liberates you from your mistakes. If you need to go back just a few stitches or just one row, simply knit backwards.

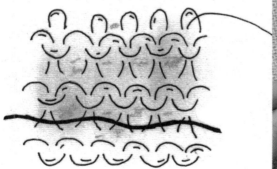

ONE WEAVE IN LIFELINE, RIP STITCHES

With a darning needle or crochet hook, pull a piece of fine scrap yarn through every stitch in the row below your mistake, with the right leg of the stitch in front of the needle, and the left leg behind. Rip out the stitches.

TWO REPLACE STITCHES ON NEEDLE

Insert the needle into the first stitch, making sure the right leg of the stitch goes in front of the needle, and the left leg behind. Repeat until every stitch is back on the needle. Pull out the lifeline if you've used one.

THE PROJECTS

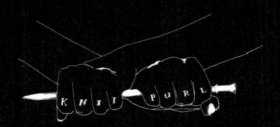

Without further ado, I bring you my dear, beloved
projects. What kind of DomiKNITrix would I be
if I didn't share some of my best designs? Each
one of these projects is like a child I nurtured
from a babe. Some sprouted up full blown and
turned out exactly as I'd thought they would, like
the L'il Red Riding Hoodie (page 152) and Sweetheart (page 184). Others required constant super-
vision and frequent punishment, like the Elfin
Bride and Gothlet (page 236) and the Devil Hat
(page 138)—the devil's in the details, after all!

Most of these developed on the needles, since
my favorite way to design is to knit and see what
happens. I wait for the yarn to tell me what it
wants to be. Of course, I'm in control, but the results are grander if the yarn has a little influence.

This is your reward for taking my lashing and
studying the techniques. This is your opportunity
to put what you've learned to the test. Enough of
the slap and tickle—let's get to the real meat!

YOU'VE GOT SKILLS
GO AHEAD, BITE OFF MORE THAN YOU CAN CHEW

I've graded the skill level involved to create each project, as well as provided a description of what each skill level means. One knitter's "easy" rates "difficult" for another, so I think it's helpful to tell you exactly what you need to know to start each project. I also include what new techniques you may learn while making each. These techniques are listed in the order they are used so you can study up. And once you know the techniques for any given project, you can use what you've learned to boot-strap another more challenging project later.

skill level

NOVICE

YOU JUST NEED TO KNOW THE BARE MINIMUM TO COMPLETE A NOVICE PROJECT. SIMPLE CAST ON, KNIT, PURL AND BIND OFF IS ALL IT TAKES, PLUS BASIC INCREASES AND DECREASES, SLIP STITCH EDGING, AND KNITTING AN I-CORD. YOU'LL NOTICE I'VE SET THE BAR RATHER HIGH, EVEN FOR "NOVICES."

APPRENTICE

YOU'LL NEED A FEW MORE ADVANCED TECHNIQUES IN YOUR REPERTOIRE TO TACKLE AN APPRENTICE PROJECT. MAKE SURE YOU KNOW HOW TO DO SHORT ROW SHAPING, AND BE FAMILIAR WITH MATTRESS AND KITCHENER STITCHES, WEAVING IN ENDS, FELTING AND INTARSIA.

DOMIKNITRIX

WELL ON YOUR WAY TO BECOMING A DOMIKNITRIX, ARE YOU? YOU'D BETTER HAVE THE SKILLS TO BACK IT UP. KNOW PICKING UP STITCHES, LACE KNITTING, TWISTED KNITTING AND STRANDED TWO-COLOR KNITTING.

size matters
KNOW YOUR SHAPE AND LOVE IT

Since well-fitted clothing is a cornerstone of the DomiKNITrix way of life, it behooves you to understand the way sizing is handled in the patterns before you get started. I know you're chomping at the bit to have stitches on your needles, but just remember…discipline is sexy and frogging is not.

SIZING FOR GARMENTS

Both sizes and relative stitch counts are represented as XS (S, M, L, XL). Stitch count is always taken at the end of the row, but it is not given for any short rows. XS, S, M, L and XL represent the varying number of sts for any particular operation based on size. If only one number is given, it is the same for all sizes. Occasionally, sizing rows are included, and these row numbers are not changed in the row count.

If no marking, the instructions are consistent across all sizes.

WOMEN'S MEASUREMENTS
Size to fit your bust-waist-hip
(in inches [and centimeters])

EXTRA SMALL: 34-26-38 [86-66-97]
SMALL: 36-28-40 [91-71-102]
MEDIUM: 38-30-42 [97-76-107]
LARGE: 40-32-44 [102-81-112]
EXTRA LARGE: 43-34-46 [109-86-117]

MEN'S MEASUREMENTS
Size to fit chest, body length and sleeve length
(in inches [and centimeters])

SMALL (MEDIUM, LARGE, EXTRA LARGE)
CHEST: 38 (40, 42, 44) [97, 102, 107, 112]
BODY LENGTH: 26 (26, 26½, 27) [66, 66, 67, 69]
SLEEVE LENGTH: 24½ (25, 25½, 26) [62, 64, 65, 66]

TASTY MORSELS
KNITTING QUICKIES

Sometimes you've just got to do it in public. The tasty projects in this chapter will help you get your stitching jollies nice and quick, and with minimal concentration, to boot.

The Thin Mint Scarf (page 100) and the Valentine Candy Pillows (page 104) are the perfect desserts for your next knitting potluck. Once you grasp knitting a tube on two circular needles, you'll be cranking Thin Mint scarves out by the foot, all the while entertaining your companions with your dizzying intellect. Cover your head without fogging up your brain when you knit the Snood and Spiral Mesh Caps (page 116), though they do demand undivided attention once you begin decreasing at the top.

Of course, there are still plenty of challenges here: The mischievous hats in this section—the Mohawk (page 120) and the Devil and Snow Devil (page 138)—will test your mettle. Sample the goods in this chapter, and you're bound to find something quite tasty indeed.

thin MINT scarf

FORMER GIRL SCOUTS, IT'S TIME TO
PLEDGE YOUR ALLEGIANCE to knitting! This
offbeat scarf is indeed a tasty morsel. Its minty blue and
rich brown colors put me in the mood to have a scoop of ice
cream or a Girl Scout cookie, and though the yarn is delicious, it is fat-free and has zero calories! (Disclaimer: This
project is not edible...but you might just look good enough
to eat wearing it...)

Knitting this tubular scarf on two circular needles is a
fun way to whip through this project, and the nifty diagonal
end gives it a clever edge. This scarf is the closest thing to
easy you'll find in this book.

WHAT YOU WILL LEARN

✘ knitting a tube (page 73)
✘ removing cast-on edge (page 65)
✘ Kitchener stitch (page 80)

YARN

2 hanks (110 yards ea) Alpaca Dream Sport alpaca in espresso by Wildwood Dream (MC)

2 balls (123 yards ea) KnitPicks Merino Style in color 23452 Tidepool (CC)

NEEDLES

two 16" (40cm) size US 6 (4mm) circular needles

NOTIONS

darning needle

GAUGE

24 sts and 28 rows = 4" (10cm) in St st

MEASUREMENTS

58" (147cm) long x 4" (10cm) wide

TERMINOLOGY

Techniques: SSK and k2tog (see page 58)

✖ *read this first* ✖

This is a great project for combining two contrasting yarns of similar gauges. Knit a gauge swatch for the main yarn, then tie on the contrast yarn and knit a few rows to check gauge. Adjust the needle size for the second yarn if the gauge varies. Or keep swatching and you may find that bringing the needle size up or down a bit for both yarns makes a more interesting fabric. You can switch back and forth between two sets of different-sized needles if you're a slave to gauge, or you could relax a bit like I did and let the subtle difference in gauge enhance the look of the scarf. See page 73 in Knitting Directions for instructions on knitting a tube with two circular needles.

This scarf is knit in two separate tubes. Each one begins at the midpoint of the scarf and ends at the pointed end. The halves of the scarf are grafted together with Kitchener stitch at the end (see page 80 in Tying Up).

SCARF HALVES (MAKE 2)

Using MC, cast on 48 sts using loop cast on and one circular needle. Sl 24 sts to a second circular needle of the same size. Fold the row in half so that 24 sts are on each needle and join, being careful not to twist sts. You will be knitting 24 sts using both ends of one needle, then the other 24 sts with both ends of the other needle. The first cast-on sts will be the first sts to knit.

WIDE STRIPE RND 1: * k24, turn work, slide working needle into place; rep from * to complete rnd. Rep rnd 15 times more (16 rnds total).

NARROW STRIPE: Join CC and rep Rnd 1 eight times.

Rep striping pattern until scarf half is approx 29" (74cm), or half the desired length, ending either 4 rows before the end of the wide stripe, or 4 rows after the beg of the wide stripe.

SCARF TIP

Cont changing colors as for main part of scarf.

DEC RND 1: Knit to 2 sts before end of first needle, SSK, turn work, knit to 2 sts before end of 2nd needle, k2tog—46 sts.

Rep Dec Rnd 1 until 2 sts rem on each needle—4 sts.

NEXT DEC RND: SSK, turn work, k2tog—2 sts.

NEXT DEC RND: SSK, pull yarn end through.

Weave in ends. Rep for second half of scarf, reversing the colors used.

FINISHING

When both halves of the scarf are complete, remove the cast-on row for each piece (see page 65) and graft the two pieces together at the cast-on edges with Kitchener stitch (see page 80).

VALENTINE CANDY PILLOWS

skill level
APPRENTICE

REMEMBER THOSE CHALKY LITTLE VAL-
ENTINE CANDIES you were willing to kick a boy down
a flight of stairs for? Those silly little hearts always had the
same antiquated phrases on them, like "DIG ME" or "BE
MINE." Yawn. To them I say, "BITE ME!" Who says ro-
mance has to be saccharine-sweet? Dare to be devilish.
And delicious.

Each of these bite-sized pillows knits up in only a
couple of hours. Embroidering your personalized message
is a lot of fun, and the sky's the limit. Be as naughty as you
like! Keep what you make for yourself, or give one away with
a choice message.

WHAT YOU WILL LEARN
✘ lifted (raised) increases (page 56)
✘ mirrored decreases (page 58)
✘ mattress stitch (page 78)
✘ Kitchener stitch (page 80)
✘ basic embroidery

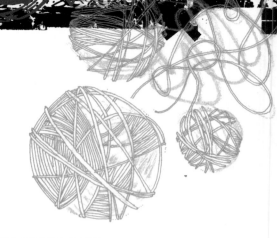

YARN

2 balls (50g each) of Goa by Muench (50% cotton, 50% acrylic) to make one pillow

Or substitute any bulky yarn.

NEEDLES

size US 10 (6mm) needles

If necessary, change needle size to obtain gauge.

NOTIONS

Baby Ull fine wool yarn from Dalegarn in color 4227 red for embroidery

darning needle

GAUGE

15 sts and 22 rows = 4" (10cm) in St st

**Gauge is tighter than recommended. Gauge recommended on ball band is 13 sts and 19 rows = 4" (10cm) on size US 8–10 (5mm–6mm) needles.

MEASUREMENTS

Pattern makes a pillow approx 7" to 8" (18 to 20cm) wide. Size of batting influences finished dimensions. Knitting will stretch to accommodate batting.

TERMINOLOGY

RLI (right lifted increase): Lift first leg of st below next st onto needle and knit this st (see page 56).

LLI (left lifted increase): Lift last leg below last knitted st onto needle and knit this st (see page 56).

SSP (slip 2, purl 2 together through back loops): Slip 2 sts, 1 at a time, to right needle as if to knit. Insert the right needle behind the left needle from left to right into the second st and then the first st and purl the 2 sts tog as 1 (see page 60).

Other techniques: k2tog and SSK (see page 58)

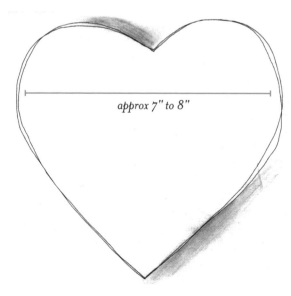

approx 7" to 8"

HEART (MAKE TWO)

Cast on 5 sts using long tail style.

ROW 1 AND ALL WS ROWS UNLESS OTHERWISE INDICATED: Purl.

ROW 2: k1, RLI, k3, LLI, k1—7 sts.

ROW 4: k1, RLI, k5, LLI, k1—9 sts.

ROW 6: k1, RLI, k1, RLI, k5, LLI, k1, LLI, k1—13 sts.

ROW 8: k1, RLI, knit to last st, LLI, k1—15 sts.

Rep Row 8 every RS row to 29 sts.

ROW 24: Knit.

ROW 26: k1, RLI, k27, LLI, k1—31 sts.

ROWS 28 AND 30: Knit.

ROW 32: k1, RLI, k29, LLI, k1—33 sts.

ROWS 34 AND 36: Knit.

ROW 38: k1, SSK, k27, k2tog, k1—31 sts.

ROW 40: k1, SSK, k25, k2tog, k1—29 sts.

ROW 41: p1, p2tog, p8, SSP, p3, p2tog, p8, SSP, p1—25 sts.

ROW 42: k1, SSK, k8, bind off 3 sts, knit to last 3 sts, k2tog, k1—10 sts left needle, 10 sts right needle.

SHAPE HEART TOP
LEFT SIDE

With WS facing, work as follows:

ROW 43: p1, p2tog, p7—9 sts.

ROW 44: sl 1, SSK, k3, k2tog, k1—7 sts.

ROW 45: p1, p2tog, p1, SSP, p1—5 sts.

ROW 46: sl2, pass first st over second st, k2tog, k1—3 sts.

Use a crochet hook to pull the yarn through sts in this order (1–3 being left to right): 2, 3, 1.

RIGHT SIDE

With WS facing, join new yarn at center of heart and shape rem side as follows:

ROW 43: p7, SSP, p1—9 sts.

ROW 44: k1, SSK, k3, k2tog, k1—7 sts.

ROW 45: p1, p2tog, p1, SSP, p1—5 sts.

ROW 46: k1, SSK, sl final st on left needle over next st to be knitted—3 sts.

Use a crochet hook to pull the yarn through sts in this order (1–3 being left to right): 2, 3, 1.

note:

To knit a slightly smaller pillow, cast on 3 sts instead of 5, and leave out Rows 36–37 as given in the pattern. Knit the side strip to 24" (61cm) long. The "Bite Me" heart pictured was knit to those smaller dimensions.

SIDE STRIP

Cast on 10 sts. Knit in Stockinette for 26" (66cm). Bind off, leaving a long yarn tail for sewing up.

ASSEMBLY
SEW PIECES OF HEART TOGETHER

Using mattress stitch worked at the edge (see page 78), begin by stitching the side strip along the edge of one heart piece, starting at the bottom of the heart and working up one side. Cont in mattress stitch all the way around the heart until the end of the straight piece meets its opposite end at the bottom of the heart. Graft the edges together with Kitchener stitch (see page 80).

Align the second heart piece symmetrically with the first side, starting at the bottom of the heart. Use mattress stitch to graft the curved top of the heart as invisibly as possible and hide the yarn ends inside the pillow. Leave one side of the heart open.

note:

As you stitch around the heart, you will notice that the stitch must jog one-half stitch to one side at the widest part of the heart, when the rounded side changes from increasing to decreasing. Look carefully to be sure you are still seaming together the legs of the sts that look like this: \ and /. If you seam together 2 legs leaning in the same direction, you need to jog one-half stitch over on one side until you reach the opposite rounded side of the heart. Try to stay as close to the edge sts as possible as you negotiate the curves.

STUFF HEART

Cut out 4 to 5 pieces of 1" (3cm)-thick batting. Stuff the pillow with enough layers of batting to get the desired fluff. Sew final seam with mattress stitch. Leave a small gap open until you have finished embroidering your message so you can knot loose yarn ends inside the pillow.

EMBROIDER HEART

Begin by outlining the first and last letters of the first word onto front of heart with embroidery yarn. Then outline remaining letters. For lettering as shown, most letters are 5 sts wide. Narrow letters such as "I" are 3 sts wide, and wider letters such as "M" and "W" are 7 sts across. Leave 1 free st between each letter, or as little as half of a stitch to fit a longer word. Leave at least 2 rows of sts between lines of text.

Once phrase is outlined, stitch loose lines diagonally criss-crossing each outline. Then weave the yarn in between the framework sts (under-over, under-over) to create a solid block of color inside each letter. Straight letters look like woven fabric on top of the knitting. Curved letters are a little trickier, and may look better filled in with a basic satin stitch. When you run short of embroidery yarn, push your darning needle inside the pillow and make a few stitches at the back of the work to secure the yarn end.

You may choose to embroider any phrase you like. Other ideas include: Bad Boy, Bad Girl, Naughty.

FLOWER PinS

skill level

APPRENTICE

THESE LOVELY FLOWERS OFFER A SASSY
FEMININE TAKE on the traditionally male bouton-
niere. And they don't wilt. Pin them where you will and go
on about your business. Wear as many or as few as you like.

They're so easy and quick to make, you can put your
knitting on auto-pilot after you've finished a few petals.
Your mind will be free to wander. Or stick yarn and needles
for this project in your knitting bag to whip out when you
want to be a knitting social butterfly. Keep one eye on your
knitting and the other on the conversation.

WHAT YOU WILL LEARN
✘ lifted (raised) increases (page 56)
✘ mirrored decreases (page 58)
✘ slip stitch edge (page 66)
✘ I-cord (page 72)
✘ felting

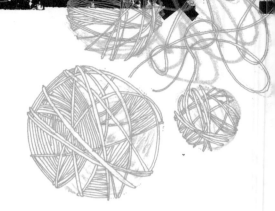

YARN

1 to 6 skeins Noro Kureyon 100% wool yarn (110 yards ea) in color 115 variegated reds and greens

NEEDLES

size US 9 (5.5mm) needles

size US 9 (5.5mm) DPNs

If necessary, change needle size to obtain gauge.

NOTIONS

sewing thread to match yarn

long hand-sewing needle

pin backs at least 1" (3cm) in length

floral wire for stem or for shaping petals (optional)

GAUGE

16 sts and 24 rows = 4" (10cm) in St st

**Gauge is not terribly important in this design since the petals are felted. A fairly loose gauge works best.

✖ *read this first* ✖

I used six balls of yarn in variegated shades of red and green, then selectively snipped the bits of color I wanted from them. I used green/ brown sections for the leaves and red sections for the petals. You might also choose to make a more rainbow-colored flower, which would require less yarn.

TERMINOLOGY

RLI (right lifted increase): Lift first leg of st below next st onto needle and knit this st (see page 56).

LLI (left lifted increase): Lift last leg below last knitted st onto needle and knit this st (see page 56).

sl 1 wyif (slip 1 with yarn in front): Slip the first st of the row while holding the yarn in front. This creates a tighter edge that allows the petal to curve naturally.

sl 1 wyib (slip 1 with yarn in back): Slip the first st of the row while holding the yarn in back.

sl2-k1-psso (slip 2, k1, psso): Slip 2 sts tog knitwise, k1, pass the 2 slipped sts over the knitted st. This double decrease shows the center st on top.

p3tog (purl 3 together): Slide the right-hand needle into the next 3 sts on the needle as if to purl. Purl all 3 sts tog as 1, just as for p2tog.

k3tog (knit 3 together): Slide the right-hand needle into the next 3 sts on the needle as if to knit. Knit all 3 sts tog as 1, just as for k2tog.

psso: Pass slipped st(s) over.

Other techniques: SSK and k2tog (see page 58)

note:

For all petals and leaf: sl first st on even rows wyif and on odd rows wyib.

FLOWER PETALS

ELONGATED POINTED PETAL FOR LILY (MAKE 7)

Cast on 5 sts.

ROW 1: k1, p3, k1.

ROW 2: sl 1, k1, RLI, k1, LLI, k1, p1—7 sts.

ROW 3: sl 1, p5, k1.

ROW 4: sl 1, k5, p1.

ROW 5: Rep Row 3.

ROW 6: sl 1, k2, RLI, k1, LLI, k2, p1—9 sts.

ROWS 7, 9 AND 11: sl 1, p7, k1.

ROWS 8 AND 10: sl 1, k7, p1.

ROW 12: sl 1, k2, sl2-k1-psso, k2, p1—7 sts.

ROW 13: sl 1, p5, k1.

ROW 14: sl 1, k5, p1.

For longer petals, rep Rows 13–14 one or two more times.

ROW 15: Rep Row 13.

ROW 16: sl 1, k1, sl2-k1-psso, k1, p1—5 sts.

ROW 17: sl 1, p3, k1.

ROW 18: sl 1, k3, p1.

ROW 19: Rep Row 17.

ROW 20: sl 1, sl2-k1-psso, p1—3 sts.

ROW 21: sl 1, p1, k1.

ROW 22: sl2-k1-psso, pull yarn end through.

ROUND PETAL FOR INNER ROSE AND CAMELLIA (MAKE AT LEAST 4 FOR BUD ROSE OR 9 FOR BLOOMING ROSE)

Cast on 7 sts.

ROW 1: k1, p5, k1.

ROW 2: sl 1, RLI, k5, LLI, p1—9 sts.

ROW 3: sl 1, p7, k1.

ROW 4: sl 1, k3, RLI, k1, LLI, k3, p1—11 sts.

ROW 5: sl 1, p9, k1.

ROW 6: sl 1, k9, p1.

ROW 7: Rep Row 5.

ROW 8: sl 1, k3, sl2-k1-psso, k3, p1—9 sts.

ROW 9: sl 1, p7, k1.

ROW 10: sl 1, SSK, k3, k2tog, p1—7 sts.

ROW 11: sl 1, p5, k1.

ROW 12: sl 1, SSK, psso, k2tog, pass first st on right needle over second st, bind off rem sts.

BLUNT OUTER PETAL FOR ROSE (MAKE 5 TO 7)

Work as for round petals for inner rose and camellia through Row 9—9 sts.

ROW 10: sl 1, k7, p1.

ROW 11: sl 1, p7, k1.

ROW 12: sl 1, SSK, k3, k2tog, p1—7 sts.

ROW 13: sl 1, k1, psso, bind off rem sts.

HEART-SHAPED PETAL FOR CAMELLIA OR FOR MIDDLE PETALS OF ROSE (MAKE A MULTIPLE OF 4 PLUS 1 FOR CENTER FOR CAMELLIA OR MAKE 3–5 FOR ROSE)

Work as for round petals for inner rose and camellia through Row 9—9 sts.

ROW 10: sl 1, SSK, k1, sl 1, k1, k2tog, p1—7 sts.

ROW 11: sl 1, p5, k1.

ROW 12: sl 1, SSK, psso, k1, pass first st on right needle over second st, k2tog, pass first st on right needle over second st, bind off last st.

LEAVES AND STEMS
LEAF FOR ROSE AND CAMELLIA

Work as for round petals for inner rose and camellia through Row 9—9 sts.

ROW 10: sl 1, k7, p1.

ROW 11: sl 1, p7, k1.

ROW 12: sl 1, k2, sl2-k1-psso, k2, p1—7 sts.

ROW 13: sl 1, p5, k1.

ROW 14: sl 1, k1, sl2-k1-psso, k1, p1—5 sts.

ROW 15: sl 1, p3tog, k1—3 sts.

ROW 16: k3tog, pull yarn end through.

I-CORD STEM

Using DPNs, cast on 3 sts and knit. Slide sts to other end of needle wyib and k3. Rep until stem is desired length, then bind off and draw the yarn end inside the stem. (See page 72 in the Knitting Directions chapter for step-by-step instructions on making an I-cord.)

ASSEMBLY
FELTING

Before sewing the flowers together, toss all of the petals, leaves and stems into a pillow case or lingerie bag, tie it securely shut, and put it through the washer. If you leave the knitted pieces loose, they will collect lint and leave their colorful lint on the rest of your wash. I recommend selecting a load of dark wash with items that won't shed fiber to prevent color from bleeding onto your laundry, and to

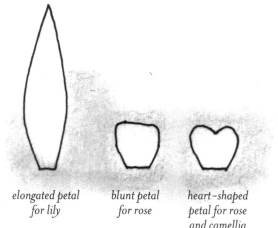

elongated petal
for lily

blunt petal
for rose

heart-shaped
petal for rose
and camellia

prevent pills from felting into your petals. Check the petals after they come out of the wash to see if they have felted to your satisfaction. One wash and dry should felt them nicely. However, if you want them to felt and shrink more, throw the bag into the dryer.

Snip off any loose yarn ends. Assemble each flower as indicated. If desired, floral wire may be inserted inside the I-cord stems and sewn onto the backs of the petals to help them hold their shape. Sew on a pin back or barrette clip, or just use a hatpin with end-cap to secure to lapel or elsewhere.

LILY

Roll one felted elongated pointed petal tightly, knit side facing out, to create the center of the flower, and secure the roll with needle and thread. Sew the rem 6 felted petals arrayed symmetrically around the core petal with knit sides facing the center and the purl sides facing out.

ROSE

To make a bud rose, use 4 round petals, and to make a blooming rose, use a minimum of 9 round petals. The more petals, the bigger the bloom. Tightly roll up a central petal and secure the roll with needle and thread. Place the next petal at the edge of the rolled petal and sew it on with the knit side facing the center and the purl side facing out. When sewn together with purl sides facing out, the petals curl in naturally just like real rose petals. Repeat until your rose is the desired size. Finish by sewing on at least one green leaf and a stem, if desired.

CAMELLIA

Tightly roll up a central petal and secure the roll with needle and thread. Arrange 4 heart-shaped petals in an X shape with the cast-on edges toward the center, knit side up. Sew the petals' side edges together in a flat shape, then sew the central petal erect in the center. For a larger flower, add one more layer of 4 petals, spacing them in between the first layer and spread out a bit more. When sewn together with knit sides up, the petals curl out naturally in the open shape of a camellia. Sew 2 green leaves together behind the flower to complete the Chanel look.

snood
+ SPiRAL MeSH CAP

skill level

ĐOMIᴙNITᴙIX

THE SNOOD'S POPULARITY DATES BACK
TO RENAISSANCE TIMES, when it was worn by
servants and nobles alike. During the Victorian period the
snood experienced a revival, and it cropped up again in the
40s. Maybe you'll be the trendsetter who helps bring it back
in the new millennium.

Whether worn by a Medieval damsel locked away in a
castle tower or by a modern Millie at the grocery store, the
snood is an elegant head covering for those days when you
want to cover your head and still look like you stepped out of
a painting. Tuck your hair inside the cap for a vintage look.

WHAT YOU WILL LEARN

✘ working in the round (page 52)
✘ picot edging
✘ simple lace (page 63)
✘ double-pointed needles (page 54)

YARN

2 balls (90 yards ea) of Crystal Palace Shimmer acrylic/nylon blend yarn in color 1737 black for Snood

2 balls (90 yards ea) of Crystal Palace Shimmer acrylic/nylon blend yarn in color 2848 periwinkle for Spiral Mesh Cap

NEEDLES

16" (40cm) size US 9 (5.5mm) circular needle

size US 9 (5.5mm) DPNs

If necessary, change needle size to obtain gauge.

NOTIONS

2 colors of ring stitch markers

darning needle

GAUGE

14 sts = 4" (10cm) in St st

MEASUREMENTS

Snood to fit sizes Medium (23" [58cm]) and Large (23½" [60cm]); Spiral Mesh Cap to fit sizes Small (21½" [55cm]), Medium and Large

✖ *read this first* ✖

Note that the mesh may be made with SSK instead of k2tog, which results in lines spiraling in the opposite direction. Combination knitters will want to do it this way, since the combination-style SSK is the same as the standard continental knitter's k2tog (that means easier!). Also, if you are trying to improve your SSK, there's no faster way than to knit the whole cap with it.

TERMINOLOGY

PM (place marker): Slide a ring marker onto the needle whenever the pattern calls for you to place a marker. When you come to the marker on subsequent rows, simply work the st before it, slip the marker, and work the subsequent st.

k3tog (knit 3 together): Slide the right-hand needle into the next 3 sts on the needle as if to knit. Knit all 3 sts tog as 1, just as for k2tog.

k4tog (knit 4 together): Slide the right-hand needle into the next 4 sts on the needle as if to knit. Knit all 4 sts tog as 1, just as for k2tog or k3tog.

[ ] (repeat operation): Rep operation in brackets the number of times indicated.

Other techniques: yo (see page 63), k2tog (see page 58)

SNOOD AND SPIRAL MESH CAPS

notes:

- *Use a different-colored marker at end of rnd than other markers.*
- *Change to DPNs when necessary.*
- *Snood is in parentheses, Spiral Mesh Cap is in brackets in gray. If only one set of numbers, it applies to all sizes or both versions.*
- *For ease in working, circle the numbers for your size.*

side view of snood and spiral mesh cap

top of spiral mesh cap

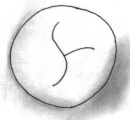

top of snood

PICOT BAND

Cast on 72 (80) [64, 72, 80] sts. PM and join for working in the rnd, taking care not to twist sts.

RNDS 1–3: Knit.

RND 4: [yo, k2tog] to end of rnd.

RNDS 5–8: Knit.

RND 9: Fold picot band in half so knit sts are on the outside. Lift first st from cast-on row and knit it tog with the st on the needle. Rep with each foll st to marker to face the band all around.

MAIN SECTION

RND 10: [yo, k2tog] to end.

RND 11: Knit, PM every 18 (20) [16, 18, 20] sts.

note:

If knitting Spiral Mesh Cap, skip to end of Crown Shaping instructions.

SNOOD ONLY

RND 12: [yo, k2, * yo, k2tog; rep from * to marker] 3 times, [yo, k2tog] to end—75 (83) sts.

If you knit your picot edging very nicely, you may even opt to wear the cap inside out, as shown here.

RND 13: Knit.

RND 14: [yo, k1, * yo, k2tog; rep from * to marker] 3 times, [yo, k2tog] to end—78 (86) sts.

RNDS 15–30: Rep Rnds 11–14 four times—102 (110) sts at end of Rnd 30.

CROWN SHAPING

RND 31 AND ALL ODD RNDS THROUGH RND 41: Knit.

RND 32: [* yo, k2tog; rep from * to 4 sts before marker, k4tog] twice, * yo, k2tog; rep from * to last 4 sts removing third marker, k4tog—93 (101) sts.

RND 34: [* yo, k2tog; rep from * to 3 sts before marker, k3tog] 3 times—87 (95) sts.

RND 36: [* yo, k2tog; rep from * to 3 sts before marker, k3tog] twice, * yo, k2tog; rep from * to last 3 sts, yo, k3tog—82 (90) sts.

RND 38: [* yo, k2tog; rep from * to 3 sts before marker, k3tog] twice, [yo, k2tog] 10 (11) times, PM, [yo, k2tog] to end—78 (86) sts.

RND 40: [* yo, k2tog; rep from * to 3 sts before marker, k3tog] twice, [* yo, k2tog; rep from * to 4 sts before marker, k4tog] twice—68 (76) sts.

MESH CAP ONLY

RNDS 12–35: Rep Rnds 10–11 twelve times more.

RND 36: [* yo, k2tog; rep from * to 4 sts before marker, k4tog] 4 times—[52, 60, 68] sts.

TOP OF CAPS
(FOR BOTH SNOOD AND SPIRAL MESH)

NEXT RND: Knit.

NEXT (DEC) RND: [* yo, k2tog; rep from * to 3 sts before marker, k3tog] 4 times—60 (68) [44, 52, 60] sts.

Rep last 2 rnds to 20 sts (5 sts in each section).

NEXT RND: Knit.

NEXT RND: [yo, k2tog, k3tog] 4 times—12 sts.

NEXT RND: [k2tog] 6 times—6 sts. Slide sts to other end of needle, holding yarn in back. Bring working yarn over front of left needle from behind and pass the sts over this yarn one at a time as if binding off, then pull the loop through so the cut end passes through to hold the sts.

FINISHING

Using a yarn needle, pull the yarn end down to the other side in the most inconspicuous way possible and run the yarn end in along one of the spiraling ribs to hide it.

mohawk Hat

skill level

DOMIKNITRIX

IF YOU'VE ALWAYS SECRETLY WANTED TO
WEAR A MOHAWK, BUT SHAVING the sides of
your head seemed too, well, drastic, this just might be the
headgear for you. This fancy-pants faux-hawk lets you make
all the statement you want with none of the stubble or up-
keep. There's no need to dip it in egg whites or use a whole
can of Aqua Net to stand it up; this yarn has a life of its own.

This hat is a real showstopper, and it will keep your
head warmer than a real Mohawk, that's for sure! Feel free
to change up the colors and let your hair live vicariously
through its yarn counterpart.

WHAT YOU WILL LEARN

✘ symmetrical increases and
decreases (pages 56–60)
✘ picking up stitches (page 64)
✘ fringe

YARN

2 balls (110 yards ea) of Lamb's Pride bulky super-wash wool in color SW05 Onyx

1 ball (190 yards ea) of Lamb's Pride bulky wool/mohair blend yarn in color M120 Limeade

Or substitute a single-ply bulky yarn, not a plied yarn that could develop split ends.

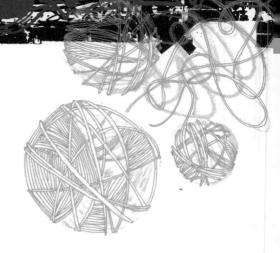

NEEDLES

24" (60cm) size US 9 (5.5mm) circular needle

Change needle size to obtain gauge, if necessary.

NOTIONS

short flexible stitch holders

2 stitch markers

crochet hook

GAUGE

16 sts and 24 rows = 4" (10cm) in St st

**Gauge is intentionally tight. Gauge recommended on ball band is 14 sts = 4" (10cm) on size US 10–10½ (6mm–6.5mm) needles.

MEASUREMENTS

to fit sizes Small (21" [54cm]), Medium (22½" [57cm]) and Large (23½" [60cm])

✖ read this first ✖

Be sure to keep the edge stitches tight. Lifted increases give the best results with this pattern. Choose other increases at your own risk. Here's how this hat is constructed:

- You will begin by knitting a shaped strip from the point of the widow's peak to the back of the head.
- Then you will pick up stitches at the top of the crown and knit the curved gusset on each side.
- Next you will knit the sides and nape of the hat.
- After the knitting is done, you will apply the bright-colored hair with a crochet hook, as you would fringe.

TERMINOLOGY

RLI (right lifted increase): Lift first leg of st below next st onto needle and knit this st (see page 56).

LLI (left lifted increase): Lift last leg below last knitted st onto needle and knit this st (see page 56).

SSP (slip 2, purl 2 together through back loop): Slip 2 sts 1 at a time as if to knit, insert left needle in back of both sts tog, and pass sts tog back to left needle, then purl 2 tog through the back loops (see page 60).

sl2-k1-psso (slip 2, knit 1, psso): Slip 2 sts together knitwise, k1, pass the 2 slipped sts over the knitted st. This double decrease shows the center st on top.

PM (place marker): Slide a ring marker onto the needle whenever the pattern calls for you to place a marker. When you come to the marker on subsequent rows, simply work the st before it, slip the marker, and work the subsequent st.

psso: Pass slipped st(s) over.

wyif or wyib: With yarn in front or back.

[ ] (repeat operation): Rep operation in brackets the number of times indicated.

Other techniques: SSK (see page 58), k2tog and p2tog (see pages 58 and 60)

WIDOW'S PEAK

Cast on 3 sts using long tail style.

ROW 1: Knit.

ROW 2: p1-k1 in first st, p1, k1-p1 in last st—5 sts.

ROW 3: k1, p1, RLI, PM, k1, LLI, p1, k1—7 sts.

ROW 4 AND REM WS ROWS THROUGH ROW 20: p1, k1, purl to last 2 sts, k1, p1.

ROW 5: K1, p1, RLI, knit to last 2 sts, LLI, p1, k1—9 sts.

ROW 7: k1, p1, RLI, knit to marker, RLI, sl marker, k1, LLI, knit to last 2 sts, LLI, p1, k1—13 sts.

ROW 8: Rep Row 4.

ROWS 9–20: Rep Rows 5–8 three times—31 sts.

note:
Over the next rows, you will break the sts into 3 groups and separate the 4 sts at each end onto a holder.

ROW 21: k1, p1, RLI, k1, sl these 4 sts to holder, k26, LLI, p1, k1—4 sts on holder, 29 on needle.

ROW 22: p1, k1, p2, sl these 4 sts to holder, p25—4 sts each holder, 25 on needle.

ROW 23: SSK, knit to marker, RLI, sl marker, k1, LLI, knit to last 2 sts, k2tog—25 sts.

ROW 24: p2tog, purl to last 2 sts, SSP—23 sts.

ROW 25: SSK, knit to last 2 sts, k2tog—21 sts.

ROW 26 AND REM WS ROWS: Purl.

ROW 27: Rep Row 23—21 sts.

ROW 29: Rep Row 25—19 sts.

ROW 31: SSK, knit to marker, RLI, sl marker, k1, LLI, knit to last 2 sts, k2tog —19 sts.

ROW 33: Knit.

ROW 34: Purl.

ROWS 35–42: Rep Rows 31–34 twice.

ROW 43: Knit to marker, RLI, sl marker, k1, LLI, knit to end—21 sts.

ROW 45: Knit.

ROW 46: Purl.

ROWS 47–50: Rep Rows 31–34—21 sts.

ROWS 51–54: Rep Rows 43–46—23 sts.

ROW 55: Rep Row 23—23 sts.

Now give the strip a firm stretch before (but not while) measuring it from the point along centerline.

Rep Rows 52–55 until piece measures 11 (12, 13)" 28 (30, 33)cm from beg. End with a RS row. If row 55 would be the last row, knit it plain instead. Sl sts to holder.

GUSSET

note:
Gussets are symmetrical for Small. Medium and Large require separate directions for each side. When picking up sts, pick up 1 st for every 2 rows (see Knitting Directions, page 64).

Fold the strip in half end-to-end and at the fold so back edge is ½" (1cm) away from front edge. Mark center where you will pick up sts for crown. Mark center st on both edges of crown.

RIGHT GUSSET

PREP ROW: With RS facing, pick up and k3 sts before center marker, and 3 sts after it. You now have an equal number of "beads" rem on either side of the picked-up sts—6 sts.

ROW 1: Turn, p6, pick up and p2—8 sts.

ROW 2: Turn, k8, pick up and k2—10 sts.

ROW 3: Turn, p10, pick up and p1 (2, 2)—11 (12, 12) sts.

ROW 4: Turn, k11 (12, 12), pick up and k1 (2, 2)—12 (14, 14) sts.

ROW 5: Turn, p12 (14, 14), pick up and p1—13 (15, 15) sts.

ROW 6: Turn, k13 (15, 15), pick up and k1 (2, 2)—14 (17, 17) sts.

ROW 7: Turn, p14 (17, 17), pick up and p1—15 (18, 18) sts.

LARGE ONLY

ROW 8: Turn, k18, pick up and k1 st at end of row—19 sts.

ROW 9: Turn, p18, sl last st, pick up and p1 st, psso—19 sts.

ROW 10: Turn, k19, pick up and k1—20 sts.

note:

The sl 1, pick up and p1 or k1, psso at the end of the following rows (and in Row 9 above) are actually joining the gusset to the hat and creating a seam perpendicular to the band, which hasn't been knitted yet. The band is created by picking up and knitting or purling a loop from the next "bead" on edge of the center strip, then passing the slipped st over.

ALL SIZES

ROW 8 (8, 11): Turn, k14 (17, 19), sl last st, pick up and k1, psso—15 (18, 20) sts.

ROW 9 (9, 12): Turn, p14 (17, 19), sl last st, pick up and p1, psso—15 (18, 20) sts.

Rep Rows 8–9 (8–9, 11–12) until the gusset is the same length as the back of the hat and the gusset meets the first of the band sts on the holder. End with RS row so yarn meets the sts on the holder. If you do not break the yarn here, you may use it to knit the band next. Place sts on holder.

LEFT GUSSET

For Small, work as for Right Gusset. Work Medium and Large sizes as follows:

PREP ROW (4): Work as for Right Gusset.

ROW 5: Turn, p14, pick up and p2—16 sts.

ROW 6: Turn, k16, pick up and k1—17 sts.

ROW 7: Turn, p17, pick up and p1—18 sts.

LARGE ONLY

ROW 8: Turn, k18, pick up and k1 st—19 sts.

ROW 9: Turn, p19, pick up and p1—20 sts.

ROW 10: Turn, k19, sl last st, pick up and k1, psso—20 sts.

ALL SIZES

Cont as for Right Gusset, ending with a WS row so yarn meets the sts on the holder. If you do not break the yarn here, you may use it to knit the nape next. Place sts on holder. There is a total of 61 (67, 71) sts: 15 (18, 20) sts for each gusset, 23 sts on center holder and 4 sts on holder on each side of center holder.

NAPE

Begin by knitting the edge sts, then turn and cont to knit the back of the hat and edge sts from opposite edge.

ROW 1: From WS of fabric and left side of hat, using the yarn from the gusset in between the sts on hold and the rest of the hat, work the 4 sts from holder as follows: p2, k1, p1.

ROW 2: k1, p1, k1, SSK, knit to last 5 sts, k2tog, k1, p1, k1—59 (65, 69) sts.

ROW 3 AND REM WS ROWS THROUGH ROW 23: p1, k1, purl to last 2 sts, k1, p1.

ROW 4: Rep Row 2—57 (63, 67) sts.

ROW 6: k1, p1, knit to last 2 sts, p1, k1.

ROW 8: Rep Row 2—55 (61, 65) sts.

ROWS 10 AND 12: Rep Row 6.

ROW 14: Rep Row 2—53 (59, 63) sts.

ROW 16: Rep Row 6.

ROW 18: k1, p1, k23 (26, 28), sl2-k1-psso, k23 (26, 28), p1, k1—51 (57, 61) sts.

ROWS 20 AND 22: Rep Row 6.

ROW 23: p1, k10, p29 (35, 39) k10, p1.

ROW 24: k11, SSK, k11 (14, 16), sl2-k1-psso, k11 (14, 16), k2tog, k11—47 (53, 57) sts.

ROW 25: Bind off 11 sts knitwise, p25 (31, 35), k11 very loosely—36 (42, 46) sts.

ROW 26: Bind off the first 10 sts as foll: pull first st tight, then: wyib, sl2 sts, pass the first st over the 2nd st, *wyif, sl 1 and pass the first st over the 2nd st, wyib, sl 1 and pass the first st over the 2nd st; rep from * until 10 sts total have been bound off, k1, psso, p1, k9 (12, 14), sl2-k1-psso, k9 (12, 14), p1, k1—23 (29, 33) sts.

ROW 27 AND REM WS ROWS THROUGH ROW 37: Rep Row 3.

ROWS 28: k1, p1, SSK, knit to last 4 sts, k2tog, p1, k1—21 (27, 31) sts.

ROW 30: Rep Row 28—19 (25, 29) sts.

ROW 32: k1, p1, k6 (9, 11), sl2-k1-psso, k6 (9, 11), p1, k1—17 (23, 27) sts.

ROW 34: Rep Row 28—15 (21, 25) sts.

ROW 36: k1, p1, k4 (7, 9), sl2-k1-psso, k4 (7, 9), p1, k1—13 (19, 23) sts.

MEDIUM AND LARGE ONLY

ROW 38: Rep Row 28—(17, 21) sts.

ROW 40: k1, p1, k(5, 7), sl2-k1-psso, k(5, 7), p1, k1—(15, 19) sts.

ALL SIZES

ROW 38 (42, 42): k1, p1, [SSK] 0 (0, 1) times, k9 (11, 11), [k2tog] 0 (0, 1) time, p1, k1.

ROW 39 (43, 43): p1, knit to last st, p1.

ROW 40 (44, 44): Knit.

ROW 41 (45, 45): Bind off knitwise.

Hat measures 16¾ (17½, 18¼)" 43 (45, 47)cm from widow's peak to base of neck when measured along centerline.

ASSEMBLY
ADD MOHAWK HAIR

Cut 150 3" to 4" (8cm to 10cm) pieces of Lamb's Pride bulky yarn for the hair. Cut hair longer than needed, then give it a haircut for the best Mohawk.

Working on the RS, insert your crochet hook through a knitted st at the front center of hat. Fold a piece of yarn in half and slide the yarn onto the crochet hook at the fold. Pull the fold through the st, creating a loop. Pull the ends of the yarn hair through the loop. Cont hooking hair onto the hat about every few rows, working from the center front to center back. The more densely you place the yarn, the more dramatic the Mohawk effect. Once all the hair is in place, you may choose to give it a trim until you're pleased with the length of your Mohawk. Don't make the Mohawk any wider than 2" (5cm), or the effect won't be as grand. Add hair 5 to 9 rows across, and taper the width at nape of neck.

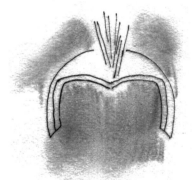

mohawk from front

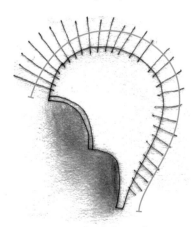

mohawk from side
16¾ (17½, 18¼)" along centerline
from widow's peak to back of neck

STRINGS OF PURLS

YOU DON'T HAVE TO BE AN IVY LEAGUE
GRADUATE TO WEAR a pearl necklace. Just knit up
this versatile novelty, making it into a short or long necklace, a belt or a drawstring cord for a hoodie; be guided by
your whim. Then vamp it up as much or as little as you want.
A string of purls can be just the thing for an informal tank
top or even a little black dress.

I encourage you to experiment with the size of the beads
and the distance between them to create something truly
unique. But don't be fooled that this is an easy project.
Closing up the beads with stuffing inside will teach your
fingers the art of contortion.

WHAT YOU WILL LEARN
✗ double-pointed needles (see page 54)
✗ I-cord (see page 72)
✗ shaping a sphere with increases and decreases

YARN

1 ball (90 yards ea) Crystal Palace Shimmer acrylic/nylon blend yarn in color 1736 white, color 1737 black or any other color of your choice

Or substitute Muench String of Pearls cotton/viscose/polyester blend yarn in color 4001 white, or any yarn with spring to it.

NEEDLES

size US 8 (5mm) DPNs for Crysal Palace yarn

size US 7 (4.5mm) DPNs for Muench yarn

If necessary, change needle size to obtain gauge.

NOTIONS

scrap yarn, cotton balls or other stuffing to fill beads (see Read This First, this page)

darning needle

GAUGE

Many different gauge yarns may be used. Regardless of the yarn selected, use needles 2–4 sizes smaller than recommended on ball band. The projects shown here are knit on needles 3 sizes smaller than recommended.

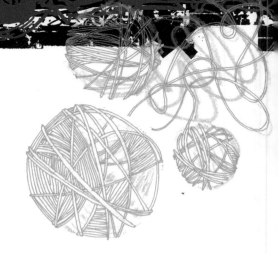

TERMINOLOGY

RLI (right lifted increase): Lift first leg of st below next st onto needle and knit this st (see page 56).

LLI (left lifted increase): Lift last leg below last knitted st onto needle and knit this st (see page 56).

sl2-k1-psso (slip 2, knit 1, pass slipped stitch over): Slip 2 sts tog as if to knit, knit 1, pass 2 slipped sts over the knitted st.

[ ] (repeat operation): Rep operation in brackets the number of times indicated.

Other techniques: SSK and k2tog (see page 58)

✖ *read this first* ✖

Stuffing each bead and then doing double decreases on DPNs while holding in the stuffing can be a real dexterity challenge. Knit one or two practice beads before you embark on this project.

For the stuffing, waste yarn from other projects in similar colors may be used, but roving or a two-ply bulky yarn works best. The finer the yarn, the more likely it will peek out through your stitches. Cotton balls and their synthetic variants also work well.

Just don't forget the beads must be stuffed before you close them up; otherwise there's no way to get anything inside!

I-CORD

With DPN, cast on 3 sts loop style.

RND 1: Knit.

RND 2: Slide sts to opposite end of DPN, pulling yarn tight across back, knit.

Rep Row 2 until cord is desired length before first bead. Stretch cord firmly before (but not while) measuring.

SMALL BEAD

noᴛe:
Work is distributed over 2 DPNs. Knit with a third needle.

RND 1: [RLI, k1, LLI] twice, pick up another DPN and RLI, k1, LLI—9 sts.

RNDS 2–4: Knit.

INSERT STUFFING: Fill bead with 12" (30cm) of super bulky yarn or with a cotton ball or other stuffing. Hold stuffing in place while you knit the next rnd.

RND 5: [sl2-k1-psso] 3 times, knitting all sts onto one DPN—3 sts. Cont working Rnd 2 of I-cord with 2 needles to desired length before next bead.

MEDIUM BEAD

RNDS 1–2: Work Rnds 1–2 as for Small Bead.

RND 3: [RLI, k3] twice; on next needle RLI, k3—12 sts.

RNDS 4–5: Knit.

INSERT STUFFING: Cut an 18" (46cm) length of super bulky yarn and roll it gently into a ball. Insert the ball into the bead firmly and hold it there while you knit the next rnd.

RND 6: [SSK, k2] 3 times—9 sts.

RND 7: Work as for Rnd 5 of Small Bead.

LARGE BEAD

RNDS 1–2: Work Rnds 1–2 as for Small Bead.

RND 3: k1, RLI, k1, LLI, k2, RLI, k1, LLI, k1; on next needle, k1, RLI, k1, LLI, k1—15 sts.

RNDS 4–6: Knit.

INSERT STUFFING: Cut a 24" (61cm) length of super bulky yarn and roll it gently into a ball. Insert the ball into the bead firmly and hold it there while you knit the next rnd.

RND 7: [SSK, k1, SSK] 3 times—9 sts.

RND 8: Work as for Rnd 5 of Small Bead.

KNITTING A LARGE BEAD FIRST

To knit a bead at the beg of the purl necklace, cast on 3 sts and work first rnd as for I-cord.

RNDS 2–9: Work as for Rnds 1–8 of Large Bead.

Be sure to tuck yarn tail inside before knitting it shut.

RND 10: sl2-k1-psso, leaving a single st. Slide st to opposite end of DPN.

RND 11: Pulling yarn tight across back, k1, p1, k1 in single st. Cont working rnd 2 of I-cord with 2 needles to desired length before next bead.

KNITTING A LARGE BEAD LAST

Use the 3 sts rem on the needle from the I-cord to knit a bead at the end of a purl necklace.

RND 1: sl2-k1-psso, leaving a single st. Slide st to opposite end of DPN wyib.

RND 2: Pulling yarn tight across back, k1, p1, k1 in single st. Slide sts to opposite end of DPN.

RND 3: Pulling yarn tight across back, k3, slide sts to opposite end of DPN.

RNDS 4–11: Work Rnds 1–8 as for Large Bead.

RND 12: sl2-k1-psso, leaving a single st.

Pull yarn through and weave in end to finish.

purls for any occasion

GATSBY NECKLACE

This classic style looks great when made overly long and looped once around the neck so you appear to be wearing a choker and a long swag at the same time. Knit 6" (15cm) of cord, then one small bead, and repeat by alternating 2" (5cm) of cord and small beads until necklace is 6" (15cm) shorter than desired length. Finish with 6" (15cm) of cord. Knot the yarn ends together and weave them in.

WILMA FLINTSTONE NECKLACE

Knit 4" (10cm) of cord, then one large bead, and repeat by alternating ¾" (2cm) of cord with large beads until you have five beads, then finish with 4" (10cm) of cord. Finish this style with a clamp-on necklace clasp, found in bead or notions stores.

GRADUATED PEARL CHOKER

Knit 4" (10cm) of cord, one small bead, ½" (1cm) cord, one small bead, ½" (1cm) cord, medium bead, ½" (1cm) cord, large bead, ½" (1cm) cord, medium bead, ½" (1cm) cord, one small bead, ½" (1cm) cord, one small bead, 4" (10cm) cord. Finish this style with a clamp-on necklace clasp.

GAUCHO'S LARIAT

Knit one large bead first, tucking the yarn end inside before stuffing and closing the bead, then 36" (91cm) of cord (or desired length) and finish with another large bead and bind off. Remember that the knot will use up 2" to 3" (5 to 8cm) of cord, so choose cord length accordingly.

BALL AND CHAIN LARIAT

Knit as for Gaucho style: 50" (127cm) of cord makes a nice lariat that reaches past the navel when knotted twice. Knot the lariat like you would begin to tie your shoes and then slip the bead of the tying end through the back of the knot. This should allow one end of cord to slide freely through the knot. Knot it twice like this for the chain look.

BEAD BELT

This works best if the chosen elastic is the same or a similar color to the yarn. Firmly knot the end of a ¼" (.6cm) wide elastic cord and insert this knot into the top of the bead before you knit the final decrease round for the cord. As you work each row of cord, be sure the working yarn wraps behind the elastic cord in order to hide it. The belt looks best with a few beads knitted at the beginning and end, but not in the middle. Beads knitted in the middle stand away from your waist, and cause the beads to flatten with wear. If you plan to wear this with belt loops, squeeze the beads through each loop.

DRAWSTRING FOR HOODIE

Knit as for Ball and Chain Lariat, with 50" (127cm) of cord. Here are two methods to thread cord through hoodie casing:

{ 1 } If you are making the hoodie yourself, leave the casing open, then lay the cord inside and sew up the casing.

{ 2 } If you are using a store-bought hoodie, or one that already has the casing closed, only knit the first bead(s) and cord, then pass live sts onto a piece of waste yarn. Cut a yarn tail at least 9 yards long and pull it through the casing along with the cord. Use this yarn tail to knit the remaining ball.

HOMEGROWN

skill level

skill level

APPRENTICE

EVERY PART OF THIS HARDY LITTLE PURSE IS TOTALLY NATURAL and sustainable, a design for my vegan friends. Plant the hemp and bamboo yourself on a farm upstate if you like. Just don't let Johnny Law catch you! Even though hemp grown for fiber has no intoxicating powers, it is illegal to grow in the United States because it is virtually indistinguishable from stony variants of the same plant.

Knit with durable hemp yarn and structurally supported by half a bamboo placemat and a pair of chopsticks, this purse is built to last and last. Carry your latest knitting project in it—your bamboo needles will look smashing poking out the top of it!

WHAT YOU WILL LEARN

✖ fabric stitch
✖ slip stitch edge (page 66)
✖ picking up stitches (page 64)
✖ I-cord (page 72)

YARN

3 balls (120 yards ea) All Hemp 6 100% hemp yarn by LanaKnits in color Sapphire

NEEDLES

32" (81cm) size US 6 (4mm) circular needle

size US 6 (4mm) DPNs

If necessary, change needle size to obtain gauge.

NOTIONS

1 bamboo or wooden button

1 pair curved bamboo purse handles

1 10½" (27cm) pair of bamboo chopsticks

1 rolled bamboo placemat or sushi roller cut to 16" x 4½" (41cm x 11cm) (Joyce Chen kitchen designs)

½ yard fabric for lining

2" (5cm) circle of cotton fabric in color to match yarn

hand-sewing needle and durable thread

darning needle

stitch holder

stitch markers

GAUGE

21 sts and 28 rows = 4" (10cm) in St st

28 sts and 41 rows = 4" (10cm) in fabric stitch

MEASUREMENTS

17" (43cm) wide at bottom x 4½" (11cm) deep x 11" (28cm) wide at opening with enclosed sides 5¼" (13cm) high

TERMINOLOGY

fabric stitch: Slip alternate sts wyif on all RS rows, slip alternate sts wyib on WS rows to create this tight fabric that looks woven (see page 135).

k3tog (knit 3 together): Insert your right needle into the next 3 sts on the left needle and knit them tog as one.

SSSK (slip 3 stitches, knit 3 together): Slip 3 sts one at a time as if to knit, then knit them tog with left needle.

SSP (slip 2, purl 2 together through back loops): Slip 2 sts knitwise, insert left needle into sts from back to front, then purl sts tog through back loops.

wyif or wyib: With yarn in front or with yarn in back.

in patt: In pattern. Cont knitting as est.

[ ] (repeat operation): Rep operation in brackets the number of times indicated.

Other techniques: SSK (see page 58), k2tog and p2tog (see pages 58 and 60)

take heed

This yarn is sold in hanks and can get quite tangled. Be sure to use a swift to wind this yarn into balls before knitting! You will be lucky if you can use your ball winder with this yarn. I needed to detangle by hand every few turns of the swift.

BASE

FABRIC STITCH

Cast on 32 sts.

ROW 1: k3, * sl 1 wyif, k1; rep from * 13 times, sl 1 wyif, k2.

ROW 2: p3, * sl 1 wyib, p1; rep from * 13 times, sl 1 wyib, p2.

ROW 3: sl2 wyib, * k1, sl 1 wyif; rep from * 14 times, sl2 wyib.

Rep Rows 2–3 until piece measure 16" (41cm) for a total of 165 rows, ending with a RS row. Do not bind off or cut yarn.

BODY

Move work to a circular needle if using straights. With RS facing, and using available yarn end, pick up and knit 1 st in each loop of slipped st edge along side of base (82 sts), 32 sts along cast on edge, and 82 sts along other side of base—228 sts total. Place a stitch marker for beg of rnd.

RNDS 1–2: Knit.

RND 3: * k82, sl2, [k1, p1] 6 times, k1, p2, k1, [p1, k1] 6 times, sl2; rep from * once more.

RND 4: Knit.

RNDS 5–10: Rep Rnds 3–4 three times.

RND 11: * k2tog, k78, SSK, sl2, [k1, p1] 6 times, k1, p2, k1, [p1, k1] 6 times, sl2; rep from * once more.

RNDS 12–19: Work even in patt as est, slipping the 2 corner sts on every other rnd and working the ribbing as est for the side panels on every rnd.

RND 20: * k2tog, k78, SSK, sl2, [k1, p1] 6 times, k1, p2, k1, [p1, k1] 6 times, sl2; rep from * once more.

RNDS 21–28: Work even in patt as est.

ROW 29: * k2tog, k74, SSK, sl2, [k1, p1] 6 times, k1, p2, k1, [p1, k1] 6 times, sl2; rep from * once more.

RNDS 30–34: Work even in patt as est.

RND 35: * k2tog, k72, SSK, sl2, [k1, p1] 6 times, k1, p2, k1, [p1, k1] 6 times, sl2; rep from * once more.

RNDS 36–40: Work even in patt as est.

RND 41: * k2tog, k70, SSK, sl2, bind off 28 sts in patt, sl2; rep from * once more.

BACK

Work the back of the bag only. Move rem sts to a holder.

ROW 42: Purl.

ROW 43: sl2, k2tog, k68, SSK, sl2.

ROW 44: Purl.

ROW 45: sl2, k2tog, k66, SSK, sl2.

ROW 46: p2, p2tog, p64, SSP, p2.

ROW 47: sl2, k2tog, k62, SSK, sl2.

ROW 48: p2, p2tog, p60, SSP, p2.

ROW 49: sl2, k2tog, k58, SSK, sl2.

ROW 50: p2, p2tog, p56, SSP, p2.

ROW 51: sl2, k3tog, k52, SSSK, sl2.

ROW 52: p2, p2tog, p50, SSP, p2.

ROW 53: sl2, k3tog, k46, SSSK, sl2.

ROW 54: p2, p2tog, p44, SSP, p2.

ROW 55: k2, k3tog, k40, SSSK, k2.

ROW 56: p2, p2tog, p38, SSP, p2.

ROW 57: k2, k3tog, k34, SSSK, k2.

ROW 58: Purl.

ROW 59: Knit.

FRONT

Rep Rows 42–59 for front of bag.

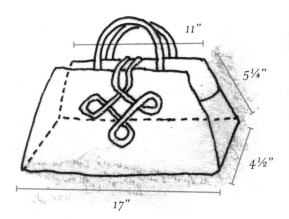

ASSEMBLY
SECURE CHOPSTICK

Cut yarn, leaving a 24" (61cm) tail. Fold the fabric over one chopstick, beg with the thicker end of the stick. It should fit snugly. Thread the yarn end through a darning needle. To prevent the chopstick from poking out either end of the casing, sew a few sts at the very end where the edge curves around, then graft down the casing around the chopstick with Kitchener stitch (see Tying Up, page 80). While grafting, make sure sts remain aligned. When you reach the last few sts, place the end of the stick in the center of the 2" (5cm) circle of cotton fabric and wrap the fabric around the thinner end of the stick. Twist the stick so the fabric lies flat. Sew a few more sts at the very end. The fabric patch will help to lock in the chopstick. Rep to secure rem chopstick.

CLOSURE

I-CORD

With DPN, cast on 4 sts.

ROW 1: Knit.

ROW 2: Without turning work, slide sts to opposite end of needle and knit.

Rep Row 2 until I-cord is 38" (96cm) long.

SECURE I-CORD

Wind the cord into the desired shape for your closure and pin it to the bag (Figure 1), leaving a loop long enough to reach around to the opposite side of the bag. Secure the end of the cord under the I-cord to keep the closure secure. Sew the I-cord closure down with a needle and matching thread.

SECURE BUTTON

Sew down the button on the opposite side of the bag with needle and thread, making sure the loop from the I-cord closure reaches securely around it.

SECURE HANDLES

Sew down the handles using the hemp yarn (see Figure 2 and Figure 3). You will only be able to pass the yarn through the hole in the handle about 3 times, but this should be enough to secure the handles. For more details on bag construction, please visit the DomiKNITrix Web site: www.domiknitrix.com.

figure 1

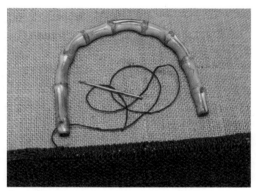

figure 2

figure 3

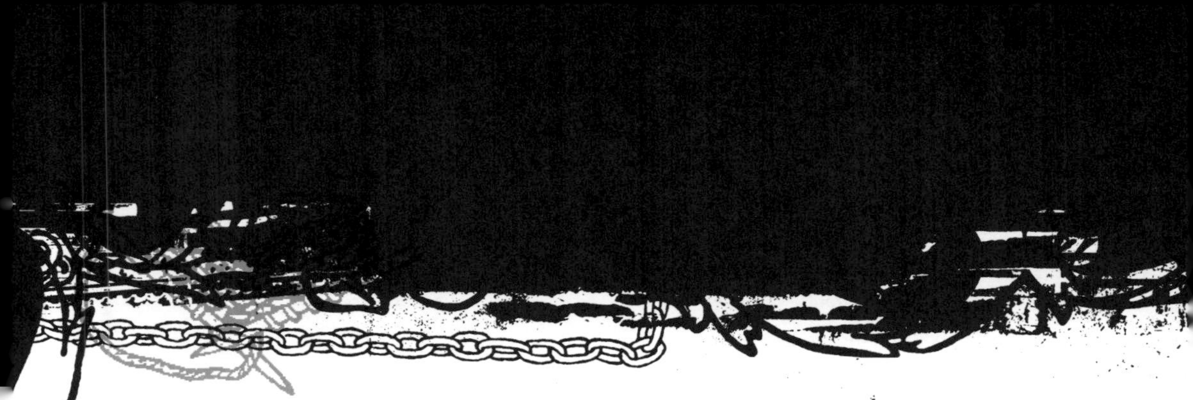

DeVIL + SnOW DEVIL HATS

skill level

ꝺOMIꝀNITꝚIX

THESE WARM HATS ARE PERFECT FOR
MARDI GRAS, CARNIVALE, HALLOWEEN or
any other time you're feeling particularly mischievous. And
they'll keep you cozy, too—stand out on the slopes in Snow
Devil with its ear flaps and pointy ties and you'll feel on top
of the world.

The Devil Hat takes just a few hours and a couple of
balls of yarn to make. You will be amazed at how people
are transformed when they put on this hat. It is a delight to
watch. Put a devilish sparkle in your eyes, you imp, and let
the mischief begin!

WHAT YOU WILL LEARN

✘ symmetrical increases and
decreases (pages 58–60)
✘ picking up stitches (page 64)
✘ double-pointed needles (page 54)
✘ short rows (page 62)
✘ Kitchener stitch (page 80)

YARN

DEVIL HAT

2 balls (60m ea) Aurora bulky cotton/acrylic blend yarn by Karabella in color 35 pink

Or substitue any bulky-weight yarn, such as Aspen by Muench or Sierra by KnitPicks.

SNOW DEVIL

approx 200 yards of any yarn listed above

NEEDLES

24" (61cm) minimum size US 9 (5.5mm) circular needle

size US 9 (5.5mm) DPNs

smaller DPNs (optional, for tightening tip of horn)

If necessary, change needle size to obtain gauge.

NOTIONS

short, flexible stitch holders

darning needle with curved tip for grafting

large safety pins

GAUGE

16 sts and 24 rows = 4" (10cm) in St st

**Gauge is intentionally tight. Recommended gauge on ball band is 13 sts and 19 rows = 4" (10cm) on US 11 (7mm) needles.

MEASUREMENTS

to fit sizes Small (21" [54cm]), Medium (22½" [57cm]) and Large (23½" [60cm])

TERMINOLOGY

RLI (right lifted increase): Lift first leg of st below next st onto needle and knit this st (see page 56).

LLI (left lifted increase): Lift last leg below last knitted st onto needle and knit this st (see page 56).

sl2-k1-psso (slip 2, knit 1, pass slipped stitch over): Slip 2 sts together as if to knit, knit one, pass 2 slipped sts over the knitted st (see page 63).

SSP (slip 2, purl 2 together through back loop): Slip 2 sts individually, insert left needle in back of both sts together, and pass sts tog back to left needle, then purl both sts together through back loop.

SSSK (slip 2, knit 3 together): Slip 3 sts 1 at a time as if to knit. Insert left needle into these 3 sts and knit them tog, as for k2tog.

PM (place marker): Slide a ring marker onto the needle whenever the pattern calls for you to place a marker. When you come to the marker on subsequent rows, simply work the st before it, slip the marker, and work the subsequent st.

wrap, turn (short row wrap): Work a partial row and pass 1 st wyif, turn the piece, then pass the same st back wyif. Knit the wrap and its st tog on the following row. The wrap prevents a hole in the knitting and keeps the fabric firm (see page 62).

wyif or wyib: with yarn in front or in back.

[ ] (repeat operation): Rep operation in brackets the number of times indicated.

Other techniques: SSK (see page 58), k2tog and p2tog (see pages 58 and 60)

✖ read this first ✖

This project is knitted tightly so horns stand up without stuffing, and so stuffing doesn't peek through if you do decide to stuff. Be sure to keep the edge stitches tight, as well as any stitches next to short row turns and at horn tips. The lifted increases give the best results, so choose other increases at your own risk. Here's how this hat is constructed:

- Begin by knitting a shaped strip from point of widow's peak to the back of the head.
- Then pick up stitches at the top of the crown and knit the curved gusset on each side.
- Next, pick up stitches from holders at the temple and knit the ribbed band, then graft it onto the hat. If knitting the Snow Devil, graft only a short piece of band on, and then knit the nape and earflaps.
- If knitting the Snow Devil, knit long ties and add arrow points.
- To finish, knit the horns and graft them onto the hat.

DEVIL HAT
WIDOW'S PEAK AND GUSSETS

Work as for Widow's Peak and Gussets of Mohawk hat, pages 123–124.

EDGING
RIGHT SIDE

ROW 1 (RS): sl4 sts from holder to needle and k2tog, p1, k1—3 sts.

ROW 2: p1, k1, p1.

ROW 3: k1, p1, k1.

Rep Rows 2–3 until the edging meets the rear gusset seam. Sl sts to holder.

LEFT SIDE

Work as for Right Side until edging is approx 11 (12, 13)" 28 (31, 33)cm and meets the Right Side edging at gusset seam. Graft sts to right side sts on holder using Kitchener stitch (see page 80).

ATTACH EDGING

Graft edging to the active sts of hat. It's best to use mattress stitch on the edging, and Kitchener stitch on the hat to keep the band elastic. The sewing yarn should form more of an S, like the knit stitch itself, instead of a whipstitch, for optimal elasticity. Do not pull the sewing yarn too tight. Weave in ends invisibly.

HORns
noTes:

- *I recommend knitting the horns at a time when you will be undisturbed for at least ½ hour. They will demand your full attention.*
- *SSK always appears at the beg of the needle, and k2tog always appears at the end of the needle. The decreases all line up to define the horns, so if they're not lining up, check your decrease technique. When you're doing the decreases correctly, you'll be able to keep your place easily since the decreases line up in a vertical row.*
- *At times, a semicolon is used to indicate the start of the next DPN.*

RIGHT HORN

RND 1: Leaving a yarn tail of 24" (61cm), cast on 24 sts onto one DPN. Knit first 9 sts, then with second DPN k8 sts, then on third DPN k6. Sl last st rem onto first DPN to join rnd, being careful not to twist the sts.

RND 2: k2tog, [k6, k2tog] twice, k5, sl last st wyif—21 sts.

SHORT ROW 1: Turn work, sl 1 wyif, p5; p6, sl last st wyif.

SHORT ROW 2: Turn work, sl 1 wyif, k6; k5, sl 1. Lift wrap onto right needle. Sl wrap and slipped st back to left needle and k2tog.

RND 3: k8, lift wrap onto needle and k2tog, [k4, k2tog] twice—19 sts.

RND 4: k6, k2tog, k6; k4, sl last st wyif—18 sts.

SHORT ROW 3: Turn work, sl 1 wyif, p4; p5, sl last st wyif.

SHORT ROW 4: Turn work, sl 1 wyif, k3, k2tog, k4, sl last st, lift wrap onto needle and k2tog.

RND 5: k7, lift wrap onto needle and k2tog, k4; k3, k2tog—16 sts.

RND 6: k5, k2tog, k5; k3, sl 1 wyif—15 sts.

SHORT ROW 5: Turn work, sl 1 wyif, p3; p4, sl last st wyif.

SHORT ROW 6: Turn work, sl 1 wyif, k2, k2tog, k2, sl

RND 15: Slide sts to other end of needle wyib, k2tog, pull yarn end through and use a darning needle to carefully draw the yarn end inside the horn through the tip.

noтe:

It is difficult to knit the last rows very tightly. You can improve the appearance of the horn tip by tightening up the sts with any pointed object once the horn is off the needle, or by knitting the last 3 rows with a smaller size needle.

LEFT HORN

RND 1: Leaving a yarn tail of 24" (61cm), cast on 24 sts onto one DPN. Knit first 9 sts, then with second DPN k7 sts, then on third DPN k7. Sl last st rem onto first DPN to join rnd, being careful not to twist the sts. SSK (slipped st with the first cast-on st) and sl new st back to left needle—23 sts.

RND 2: k8, [SSK, k5] twice, sl last st wyif—21 sts.

SHORT ROW 1: Turn work, sl 1 wyif, p6; p5, sl last st wyif.

SHORT ROW 2: Turn work, sl 1 wyif, k5; k6, lift wrap onto needle and k2tog.

RND 3: k8, lift wrap onto needle and SSSK, k4, SSK, k5—19 sts.

RND 4: SSK, k6; k5; k5, sl last st wyif—18 sts.

SHORT ROW 3: Turn work, sl 1 wyif, p5; p4, sl last st wyif.

SHORT ROW 4: Turn work, sl 1 wyif, k4, SSK, k3, lift wrap onto needle and k2tog.

RND 5: k7, lift wrap onto needle and SSSK, K3; k5—16 sts.

RND 6: SSK, k5; k4, SSK, k2, sl last st wyif—14 sts.

SHORT ROW 5: Turn work, sl 1 wyif, p3; p2, SSP, sl st on next needle wyif, and sl back to left needle wyib.

SHORT ROW 6: Turn work, k3; k3, lift wrap onto needle and k2tog.

RND 7: k5, lift wrap onto needle and k2tog, k3, SSK, k2—12 sts.

RND 8: SSK, k4, SSK, k1, drop left needle and k3—10 sts.

RND 9: [k5] twice.

RND 10: k5, SSK, k3—9 sts.

RND 11: SSK, k3; k1, SSK, k1—7 sts.

next 2 sts as if to k2tog, then lift wrap onto needle and k3tog.

RND 7: k6, lift wrap onto needle and k2tog, k3; k3—13 sts.

RND 8: k4, k2tog, k2, k2tog, drop left needle and cont to knit next sts onto right needle, k1, k2tog—10 sts.

RND 9: [k5] twice.

RND 10: k3, k2tog, k5—9 sts.

RND 11: k2, k2tog, k3, k2tog—7 sts.

RND 12: k3, k1, k2tog, k1, drop left needle and use next DPN to k1, k2tog.

RND 13: Slide sts to other end of needle wyib, k1, k2tog, k2—4 sts.

RND 14: Slide sts to other end of needle wyib, [k2tog] twice—2 sts.

RND 12: SSK, k2; k3—6 sts.

RND 13: k3, drop needle, SSK, k1—5 sts.

RND 14: Slide sts to other end of needle wyib, SSK, k3—4 sts.

RND 15: Slide sts to other end of needle wyib, [SSK] twice.

RND 16: Slide sts to other end of needle and k2tog. Pull yarn end through and use a darning needle to carefully draw the yarn end inside the horn through the tip.

See note at end of Right Horn for tips on keeping the last rows tight.

ASSEMBLY
STUFF HORNS

If desired, cut out 2 small pieces of batting in approx the same size and shape as the horn profile. Gently insert the batting into the horns. Do not overstuff or use stuffing not cut to shape.

GRAFT HORNS TO HAT

Graft the horns onto the hat with Kitchener stitch. I recommend pinning the horns on first with large safety pins and trying on the hat before stitching them in place. The horns should be placed symmetrically, 3" (8cm) apart from each other for Small/Medium, and 3½" (9cm) apart for Large, and ½" (1cm) from the edging for all sizes.

SNOW DEVIL HAT
WIDOW'S PEAK AND GUSSETS

Work as for Widow's Peak and Gussets of Mohawk hat, pages 123–124.

SHORT TEMPLE EDGING

Work both sides as for Devil Hat for a total of 6 (8, 10) rows. Sl sts to holder.

ATTACH EDGING AT TEMPLE

Graft the front 5 (7, 8) sts from each gusset to the side of both edgings. This join will be concealed by the horn later, so technique is less important. The edging should now be the same length as the back of the hat. Sl edging, gusset and center sts to the same needle so you can knit them as one piece—49 (51, 53) sts. Do not cut the sewing yarn here, because this is a stress point. Weave this yarn in invisibly and secure it. If the yarn end is long, you may cont knitting with it for several sts before splicing in a new ball.

devil from front

devil from side

NAPE

ROW 1: k1, p1, knit to last 2 sts, p1, k1.

ROW 2 AND ALL WS ROWS THROUGH ROW 10: p1, k1, purl to last 2 sts, k1, p1.

ROW 3: k1, p1, k21 (22, 49), [sl2-k1-psso] 1 (1, 0) time, knit to last 2 sts, p1, k1—47 (49, 53) sts.

ROWS 5 AND 7: Rep Row 1.

ROW 9: k1, p1, k20 (21, 23), sl2-k1-psso and mark as center st, knit to last 2 sts, p1, k1—45 (47, 51) sts.

ROW 11: k1, p1, k10 (11, 13), PM, RLI, k21, LLI, PM, knit to last 2 sts, p1, k1—47 (49, 53) sts.

ROW 12: p1, k1, purl to last 2 sts, k1, p1.

ROW 13: k1, p1, knit to marker and sl marker, RLI, knit to 1 st before center marked st, sl2-k1-psso, knit to marker, LLI, sl marker, knit to last 2 sts, p1, k1—47 (49, 53) sts.

ROW 14: p1, k1, purl to last 2 sts, k1, p1.

ROW 15: k1, p1, knit to marker and sl, RLI, knit to last marker, LLI, sl marker, knit to last 2 sts, p1, k1—49 (51, 55) sts.

ROWS 16–31: Rep Rows 12–15 four times—55 (57, 61) sts.

LEFT FLAP

Split at nape for left flap as follows:

PREP ROW (WS): p1, k1, p21 and sl those 23 sts to a holder; bind off 9 (11, 15) sts loosely, purl to last 2 sts, k1, p1—23 sts each flap.

ROW 1 (RS): k1, p1, knit to last 4 sts, k2tog, p1, k1—22 sts.

ROW 2 AND ALL WS ROWS THROUGH ROW 16: p1, k1, p2tog, purl to last 2 sts, k1, p1.

ROW 3: k1, p1, k9, RLI, k6, k2tog, p1, k1—21 sts.

ROW 5: k1, p1, knit to last 4 sts, k2tog, p1, k1—19 sts.

ROW 6: p1, k1, p2tog, purl to last 2 sts, k1, p1—18 sts.

ROWS 7–12: Rep Rows 5–6 three times—12 sts.

ROWS 13 AND 15: k1, p1, SSK, knit to last 4 sts, k2tog, p1, k1—7 sts at end of Row 15.

ROW 17: K1, p1, SSK, p1, k1—5 sts.

ROW 18: p1, SSP, k1, p1—4 sts.

ROW 19: k1, p1, k2tog—3 sts.

RIBBED CORD TIE

ROW 20: p1, k1, p1—3 sts.

ROW 21: k1, p1, k1.

Rep Rows 20–21 until piece is 8" (21cm) long or desired length, ending with a Row 20.

ARROW POINT

Beg with 3 sts rem on needles from tie, work points as foll:

PREP ROW: * p1, but do not remove st from needle; sl the st you just made back to the left needle; rep from * twice more—3 new sts, 6 sts total.

ROW 1: [k1, p1] 3 times, insert left needle into bead of st below last st worked and purl it. Cast on 2 more sts before turning—9 sts.

ROW 2: [p1, k1] twice, LLI, p1, RLI, [k1, p1] twice—11 sts.

ROW 3: SSK, k1, p1, k3, p1, k1, k2tog—9 sts.

ROW 4: p2, k1, p3, k1, p2.

ROW 5: SSK, [p1, k1] twice, p1, k2tog—7 sts.

ROW 6: p1, k2, p1, k2, p1.

ROW 7: SSK, sl2-k1-psso, k2tog—3 sts.

ROW 8: p3.

ROW 9: sl2-k1-psso. Cut yarn and pull end through. Weave end in.

RIGHT FLAP

Sl sts from holder to needle.

ROW 1: Join yarn at center back and k1, p1, SSK, k17, p1, k1—22 sts.

ROW 2 AND ALL WS ROWS THROUGH ROW 16: p1, k1, purl to last 4 sts, SSP, k1, p1—21 sts.

ROW 3: k1, p1, SSK, k6, LLI, k9, p1, k1—21 sts.

ROW 5: k1, p1, SSK, knit to last 2 sts, p1, k1—19 sts.

ROW 6: p1, k1, purl to last 4 sts, SSP, k1, p1—18 sts.

ROWS 7–12: Rep Rows 5–6 three times—12 sts at end of Row 12.

ROWS 13 AND 15: k1, p1, SSK, knit to last 4 sts, k2tog, p1, k1—7 sts at end of Row 15.

ROW 17: k1, p1, k2tog, p1, k1—5 sts.

ROW 18: p1, k1, k2tog, p1—4 sts.

ROW 19: k1, p2tog, k1—3 sts.

RIBBED CORD TIE

Knit as for first ribbed tie, but cont to rep Rows 20–21 until tie measures 11" (28cm). The ties are different lengths just to be a little more devilish! Finish with arrow point as for left flap. Work horns and attach as for Devil Hat.

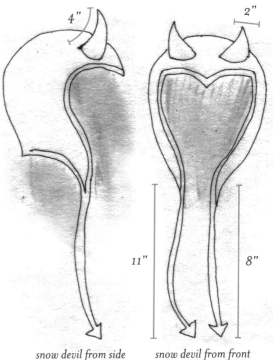

snow devil from side   *snow devil from front*

STAR pillow

skill level
skill level
APPRENTICE

ENOUGH OF THAT POTTERY BARN, CRATE AND BARREL SAMENESS! Who says your sofa can't wear your knitting too? I chose the star because it rings true in so many cultures: It's a symbol of the light of dying suns, of the goddess Venus, of Christ's wounds and of pagan faith. Lounge on this pillow and get in touch with your spiritual self, be ye heathen or Christian or whatever lies betwixt.

There's no need to toil in eternal purgatory with this project, either. The chunky yarn makes for a happy introduction to intarsia, and it's easy to untangle. It's quick to knit at this gauge, too: Go ahead, worship at the Church of Instant Gratification. Just this once.

WHAT YOU WILL LEARN

✗ intarsia (page 68)
✗ installing a zipper (page 86)
✗ mattress stitch (page 78)
✗ Kitchener stitch (page 80)

YARN

5 balls (60 yards ea) Tahki Yarns Baby 100% merino super bulky in color 16 black (MC); 3 balls in color 20 red (CC)

If ommitting star on back side, use 1 additional ball of MC and 1 less of CC.

NEEDLES

size US 13 (9mm) needles

If necessary, change needle size to obtain gauge.

NOTIONS

18" (46cm) zipper to match MC

cloth to cover zipper

20–22" (51–56cm) pillow form or batting

finer yarn for seaming pillow together

darning needle

GAUGE

9 sts and 13 rows = 4" (10cm) in St st

**Gauge is intentionally tight. Recommended gauge on ball band is 10 sts = 4" (10cm) on US 17 (12.5mm) needles.

MEASUREMENTS

18" (46cm) x 22" (56cm)

BACK AND FRONT (MAKE 2)

Cast on 41 sts with MC. Beg with a WS row, work 13 rows St st. Work 46 rows of Star Chart, then work 13 rows St st with MC. Bind off. For second side, you may omit the star if desired. Both pieces should measure 18" (46cm) wide and 22" (56cm) long. If your pieces are larger in size, you may wish to stuff with a larger pillow form or use batting instead, since it can be cut to any size.

ASSEMBLY
ORIENT BACK AND FRONT OF PILLOW

On one side of this pillow, the knitted Stockinette rows run vertically, and on the other side they run horizontally. When preparing to install the zipper, make sure the back and front pieces are oriented so the Stockinette rows run vertically on one side and horizontally on the other.

INSTALL ZIPPER

If unable to find a matching zipper, cover the RS of the zipper with ¾" (2cm) wide ribbon to conceal the zipper tape and teeth. (See Tying Up page 86 for step-by-step instructions on installing a zipper.)

Use sewing needle and thread to sew one side of the zipper to the cast-on edge of one of the pillow pieces, making sure the zipper pull is facing out. Open the zipper, and center it along a long (side) edge of the other piece with 2" (5cm) of fabric on each end of the zipper. Sew this ribbon-covered edge (with zipper pull facing out) to the side edge. The zipper teeth will be approximately ½" (1cm) away from the edge of the pillow.

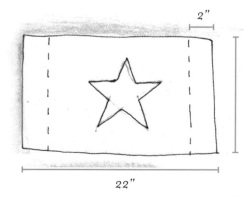

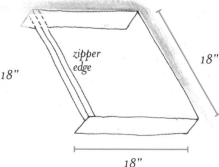

SEW PILLOW TOGETHER

Thread a darning needle with a length of matching yarn finer than the yarn used to knit the pillow. Beg in the corner near the end of the zip, sew along the side edge to the next corner. Because you are sewing the 2 pieces together at different orientations, it's best to pin the edges to be sewn together in at least 4 places on each edge.

When you reach the end of the narrower piece, knot your thread securely at the corner and anchor it in the knitting. Now fold the narrower piece over the other piece so that it looks like a small plus sign (+) with the sewn edge appearing a little shorter than the others. It will look like a flattened box.

Match up the side edges to the left and right of the seam you just sewed, leaving a 2½" (7cm) gap at top and bottom where the corners will be sewn together. Now sew the side seams in the same manner, starting at the end opposite the first seam and cont to sew up the 2½" (7cm) corner of the box edge. Once you have sewn both sides, you will have a box shape with an open flap ending with the bound-off row.

STUFF PILLOW

If using a pillow form, simply insert form into pillow and zip up. If using batting, measure at least 4 squares of batting in the same dimensions as the pillow. Stack them and insert into pillow. Keep squares lined up with edges of pillow. If this does not give enough fill, cut 2 to 4 more squares and add squares until pillow is desired volume.

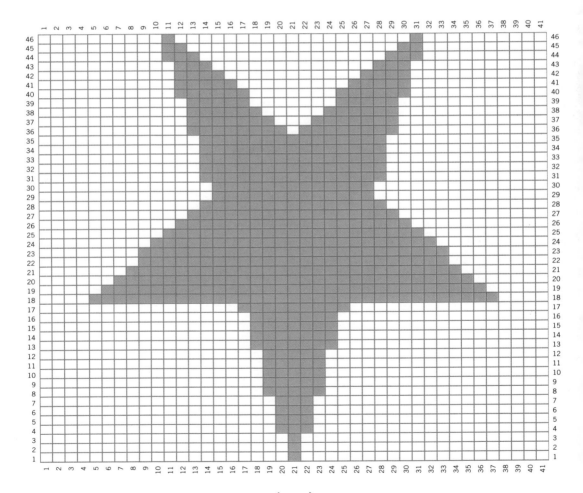

ON THE LEVEL
KNITTING IN THE MISSIONARY POSITION

Sometimes you prefer things simple, straightforward and easy to understand. No jumping through hoops, walking on fire or contortions, nuh-uh, no way. Well, that's just what these projects offer—knitting you can do flat on your back. All the projects in this chapter are knit from the bottom up. So, er...bottoms up!

Here are eight great first-sweater projects for newer knitters. Basic knit and purl textures are carved into sexy shapes with increase/decrease shaping so each piece fits your shapely figure. Intarsia and duplicate stitch are great ways to customize many of these designs, but you might just as easily knit them without the charts for basics you can wear more often.

Mostly larger-gauge yarns will help you fly through the sexy new wardrobe you are about to knit. Don't forget, when asked where you got that hot sweater, you tell 'em it's a DomiKNITrix design and you are a DomiKNITrix in training.

L'il RED RIDING HOODiE

skill level
APPRENTICE

YOU'LL BE MORE WOLF THAN BAIT IN
THIS HOT LITTLE HOODIE. If you haven't seen
Freeway, I urge you to sit down with some popcorn and watch
Little Red Riding Hood kick some serious wolf ass. This
sweater is dedicated to Reese Witherspoon.

If you prefer, knit it up in black with the white skull,
red stiletto, or golden fleur-de-lys on the back. You don't
have to play the part in someone else's fairytale. Make up
your own story (or rewrite one to suit you) and play your
starring role wearing a sweater that fits the part.

WHAT YOU WILL LEARN
✘ symmetrical increases and
decreases (pages 58–60)
✘ twisted knitting (page 67)
✘ picking up stitches (page 64)
✘ pockets (page 88)
✘ Kitchener stitch (page 80)

YARN

20 (21, 22, 23, 24) skeins (56 yards ea) Karabella Aurora bulky merino yarn in color 19 crimson

Or substitute any bulky wool yarn or other yarn that knits to gauge.

NEEDLES

size US 10½ (6.5mm) needles

NOTIONS

24" (61cm) long separating zipper

6 buttons (optional)

hand-sewing needle and thread

darning needle

GAUGE

15 sts and 22 rows = 4" (10cm) in St st

✗ *read this first* ✗

The body of this sweater is knit flat and begins with St st on right and left sides (fronts), with k1-p1 rib in the center (back). After ribbing, the body is worked in St st with raised increase shaping up to armhole gussets; the fronts are then knit up to the neck one side at a time. Then the back is knit up to the neck. Sleeves are knit separately, with a ribbed cuff and twisted knit elbow patch, tapered into raglan at the top, and then sewn onto body with mattress stitch. Stitches from body and sleeves are placed onto one needle and hood is knit up to a central strip that is then sewn together to close the top of the hood. Bands are knitted in k1, p1 rib separately to prevent frilling and then sewn on with mattress stitch. Pockets are picked up and knit from cast-on edge, then grafted at top and sides.

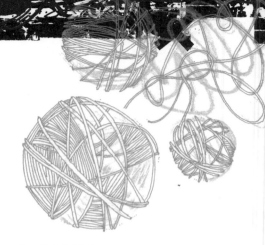

TERMINOLOGY

RLI (right lifted increase): Lift first leg of st below next st onto needle and knit this st (see page 56).

LLI (left lifted increase): Lift last leg below last knitted st onto needle and knit this st (see page 56).

KFB (knit 1 front and back): Knit into front and back of st to increase (see page 57).

SSP (slip 2, purl 2 together through back loop): Slip 2 sts individually, insert left needle in back of both sts together, and pass sts tog back to left needle, then purl both sts together through back loop.

SSSK (slip 2, knit 3 together): Slip 2 sts tog, slip another st, and knit these 3 sts tog.

k3tog (knit 3 together): Slide the right-hand needle into the next 3 sts on the needle as if to knit. Knit all 3 sts tog as one, just as for k2tog.

Other techniques: SSK and k2tog (see page 58)

BODY

Cast on 111 (115, 119, 123, 131) sts using long tail style.

ROW 1 (RS): k28 (29, 30, 31, 33), PM, p1, [k1, p1] until 55 (57, 59, 61, 65) sts have been knitted in rib, PM, k28 (29, 30, 31, 33)—111 (115, 119, 123, 131) sts.

ROW 2: p28 (29, 30, 31, 33), work in k1, p1 rib to next marker, purl to end.

Cont in St st on the side panels and rib in the center until piece measures approx 3" (8cm), ending with a WS row.

NEXT ROW (RS): Working in St st, k28 (29, 30, 31, 33); between markers: dec 13 sts evenly spaced to 42 (44, 46, 48, 52) sts; k28 (29, 30, 31, 33)—98 (102, 106, 110, 118) sts.

Removing markers, work even in St st until piece measures 5 (5¼, 5¼, 5½, 5¾)" 13 (13, 13, 14, 15)cm from beg, ending with a WS row.

NEXT ROW: PM, k9, PM, k9 (10, 11, 12, 14), PM, k14, PM, k34 (36, 38, 40, 44), PM, k14, PM, k9 (10, 11, 12, 14), PM, K9.

Purl 1 row even.

BODY SHAPING

NOTE:

Work all inc to shape body to right of center as LLI after the last st before the marker. Work all inc to the left of center as RLI before the first st after the marker. Inc worked in this manner create the illusion of seams slanting away from centerline.

NEXT ROW: k9, LLI, k9 (10, 11, 12, 14), LLI, k14, LLI, k34 (36, 38, 40, 44), RLI, k14, RLI, k9 (10, 11, 12, 14), RLI, k9—104 (108, 112, 116, 124) sts.

Knit 5 rows in St st, ending with a WS row, removing first and last markers.

Working in St st, cont to inc at the 4 rem markers as est on the foll row and every 6th row 5 more times—128 (132, 136, 140, 148) sts.

Work 5 rows in St st, ending with a WS row. Piece measures approx 12¾ (13, 13, 13¼, 13½)" 33 (33, 33, 34, 35)cm from cast-on row.

BUST DART AND UNDERARM BIND-OFF

NEXT ROW: k18, SSK, k5 (6, 7, 8, 10), k2tog, k3, bind off 12, k2, SSK, k34 (36, 38, 40, 44), k2tog, k3, bind off 12, k2, SSK, k5 (6, 7, 8, 10), k2tog, k18—28 (29, 30, 31, 33) active sts each front, 42 (44, 46, 48, 52) back sts resting.

LEFT FRONT

RAGLAN SHAPING (AND BUST DART)

Beg at left front edge, work as foll:

ROW 1 (WS): Purl to last 5 sts, SSP, p3—27 (28, 29, 30, 32) sts.

ROW 2: k3, SSK, k3 (4, 5, 6, 8), k2tog, k17—25 (26, 27, 28, 30) sts.

ROW 3: Rep Row 1—24 (25, 26, 27, 29) sts.

ROW 4: k3, SSK, k0 (1, 2, 3, 5), k2tog, k17—22 (23, 24, 25, 27) sts.

ROW 5: Rep Row 1—21 (22, 23, 24, 26) sts.

ROW 6: k3, SSK, k0 (0, 0, 0, 2), (k2tog for XL only), k16 (17, 18, 19, 17)—20 (21, 22, 23, 24) sts.

ROW 7: p15 (16, 17, 18, 24), [SSP, p3] 1 (1, 1, 1, 0) time—19 (20, 21, 22, 24) sts.

ROW 8: k3, SSK, knit—18 (19, 20, 21, 23) sts.

ROW 9 AND ALL WS ROWS: Purl.

Cont to dec on foll row as est, then every 4th row once, then every 6th row 4 times—12 (13, 14, 15, 17) sts.

Work 5 rows even in St st.

NECK SHAPING

SHORT ROW 1: k3, SSK, k3 (4, 5, 6, 8), wrap, turn.

WS ROWS: Purl.

SHORT ROW 3: k5 (6, 7, 8, 10), wrap, turn.

SHORT ROW 5: k3 (4, 5, 6, 8), wrap, turn.

NEXT ROW: Knit, lifting each wrap onto needle and knit it tog with st it wraps. k2, k2tog, k7 (8, 9, 10, 12)—10 (11, 12, 13, 15) sts.

If necessary, cont in St st until piece measures 21½ (21¾, 22, 22½, 23¼)" 55 (56, 56, 57, 59)cm from cast-on edge. Move sts to a holder.

RIGHT FRONT

Tie on a new ball at the right front underarm. Work Right Side as for Left Side, replacing SSP with p2tog, replacing k2tog with SSK, and replacing SSK with k2tog.

NECK SHAPING

SHORT ROW 1: p7 (8, 9, 10, 12), wrap, turn.

RS: k2 (3, 4, 5, 7), k2tog, k3.

SHORT ROW 3: p5 (6, 7, 8, 10), wrap, turn.

RS: k5 (6, 7, 8, 10).

SHORT ROW 5: p3 (4, 5, 6, 8), wrap, turn.

RS: k3 (4, 5, 6, 8).

NEXT ROW: Purl all sts while lifting each wrap onto needle and purl tog with st it wraps—11 (12, 13, 14, 16) sts.

RS: k7 (8, 9, 10, 12) SSK, k2—10 (11, 12, 13, 15) sts.

Finish as for Left Side, reversing shaping, and place sts on a holder.

BACK

RAGLAN SHAPING

ROW 1 (WS): Tie on new yarn at left underarm and purl—42 (44, 46, 48, 52) sts.

ROW 2: k3, PM, SSK, k32 (34, 36, 38, 42), k2tog, PM, k3—40 (42, 44, 46, 50) sts.

ROWS 3–5: Work even in St st.

ROW 6: k3, SSK, knit to 2 sts before marker, k2tog, k3—38 (40, 42, 44, 48) sts.

ROWS 7–9: Work even.

Cont to dec as est every fourth row 12 more times—14 (16, 18, 20, 24) sts.

Work even in St st for 3 rows.

LAST ROW (RS): k3, (XS: SSK, k4, k2tog; S: SSK, k6, k2tog; M: SSK, k8, k2tog; L: SSSK, k8, k3tog; XL: SSSK, k2, SSSK, k2, k3tog, k2, k3tog), k3—12 (14, 16, 16, 16) sts.

Piece measures approx 21¾ (22, 22¼, 22¾, 23½)" 56 (56, 57, 58, 59)cm from cast-on row. Move sts to a holder.

SLEEVES

LEFT SLEEVE

Cast on 31 (33, 35, 37, 39) sts long tail style. Beg and ending row with p1, work in k1, p1 ribbing until piece measures 3 (3¼, 3½, 3¾, 4)" 8 (8, 9, 10, 10)cm, ending with WS row.

ROW 1: k1, RLI, knit—32 (34, 36, 38, 40) sts.

ROWS 2–6: Work even in St st.

ROW 7: Knit to last st, LLI, k1—33 (35, 37, 39, 41) sts.

ROWS 8–10: Work even.

ROW 11: Rep Row 1—34 (36, 38, 40, 42) sts.

ROWS 12–14: Work even.

ROW 15: Rep Row 7—35 (37, 39, 41, 43) sts.

ROWS 16–18: Work even.

ROW 19: Rep Row 1—36 (38, 40, 42, 44) sts.

ROW 20: Purl.

Sleeve measures approx 7½ (7¾, 8, 8¼, 8½)" 19 (20, 21, 21, 22)cm from cast-on edge.

LEFT ELBOW PATCH

ɴᴏᴛᴇ:
See page 67 in the Knitting Directions chapter for instructions on twisted knitting. Work the elbow patch sts in twisted knitting, and all other sts in St st. If desired, use an open-ended stitch marker at each edge of the patch, and move them into position for the next row after completing each row.

ROW 21: k1 (2, 3, 4, 5) PM, work row 1 of chart, PM, k20 (21, 22,23, 24)

ROW 22 AND ALL WS ROWS: Purl, working next row of chart.

ROW 23: Knit, working next row of chart.

ROW 25: Working next row of chart, knit to last st, LLI, k1—37 (39, 41, 43, 45) sts.

ROW 27 AND 29: Rep Row 23.

ROW 31: k1, RLI, work next row of chart—38 (40, 42, 44, 46) sts.

ROWS 33–37: Rep Rows 21–25—39 (41, 43, 45, 47) sts.

ROWS 39–43: Rep Rows 27–31—40 (42, 44, 46, 48) sts.

ROWS 45–49: Rep Rows 21–25—41 (43, 45, 47, 49) sts.

ROW 50: Purl, working last row of chart.

Work even in St st until sleeve measures approx 16¼" (42cm) from cast-on edge.

LEFT GUSSET AND SHOULDER

note:

Gusset inc are worked at beg of sleeve with 2 inc on every RS row. Inc move away from each other, creating a triangle shape. Work KFB in first st loosely to make sts elastic and reduce strain on underarm seam.

Purl all WS rows.

ROW 1: KFB in first st, LLI under st just worked, knit to end—gusset 3, sleeve 40 (42, 44, 46, 48) sts.

ROW 3: Knit.

ROW 5: KFB, k2, LLI, knit to end—gusset 5, sleeve 40 (42, 44, 46, 48) sts.

ROW 7: k8, RLI, k34 (36, 38, 40, 42), PM, k3—gusset 5, sleeve 41 (43, 45, 47, 49) sts.

ROW 9: KFB, k4, LLI, knit to end—gusset 7, sleeve 41 (43, 45, 47, 49) sts.

ROW 11: Knit.

ROW 13: KFB, k6, LLI, knit to marker, LLI, k3—gusset 9, sleeve 42 (44, 46, 48, 50) sts.

ROW 15: Knit.

ROW 17: KFB, k8, LLI, knit to end—gusset 11, sleeve 42 (44, 46, 48, 50) sts.

ROW 19: (XS only): bind off 11 sts; all larger sizes, k11, k3, RLI, knit to end—gusset 11, sleeve 43 (45, 47, 49, 51) sts.

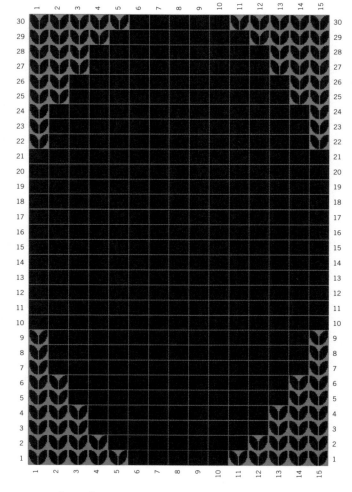

ROW 21: (S only): Bind off 11 sts; all larger sizes, KFB, k10, LLI, k3, RLI, knit to marker, LLI, k3—gusset 13, sleeve 45 (47, 49, 51, 53) sts.

ROW 23: (M only): Bind off 13 sts; L and XL: knit to marker, LLI, k3—gusset 13, sleeve 46 (48, 50, 52, 54) sts.

ROW 25: (L only): Bind off 13 sts; XL: knit to end—gusset 13, sleeve 46 (48, 50, 52, 54) sts.

ROW 27: (XL only: Bind off 13 sts), k3, SSK, knit to marker, LLI, k3—46 (48, 50, 52, 54) sts.

ROW 29: Knit.

ROW 31: Knit to marker, LLI, k3—47 (49, 51, 53, 55) sts.

ROW 33: k3, PM, SSK, knit to end—46 (48, 50, 52, 54) sts.

ROW 35: Knit to 2 sts before second marker, k2tog, k3—45 (47, 49, 51, 53) sts.

ROW 37: Knit to first marker, SSK, knit to 2 sts before second marker, k2tog, k3—43 (45, 47, 49, 51) sts.

ROW 39: Knit to 2 sts before second marker, k2tog, k3—42 (44, 46, 48, 50) sts.

Place new markers 1 to 4 from left to right on next row.

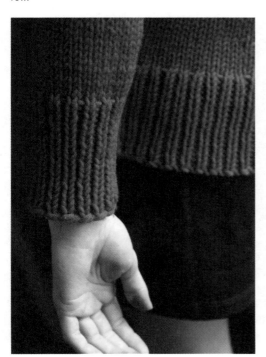

ROW 41: k3, SSK, k9 (10, 11, 12, 13), k2tog, PM, k5, PM, SSK, k14 (15, 16, 17, 18), k2tog, k3—38 (40, 42, 44, 46) sts.

ROW 43: Knit to 2 sts before fourth marker, k2tog, k3—37 (39, 41, 43, 45]

ROW 45: Knit to first marker, SSK, knit to 2 sts before second marker, k2tog, knit to third marker, SSK, knit to 2 sts before fourth marker, k2tog, k3—33 (35, 37, 39, 41) sts.

ROWS 47–58: Rep Rows 43–46 three times—18 (20, 22, 24, 26) sts.

ROW 59: Rep Row 43—17 (19, 21, 23, 25) sts.

ROW 61: k3, SSK, k1 (0, 1, 2, 3), k2tog (XS: skip k2tog), k5, SSK (XS: skip SSK), k1 (0, 1, 2, 3), k2tog, k3—15 (15, 17, 19, 21) sts.

ROW 63: Rep Row 43—14 (14, 16, 18 20) sts.

ROW 65: k3, SSK, k4 (4, 6, 8, 10), k2tog, k3—12 (12, 14, 16, 18) sts.

ROW 67 AND 71: Knit.

ROW 69 AND 73: Rep Row 43—10 (10, 12, 14, 16) sts at end of Row 73.

ROW 75: XS, S: Knit. M, L: k3, SSK, k0 (0, 2, 4, 0), k2tog, k3. XL: k3, SSSK, k0 (0, 0, 0, 4), k3tog, k3—10 (10, 10, 12, 12) sts.

Place rem sts on a holder.

RIGHT SLEEVE

Work as for Left Sleeve, working Rows 1 and 7 as follows. Work all other rows as given for Left Sleeve.

ROW 1: Knit to last st, LLI, k1—32 (34, 36, 38, 40) sts.

ROW 7: k1, RLI, knit to end—33 (35, 37, 39, 41) sts.

Finish Right Sleeve as for Left Sleeve.

RIGHT ELBOW PATCH

Work as for Left Elbow Patch, working Rows 21, 25, and 31 as foll. Work all other rows as given for Left Elbow Patch.

ROW 21: k20 (21, 22, 23, 24), PM, work Row 1 of chart, PM, k1 (2, 3, 4, 5).

ROW 25: Working next row of chart, k1, RLI knit to end—37 (39, 41, 43, 45) sts.

ROW 31: Working next row of chart, knit to last st, LLI, k1—38 (40, 42, 44, 46) sts.

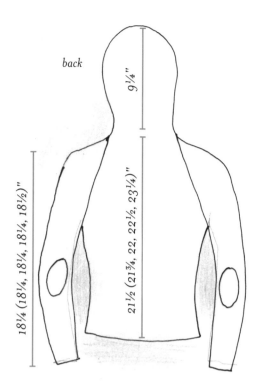

back

9¼"

21½ (21¾, 22, 22½, 23¼)"

18¼ (18¼, 18¼, 18¼, 18½)"

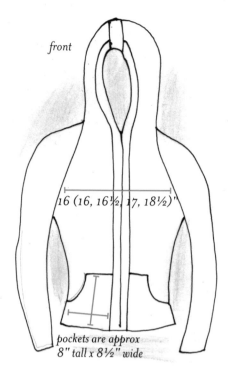

front

16 (16, 16½, 17, 18½)"

*pockets are approx
8" tall x 8½" wide*

RIGHT GUSSET AND SHOULDER

*Gusset inc are worked as 2 inc at end of every
RS row. See notes for Left Gusset.*

Purl all WS rows. Work as for Left Shoulder and
Gusset, reversing shaping. Beg at Row 20 (22, 24,
26, 28), bind off sts at beg of WS row. Reverse
shaping for Left Shoulder to Row 75. Place all sts
on a holder.

FINISHING

Use mattress stitch to sew the sleeve seams (see
Tying up page 78). Making sure the elbow patches
and gussets are toward the back of the sweater, sew
the sleeves onto the body all the way up to the neck
with mattress stitch. Once the seams are sewn,
slide all of the resting sts of the neck onto one
needle: 10 (11, 12, 13, 15 sts from Right Front,
10 (10, 10, 12, 12) from Right Sleeve, 12 (14,
16, 16, 16) sts from Back, 10 (10, 10, 12, 12) sts
from Left Sleeve, and 10 (11, 12, 13, 15) sts from
Left Front—52 (56, 60, 66, 70) sts.

HOOD

With RS up, tie on yarn at right front.

ROW 1:

XS: Knit

S: k10, SSK, k32, k2tog, k10—54 sts.

M, L AND XL: k(11, 12, 14) SSK, k(8, 10, 10),
SSK, k14, k2tog, k(8, 10, 10) k2tog, k(11, 12,
14)—(56, 62, 66) sts.

ROW 2 AND ALL WS ROWS: Purl.

ROWS 3–6: Work even.

ROW 7: k20 (21, 22, 25, 27), LLI, PM, k12, RLI,
knit to end—54 (56, 58, 64, 68) sts.

ROW 8–16: Work even.

ROW 17: Knit to marker, LLI, sl marker, k12, RLI,
knit to end—56 (58, 60, 66, 70) sts.

ROW 18–26: Work even.

ROWS 27–56: Rep Rows 17–26 three times—62
(64, 66, 72, 76) sts.

Hood measures approx 11" (28)cm from Row 1.

ROW 57: Bind off 25 (26, 27, 30, 32) sts, LLI and bind it off. Knit remainder of row as foll, do not bind off: k12, RLI, knit—39 (40, 41, 43, 46) sts.

ROW 58: Bind off 26 (27, 28, 31, 33) sts purlwise, purl rem sts—12 sts.

ROWS 59 AND BEYOND: Knit in St st until strip measures 9¼ (9½, 9¾, 10, 10¼)" 24 (24, 25, 26, 26)cm. Work [p1, k1] twice, inc 1 st in purl, [k1, p1] twice more. Cont in rib until strip measures 10½ (10¾, 11, 11¼, 11½)" 27 (28, 28, 29, 29)cm. Bind off. Strip is 1¼" longer than hood when folded to meet the top of the hood. Zipper bands will meet the top strip of the hood in a T when sewn on. Graft or sew the top of the hood.

POCKETS
LEFT POCKET

Working in the base of each st on the sweater's Left Front, pick up and k30 sts at the cast-on row. Knit in St st for approx 22 rows or 4" (10cm), ending with a WS row.

NEXT ROW: k1, SSK, knit across—29 sts.

NEXT ROW: Purl to last 3 sts, SSP, p1—28 sts.

Cont to work in St st, working dec 1 st in from the edge as est (using SSK on odd rows, and SSP on even-numbered dec rows) once every row 3 times, then every other row 3 times, then 2 times every 4th row—19 sts.

Work even in St st for 4 more rows, until pocket measures approx 8" (20cm) from beg. Cut yarn, leaving a long tail and use to graft active sts to front of sweater. Sew long side of pocket to front edge (now, or while sewing on the zipper bands later), and short straight side next to back ribbing.

RIGHT POCKET

Work as for Left Pocket, reversing shaping and dec as k2tog on RS rows and p2tog on WS rows.

ZIPPER BANDS (KNIT TWO)

Use a smaller gauge needle if desired. Cast on 11 sts.

ROW 1 (RS): [k1, p1], rep to end, k1.

ROW 2: [p1, k1], rep to end, p1.

Rep these 2 rows until pieces measure 33 (33½, 33¾, 34, 34½)" 84 (85, 86, 87, 88)cm from cast-on edge. Give them a good stretch and let bounce back before measuring. Ribbing can stretch, and you want it to stretch before sewing, or later it will look like a frill instead of a band.

Bind off or leave sts on the needle or a holder until you have completed the sewing up, in case you need to adjust the length to make things meet perfectly at the top of the hood.

BUTTON BANDS (OPTIONAL)

If you'd rather knit a button band for your sweater, work as follows. This band is knitted 1½ times wider than the zipper band to provide an overlap for buttoning up. This extra width is knit in St st to be sewn to front of sweater. Buttons are placed close together to minimize gapping.

BUTTONHOLE BAND

Cast on 17 sts.

ROW 1 (RS): [k1, p1], rep 4 more times, k7.

ROW 2: p7, [k1, p1] to end.

Rep Rows 1–2 twice before first buttonhole.

BUTTONHOLE ROW 1: k1, p1, k1, bind off 3 sts, [k1, p1] once, k7.

BUTTONHOLE ROW 2: p7, [k1, p1] once, cast on 3 sts, p1, k1, p1.

Rep Rows 1–2 eight times. Rep Buttonhole Rows.

Cont until Buttonhole Band measures 21¾ (22, 22¼, 22½, 23)" 56 (56, 57, 57, 59)cm, ending with a WS row. Finish band as follows:

DECREASE ROWS

ROW 1: [k1, p1] 5 times, SSK, k5.

ROW 2: p6, [k1, p1] to end.

ROW 3: [k1, p1] 5 times, SSK, k4.

ROW 4: p5, [k1, p1] to end.

ROW 5: [k1, p1] 5 times, SSK, k3.

ROW 6: p4, [k1, p1] to end.

ROW 7: [k1, p1] 5 times, SSK, k2.

ROW 8: p3, [k1, p1] to end.

ROW 9: [k1, p1] 5 times, SSK, k1.

ROW 10: p2, [k1, p1] to end.

ROW 11: [k1, p1] 5 times, SSK.

ROW 12: p1, [k1, p1] to end.

ROW 13: [k1, p1] 5 times, k1.

Rep Rows 12–13 until piece measures 33 (33½, 33¾, 34, 34½)" 84 (85, 86, 87, 88)cm.

Knit in rib until piece measures 33 (33½, 33¾, 34, 34½)" 84 (85, 86, 87, 88)cm.

BUTTON BAND

Cast on 17 sts.

ROW 1 (RS): k7, [p1, k1] to end.

ROW 2: [p1, k1] 5 more times, k7.

Rep Rows 1–2 until button band measures same length as Buttonhole Band before dec.

DECREASE ROWS
Work Button Band dec as for Buttonhole Band dec, reversing shaping through Row 11 and dec as k2tog.

Follow pattern from Rows 12–13 to end as given for Buttonhole Band.

FINAL ASSEMBLY

Pin pockets to fronts, and sew the bands onto the sweater with mattress stitch (see page 78). If using button bands, place the buttonhole band on the right side and the button band on the left side of the sweater. The bands should butt up against the sweater and pocket edge.

Sew the band to the pocket first by working from top corner of the pocket to bottom pocket corner, then turn it over and cont sewing the sweater to the band on the back side. Count sts on each side and pin it so you get it right the first time. If the number of rows to be stitched together is not equal, you will end up with a pucker at the pocket corner. You may prefer to sew the sweater body to the pocket first, and then sew the band on top of it. Either way is fine, but be sure to place the bands so the bind-off end is up at the hood, just in case you need to make any length adjustment to the band as you sew it to the hood.

Cont sewing the band to the sweater fronts all the way up to the hood, lining up the bands so they meet perpendicular to the strip along the top of the hood. Graft the joins together, and you're done!

BiG BAD WOLF PULlover

skill level

APPRENTICE

WHETHER YOUR MAN IS A LONE WOLF
OR ONE WHO RUNS WITH A PACK, I'll bet
he likes to get out at night and howl from time to time. This
pullover will keep him warm while he's on the prowl. And
when he comes home, you'll get to snuggle in with your Big
Bad Wolf. If you're lucky, he might bite.

This sweater is a basic wardrobe piece with garter gaunt-
lets and collar for a very masculine touch. Grrr. I've sup-
plied a variety of charts (see Bob Dobbs on page 175, Skull
on page 177 and more charts on pages 249–251) so you can
give this sweater his own personal stamp (or yours).

WHAT YOU WILL LEARN

✖ intarsia (page 68)
✖ short rows (page 62)
✖ seaming garter (page 82)
✖ mattress stitch (page 78)
✖ Kitchener stitch (page 80)

YARN

6 (6, 7, 7) skeins (190 yards ea) of Lamb's Pride wool/mohair blend bulky yarn in color M01 Sandy Heather (MC)

1 skein (190 yards ea) of Lamb's Pride wool/mohair blend bulky yarn in color M04 Charcoal Heather (CC)

NEEDLES

16" (40cm) size US 10 (6mm) circular needle

29" (74cm) size US 10 (6mm) circular needle

If necessary, change needle size to obtain gauge.

NOTIONS

stitch markers

stitch holders

darning needle

GAUGE

14 sts and 20 rows = 4" (10cm) in St st

14 sts and 28 rows = 4" (10cm) in garter st

If your garter st row gauge differs from your St st gauge, you may need to change needle size when switching between stitches.

MEASUREMENTS

To fit chest 38 (40, 42, 44)" 97 (102, 107, 112)cm

See schematics on page 165 for additional measurements.

✕ *read this first* ✕

The garter cuffs and the band at the waist are not intended to draw in like ribbing. Make double sure to knit a gauge swatch with both Stockinette and garter, so you can be sure.

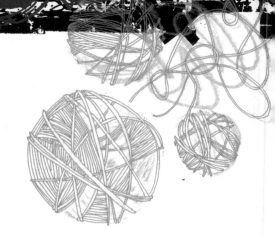

TERMINOLOGY

wrap, turn (short row wrap): Work a partial row and pass 1 st wyif, turn the piece, then pass the same st back wyif. Knit the wrap and its st tog on the following row. The wrap prevents a hole in the knitting and keeps the fabric firm (see page 62).

SSP (slip 2, purl 2 together through back loops): Slip 2 sts 1 at a time as if to knit, insert left needle in back of both sts tog, and pass sts tog back to left needle, then purl 2 tog through the back loops (see page 60).

PM (place marker): Slide a ring marker onto the needle whenever the pattern calls for you to place a marker. When you come to the marker on subsequent rows, simply work the st before it, slip the marker, and work the subsequent st.

Other techniques: SSK and k2tog (see page 58)

SLEEVES (MAKE TWO)
CUFF

Cast on 29 (29, 31, 33) sts using long tail style.

ROW 1 (RS): Purl.

ROWS 2–15: Knit 14 rows in garter st. On Row 15, PM after first 2 sts and before last 2 sts.

NEXT ROW: Cont in garter st, inc before first marker and after last marker this row, then every 16 rows once, then every 8 rows twice—37 (37, 39, 41) sts.

REMAINDER

(WS) Beg with a purl row, work 7 rows St st.

NEXT ROW (RS): Cont in St st, inc before first marker and after last marker this row, then every 6 rows 4 times more, then every 8 rows 8 times—63 (63, 65, 67) sts.

Knit 3 (5, 5, 7) rows even in St st; end with WS row.

SHAPE CAP

(RS) Dec this row and every 4 rows twice more as k1, SSK, knit to last 3 sts, k2tog, k1—57 (57, 59, 61) sts. Knit 0 (2, 5, 6) rows in St st, bind off.

BODY

Using circular needle, loosely cast on 133 (140, 147, 155) sts. PM for beg of rnd and join, being careful not to twist sts. Work in garter st (knit 1 rnd, purl 1 rnd) until piece measures 2" (5cm) from beg.

Work in St st (knit every round) until piece measures 6½ (6½, 7, 7½)" 17 (17, 18, 19)cm from beg.

DIVIDE FOR FRONT AND BACK

k67 (70, 73, 77) for Back, PM and turn, leaving rem 66 (70, 74, 78) sts unworked for Front.

note:

To avoid transferring sts to a holder, you may keep all the sts on the same needle and work only between the markers. However, you may move the Front sts to another needle so you don't knit them by mistake.

BACK

k1, inc 1, knit to last st, inc 1, k1—69 (72, 75, 79) sts. (These extra sts are needed so you can seam the sweater later without affecting the fit.)

Cont working even in St st until piece measures 15¾" (40cm) from beg, ending with a WS row.

UNDERARM SHAPING

ROW 1 (RS): k1, SSK, knit to last 3 sts, k2tog, k1—67 (70, 73, 77) sts.

ROW 2: p1, p2tog, purl to last 3 sts, SSP, p1—65 (68, 71, 75) sts.

Rep Rows 1 and 2 one (1, 2, 2) time(s) more—61 (64, 63, 67) sts.

M & XL SIZES ONLY: Rep Row 1 once more.

ALL SIZES: Cont working even in St st until armhole measures 4¾ (5¼, 5¼, 5½)" 12 (14, 14, 14)cm, ending with a WS row—61 (62, 63, 65) sts.

NEXT (INC) ROW (RS): k1, inc 1, knit to last st, inc 1, k1—63 (64, 65, 67) sts.

Cont working even in St st until armhole measures 8¾ (9¼, 9¼, 9½)" 22 (24, 24, 24)cm, ending with a WS row. Rep Inc Row once more—65 (66, 67, 69) sts.

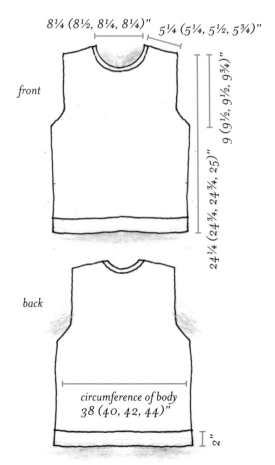

8¼ (8½, 8¼, 8¼)" 5¼ (5¼, 5½, 5¾)"

front

9 (9½, 9½, 9¾)"

24¼ (24¾, 24¾, 25)"

back

circumference of body
38 (40, 42, 44)"

2"

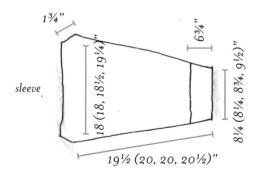

1¾"

sleeve

18 (18, 18½, 19¼)"

6¾"

8¼ (8¼, 8¾, 9½)"

19½ (20, 20, 20½)"

LEFT SHOULDER

SHORT ROW 1: p22 (22, 23, 24), wrap, turn.

SHORT ROW 2: k19, wrap, turn.

SHORT ROW 3: p16, wrap, turn.

SHORT ROW 4: k10, wrap, turn

SHORT ROW 5: p9, wrap, turn.

SIZE XL ONLY: k20, lifting each short row wrap onto your needle and knitting tog with the st above it as you do. You may disregard direction to lift wrap in bind-off row since you have done it here.

ALL SIZES: Loosely bind off 18 (18, 19, 20) sts, lifting each short row wrap onto your needle and knitting tog with the st above it as you do. If you prefer, instead of binding off, you may cut this yarn and sl the sts on a holder to graft later rather than sew tog bound-off edges at the end.

RIGHT SHOULDER

With RS facing, join yarn at right shoulder. Work as for Left Shoulder, knitting the odd short rows and purling the even short rows. Bind off in purl for all sizes except XL: XL bind off in knit. Place rem 29 (30, 29, 29) sts for collar on a holder.

FRONT

ROW 1 (RS): k10 (12, 14, 16), PM for chart, work 46 sts of chart Row 1, PM, knit to end—66 (70, 74, 78) sts. Cont even in St st, working the chart between markers, until piece measures 15¾" (40cm) from beg, ending with a WS row.

UNDERARM SHAPING

Cont working chart until finished and AT THE SAME TIME, work underarm shaping as for Back until armhole measures 7½ (8, 8, 8)" 19 (21, 21, 21)cm, ending with a WS row—60 (62, 64, 66) sts.

LEFT NECK AND SHOULDER SHAPING

SHORT ROW 1 (RS): k24 (24, 25, 26), wrap, turn; purl back.

SHORT ROW 2: k22 (22, 23, 24), wrap, turn; purl back.

SHORT ROW 3: k20 (20, 21, 22), wrap, turn; purl back.

SHORT ROW 4: k1, inc 1, k18 (18, 19, 20), wrap, turn.

SHORT ROW 5: p17 (17, 18, 19), wrap, turn. (Note: this begins the shoulder shaping.)

SHORT ROW 6: k16 (16, 17, 18), wrap, turn.

SHORT ROW 7: p10 (10, 11, 12), wrap, turn.

SHORT ROW 8: k9 (9, 10, 11), wrap, turn.

SIZE XL ONLY: Purl to end, lifting each short wrap onto your needle and purling tog with the st above it as you do. Disregard directions to do same in the bind-off row.

ALL SIZES: Loosely bind off 18 (18, 19, 20) sts, lifting each short wrap onto your needle and purling tog with the st above it as you do.

RIGHT NECK AND SHOULDER SHAPING

With WS facing, join yarn at right shoulder. Work as for Left Neck and Shoulder, purling then knitting back for Short Rows 1–3, then knitting the rem odd short rows and purling the rem even short rows. Bind off in knit for all sizes except XL: XL bind off in purl. Place rem 26 (28, 28, 28) sts for collar on a holder. If you do not cut the yarn here, you may use it to knit the collar after the shoulders are seamed.

FINISHING

Loosely graft shoulder seams together with Kitchener stitch (see Tying Up, page 80). Set in sleeves. Sew side seams using mattress stitch (see Tying Up, page 78), then sleeve seams.

COLLAR

Sl 29 (30, 29, 29) back neck sts, then 26 (28, 28, 28) front neck sts from holders onto 16" (40cm) circular needle, ready to beg at right shoulder seam.

RND 1: * Pick up and k1 in shoulder seam, knit every st to other shoulder seam, and AT THE SAME TIME, pick up and k1 in every short row wrap; rep from *, PM—75 (78, 77, 77) sts (38 (40, 40, 40) front neck, 35 (36, 35, 35) back neck, and 1 st each shoulder seam.

RND 2: Purl.

RND 3: SSK, knit to 1 st before shoulder seam, k2tog, SSK, knit to 2 sts before marker, k2tog—71 (74, 73, 73) sts.

RNDS 4 AND 6: Purl.

RND 5: Knit.

RND 7: k10, SSK, k12 (14, 14, 14), k2tog, knit to end—69 (72, 71, 71) sts

Purl 1 row. Bind off in knit.

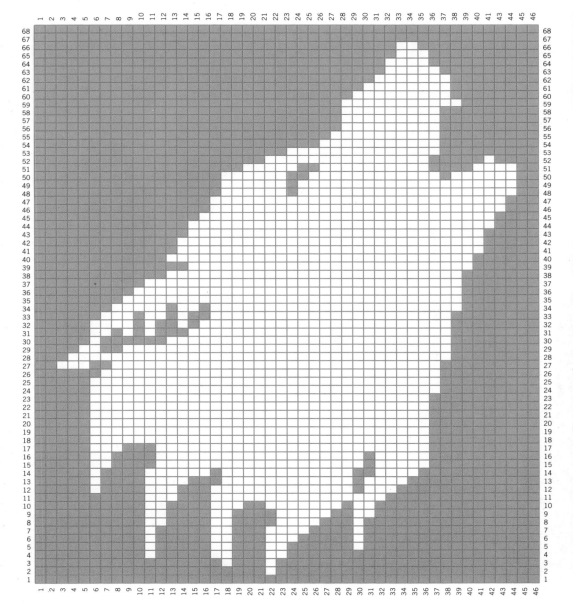

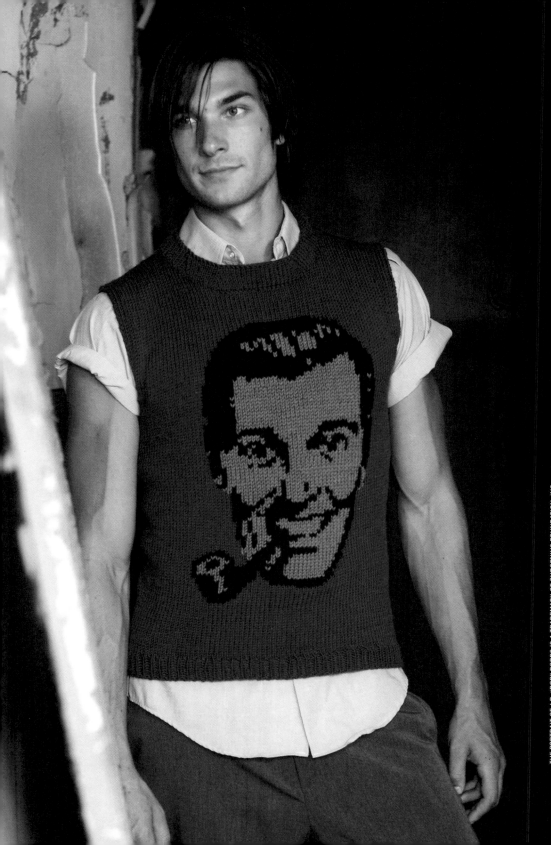

BOB DOBBS + skull vests

skill level

DOMIKNITRIX

EVERY MAN SHOULD HAVE A BASIC
PULLOVER VEST IN HIS WARDROBE.
This vest has just enough ribbing to make the edges lie flat,
and a plain crew-neck collar with elastic inside the casing
helps it hold its shape. The designs on these vests may be
added with duplicate stitch or with intarsia.

The Bob Dobbs Vest is dedicated to Bob Dobbs, a regis-
tered trademark of the Church of the Subgenius, an orga-
nization for "mutants, blasphemers, disbelievers, rebels,
outcasts, hackers, freethinkers" and people who generally
consider themselves outside of "mainstream" society. Cheers
to miscreants and misfits. Or choose to emblazon your guy's
vest with the grim skull. It's the perfect excuse for calling people "Mate" around the office. But watch out for the boyfriend
curse...read on to find out if it's fact or fiction.

WHAT YOU WILL LEARN

✘ working in the round (page 52)
✘ short rows (page 62)
✘ picking up stitches (page 64)
✘ grafting facings (page 84)
✘ duplicate stitch (page 69)

YARN

BOB DOBBS

9 (9, 10, 10) balls (90m ea) of Karabella Aurora 8 yarn in color 14 muted blue

1 ball Lana Grossa Numero Uno (125m ea) in color 35 charcoal gray; 1 ball in color 130 medium gray

SKULL

The yarn used for Skull has been discontinued. Use same yarn as used for Bob Dobbs in black or dark gray.

1 ball Lana Grossa Numero Uno (125m ea) in a cream color for skull

NEEDLES

two size US 9 (5.5mm) circular needles

If necessary, change needle size to obtain gauge.

NOTIONS

elastic for neckline

sewing thread and needle

darning needle

stitch markers

large safety pin or bodkin

GAUGE

18 sts and 24 rows = 4" (10cm) in St st

MEASUREMENTS

To fit chest 38 (40, 42, 44)" 97 (102, 107, 112)cm

See schematics on page 173 for complete measurements.

TERMINOLOGY

wrap, turn (short row wrap): Work a partial row and pass 1 st wyif, turn the piece, then pass the same st back wyif. Knit the wrap and its st tog on the following row. The wrap prevents a hole in the knitting and keeps the fabric firm (see page 62).

In patt: In pattern. Cont knitting as est.

RLI (right lifted increase): Lift first leg of st below next st onto needle and knit this st (see page 56).

LLI (left lifted increase): Lift last leg below last knitted st onto needle and knit this st (see page 56).

PM (place marker): Slide a ring marker onto the needle whenever the pattern calls for you to place a marker. When you come to the marker on subsequent rows, simply work the st before it, slip the marker, and work the subsequent st.

[ ] (repeat operation): Rep operation in brackets the number of times indicated.

Other techniques: SSK and k2tog (see page 58)

✖ *read this first* ✖

The ribbing at the waist is not intended to draw in like most sweaters, which is why you find decreases after the ribbing instead of increases as in most patterns. If your gauge on ribbing differs much from the given gauge, you may need to change needle size when switching between garter and Stockinette. Your gauge swatch will tell you for sure.

Since the base yarn I used to knit the Skull vest is from Germany (thirteen years ago!), and since I don't have any information about it beyond that it's 100 percent virgin wool, worsted weight, I'm recommending you make the Skull with the same yarn used for the Bob Dobbs vest. Be aware that the difference in gauge used for my sample and the yarn I'm recommending, will create a slightly smaller skull than the one pictured.

BODY

Cast on 180 (190, 200, 210) sts and join on circular needle, taking care not to twist sts. PM at the start of the rnd.

Knit 8 rounds in k1, p1 rib, or until piece measures 1¼" (3cm). Switch to St st and dec 10 sts evenly in the first rnd.

FOR SIZE S ONLY: [SSK, k16] 10 times—170 sts.

FOR SIZE M ONLY: k6, [SSK, k16] 10 times, k4—180 sts.

FOR SIZE L ONLY: [SSK, k18] 10 times—190 sts.

FOR SIZE XL ONLY: k6, [SSK, k18] 10 times, k4—200 sts.

Knit even until piece measures 15½ (15½, 15½, 15¾)" 39 (39, 39, 40)cm from cast-on edge, ending 6 sts before the marker for start of rnd.

PREP FOR UNDERARM BIND OFF

RND 1: Beg 6 sts before the marker for the rnd, [p1, k1] 6 times, p1, k70 (76, 80, 86) across front, [p1, k1] 6 times, p1, k74 (78, 84, 88) across back, ending 6 sts before marker.

RNDS 2–5: Rep Row 1 four more times or until piece measures 16 (16, 16, 16¼)" 41 (41, 41, 42)cm from cast-on edge—170 (180, 190, 200) sts. Do not break yarn.

UNDERARM BIND OFF

RND 6: Beg 6 sts before the marker for the rnd, [p1, k1] twice, bind off 5 sts in patt, p1, k1, p1, k66 (72, 76, 82), [p1, k1] twice, bind off 5 sts in patt, p1, k1, p1, k74 (78, 84, 88), [p1, k1] twice—74 (80, 84, 90) sts for Front; 82 (86, 92, 96) sts for Back.

BACK

Work Back only as foll:

ROW 7 (WS): [p1, k1] twice, p74 (78, 84, 88), [k1, p1] twice.

ROW 8: [p1, p1] twice, k74 (78, 84, 88), [p1, k1] twice.

Repeat Rows 7–8 until piece measures 8¾ (9, 9¼, 9¾)" 22 (23, 24, 25)cm from underarm bind off, ending with a RS row.

SHOULDER SHAPING

ROW 1 (WS): [p1, k1] twice, p70 (74, 80, 84), wrap, turn.

ROW 2: k66 (70, 76, 80), wrap, turn.

ROW 3: p62 (66, 72, 76), wrap, turn.

ROW 4: k58 (62, 68, 72), wrap, turn.

ROW 5: p54 (58, 64, 68), wrap, turn.

ROW 6: k50 (54, 60, 64), wrap, turn.

ROW 7: p46 (50, 56, 60), wrap, turn.

ROW 8: k42 (46, 52, 56), wrap, turn.

SIZES M (L, XL) ONLY

ROW 9: p43 (48, 52), wrap, turn.

ROW 10: k40 (45, 48), wrap, turn.

SIZES L (XL) ONLY

ROW 11: p42 (44), wrap, turn.

SIZE XL ONLY

ROW 12: k40.

Move Back sts to a holder and break yarn—42 (40, 42, 40) sts. The shoulders will be grafted when the Front is finished.

FRONT

With WS facing, rejoin yarn.

ROW 1 (WS): [p1, k1] twice, p66 (72, 76, 82), [k1, p1] twice.

ROW 2: [k1, p1] twice, k66 (72, 76, 82), [p1, k1] twice.

Rep Rows 1–2 until piece measures 4" (10cm) from underarm bind off, ending with Row 1.

INC ROW (RS): [k1, p1] twice, k2, RLI, k62 (68, 72, 78), LLI, k2, [p1, k1] twice—76 (82, 86, 92) sts.

Rep Rows 1-2 until piece measures 5½" (14cm) from underarm bind off, ending with Row 2.

NECK SHAPING

ROW 1 (RS): [k1, p1] twice, k25 (28, 30, 33), PM for neck sts, k18, PM, k25 (28, 30, 33), [p1, k1] twice. The neck sts will not be knit again until you pick up sts for the casing. 29 (32, 34, 37) active sts on needle for Right Front Shoulder.

RIGHT FRONT SHOULDER

ROW 2: [p1, k1] twice, p22 (25, 27, 30), wrap, turn.

ROW 3: k22 (25, 27, 30), [p1, k1] twice.

ROW 4: [p1, k1] twice, p20 (23, 25, 28), wrap, turn.

ROW 5: k20 (23, 25, 28), [p1, k1] twice.

ROW 6: [p1, k1] twice, p18 (21, 23, 26), wrap, turn.

ROW 7: k18 (21, 23, 26), [p1, k1] twice.

ROW 8: [p1, k1] twice, p17 (20, 22, 25), wrap, turn.

ROW 9: k17 (20, 22, 25), [p1, k1] twice.

ROW 10: [p1, k1] twice, p16 (19, 21, 24), wrap, turn.

ROW 11: k16 (19, 21, 24), [p1, k1] twice.

ROW 12: [p1, k1] twice, p16 (19, 21, 24).

ROWS 13–16: Rep Rows 11–12 twice.

ROW 17: Repeat Row 11.

LEFT FRONT SHOULDER

With RS facing, join yarn at left side neck marker.

ROW 2: [k1, p1] twice, k22 (25, 27, 30), wrap, turn.

ROW 3: p22 (25, 27, 30), [p1, k1] twice.

ROW 4: [k1, p1] twice, k20 (23, 25, 28), wrap, turn.

ROW 5: p20 (23, 25, 28), [p1, k1] twice.

ROW 6: [k1, p1] twice, k18 (21, 23, 26), wrap, turn.

ROW 7: p18 (21, 23, 26), [p1, k1] twice.

ROW 8: [k1, p1] twice, k17 (20, 22, 25), wrap, turn.

ROW 9: p17 (20, 22, 25), [p1, k1] twice.

ROW 10: [k1, p1] twice, k16 (19, 21, 24), wrap, turn.

ROW 11: p16 (19, 21, 24), [p1, k1] twice.

ROW 12: [k1, p1] twice, k16 (19, 21, 24).

ROWS 13–16: Rep Rows 11–12 twice.

ROW 17: Rep Row 11.

When short rows are completed, there are 29 (32, 34, 37) sts total for each side on the needle, but only 20 (23, 25, 28) active sts for each side. The sts along front side edge are for neck, and are not part of shoulder.

5¼ (5¼, 5½, 5¾)"   8¼"

8¾ (9, 9¼, 9¾)"

front

circumference of body
38 (40, 42, 44)"

16 (16, 16, 16¼)"

back

24¾ (26, 26¼, 27)"

GRAFT SHOULDER STITCHES TOGETHER

Graft the 20 (23, 25, 28) shoulder sts on Front and Back tog to complete each shoulder, placing the rem neck sts on a circular needle.

NECK FACING

RND 1: With RS facing and circular needle of same size, tie on a new ball of yarn before the first of the neck sts and k42 (40, 42, 40) across back neck. Pick up and knit 7 new sts along side neck, [k1, pick up and k1] 3 times, [k2, pick up and k1] twice, k18 across front neck, [pick up and k1, k2] twice, [pick up and k1, k1] 3 times, pick up and knit 7 new sts along side neck. Join with sts from back neck. PM for beg of rnd—98 (96, 98, 96) sts.

RND 2: Knit.

RND 3: SSK, k38 (36, 38, 36), k2tog, k11, k2tog, k4, SSK, k18, k2tog, k4, SSK, k11—92 (90, 92, 90) sts.

RND 4: Knit.

RND 5: SSK, k36 (34, 36, 34), k2tog, k10, k2tog, k4, SSK, k16, k2tog, k4, SSK, k10—86 (84, 86, 84) sts.

RND 6: Knit.

RND 7: SSK, k34 (32, 34, 32), k2tog, k9, k2tog, k4, SSK, k14, k2tog, k4, SSK, k9—80 (78, 80, 78) sts.

RND 8: Knit.

RNDS 9–10 (TURNING RIDGE): Purl.

RND 11: Knit.

RND 12: Inc, k36 (34, 36, 34), inc, k10, inc, k4, inc, k16, inc, k4, inc, k10—86 (84, 86, 84) sts.

RND 13: Knit.

RND 14: Inc, k38 (36, 38, 36), inc, k11, inc, k4, inc, k18, inc, k4, inc, k11—92 (90, 92, 90) sts.

RND 15: Knit.

RND 16: Inc, k40 (38, 40, 38), inc, k12, inc, k4, inc, k20, inc, k4, inc, k12—98 (96, 98, 96) sts.

RND 17: Knit.

RND 18: Inc, k42 (40, 42, 40), inc, k13, inc, k4, inc, k22, inc, k4, inc, k13—104 (102, 104, 102) sts.

FINISHING
SECURE FACING

Graft or sew down the neck facing (see page 84), leaving a small open gap to insert the elastic to fit your guy's neck, leaving enough yarn to sew it up later. Insert elastic and stitch ends together with thread, being careful not to twist. Close gap in facing.

APPLY DUPLICATE STITCH DESIGN

Follow the chart on opposite page to add the Bob Dobbs face to your sweater vest. Begin with the color covering the most area, and end with the outline sts. See Knitting Directions page 69 for step-by-step instructions on working duplicate stitch. See page 177 for the Skull chart.

Try adding the Skull or Bob with intarsia if you're feeling adventurous. See page 68 in the Knitting Directions chapter for step-by-step instructions for working intarsia.

KNITTING FOR YOUR MAN:
THE SWEATER CURSE

myth: IF YOU KNIT HIM A SWEATER, IT WON'T WORK OUT.

reality: ANY TIME YOU AND YOUR PARTNER HAVE WILDLY DIFFERENT PERSPECTIVES ABOUT HOW THE RELATIONSHIP IS GOING, IT'S A PROBLEM. KNITTING A SWEATER FOR YOUR MAN IS A SURE SIGN YOU'RE INTO HIM. BUT WHAT IF HE'S REALLY NOT THAT INTO YOU?

If you are seriously planning to knit something for your sweetie, here's a checklist:

✘ *Make sure he's into you.* If you have any doubts whatsoever, don't waste a minute knitting for him. Don't entertain the delusion that you're weaving a spell with each stitch. If you haven't won him yet, the sweater will confirm he's not worthy and send him packing. If you're certain about him, please do entertain above delusion.

✘ *Make sure he actually wears sweaters.* Some men just don't. Carefully observe the type and color knits he wears. Some guys like sweaters with zippers, while others prefer pullovers. Don't send him into un-chartered fashion terri-tory. He is a man.

✘ *Plan a project you can finish quickly.* Save the creative fiber masterpiece for your hippie aunt or mom. Stick with something simple you know you can finish in a reasonable amount of time. If you're at all unsure about your fella, start with a hat. Let him earn a sweater.

And if you insist on being superstitious, stave off the curse by knitting in a strand of your hair. For most of us, knitted-in hair is un-preventable, so I hardly need to instruct you. Snipping off the root and catching the strand in every stitch will anchor it in your knitting. Just don't get carried away. Remember, hair shirts were worn for penance.

winged heart bralet

skill level
DOMIKNITRIX

WEAR THIS SEXY HALTER TO THE BEACH
OR OUT ON THE TOWN if you dare. The tattoo-
esque winged heart lace motif is a nod to the Harley-David-
son logo, and it draws the eye directly to dramatic décol-
letage. This halter top lets everybody know you're a bad,
bad girl. Heck, if you've got it, you might as well flaunt it.
Ooo-la-la, lusty lady.

I call this hot little number a bralet because it is recommended for women with cup sizes A and B. Unless you
have impressive, shall we say, self-control, it may not offer
adequate support for larger cup sizes.

WHAT YOU WILL LEARN

✘ grafting facings (page 84)
✘ short rows (page 62)
✘ lace knitting (page 63)

YARN

2 (3) balls (104 yards ea) Zodiac viscose/nylon blend yarn by ArtFibers in color 2 variegated deep purple, burgundy and black (MC)

1 ball (108 yards ea) Tahki Stacy Charles Cotton Classic in your choice of complementary color (CC)

NEEDLES

size US 8 (5mm) needles

size US 6 (4mm) needles

If necessary, change needle size to obtain gauge.

NOTIONS

29 (31, 33, 35)" 74 (79, 84, 89)cm of 1" (3cm) wide elastic for bra band in color to blend with yarn

S-hook swimsuit closure

sewing needle and thread to match MC

stitch markers

GAUGE

24 sts and 32 rows = 4" (10cm) in St st with size US 8 (5mm) needles

MEASUREMENTS

to fit cup size A/B and finished band measurement 29 (31, 33, 35)" 74 (79, 84, 89)cm

TERMINOLOGY

RLI (right lifted increase): Lift first leg of st below next st onto needle and knit this st (see page 56).

LLI (left lifted increase): Lift last leg below last knitted st onto needle and knit this st (see page 56).

psso: Pass slipped st(s) over.

wrap, turn (short row wrap): Work a partial row and pass 1 st wyif, turn the piece, then pass the same st back wyif. Knit the wrap and its st tog on the following row. The wrap prevents a hole in the knitting and keeps the fabric firm (see page 62).

PM (place marker): Slide a ring marker onto the needle whenever the pattern calls for you to place a marker. When you come to the marker on subsequent rows, simply work the st before it, slip the marker, and work the subsequent st.

SSP (slip 2, purl 2 together through back loops): Slip 2 sts 1 at a time as if to knit, insert left needle in back of both sts tog, and pass sts tog back to left needle, then purl 2 tog through the back loops (see page 60).

sl2-k1-psso (slip 2, knit 1, psso): Slip 2 sts together knitwise, k1, pass the 2 slipped sts over the knitted st. This double decrease shows the center st on top.

[ ] (repeat operation): Rep operation in brackets the number of times indicated.

Other techniques: SSK and k2tog (see page 58), yo (see page 63)

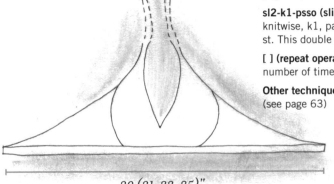

29 (31, 33, 35)"

BAND AND FACING

With MC and larger needles, cast on 157 (169, 183, 195) sts using long tail style.

ROW 1 (WS): p75 (81, 88, 94), k7, purl to end.

ROW 2 AND ALL RS ROWS THROUGH ROW 6: Purl.

ROW 3: p76 (82, 89, 95), k5, purl to end.

ROW 5: p77 (83, 90, 96), k3, purl to end.

ROW 7: p78 (84, 91, 97), k1, purl to end.

ROW 8: Purl for turning ridge.

ROW 9: Join CC for facing and purl. Do not cut MC; drop.

ROWS 10–15: With CC, beg with a knit row, work 6 more rows St st. Cut CC, leaving a tail.

ROW 16: Fold band in half at turning ridge, with RS out. With MC, lift the first st from the cast-on row onto the left needle and SSK with the active st. After joining a few sts in this manner, insert the elastic into the casing you are making, leaving about 1" (3cm) extending out on your right. Cont joining the casing closed in this manner until 75 (81, 88, 94) sts have been worked. Work SSP 7 times to join the next 7 pairs of cast-on sts and active sts, then cont as before with SSK to end, enclosing the elastic as you go—157 (169, 183, 195) sts. When complete, stretch the elastic a bit so it extends outside the casing on each end.

BEGIN BRA CUPS AND LACE MOTIF

ROW 17 (RS): k75 (81, 88, 94), p7, knit to end.

ROWS 18 AND 20: Purl.

ROW 19: k74 (80, 87, 93), p9, knit to end.

ROW 21: k60 (65, 71, 76), PM, RLI, k14 (15, 16, 17), p4, yo, k1, LLI, yo, p4, k14 (15, 16, 17), LLI, PM, knit to end—162 (174, 188, 200) sts.

ROW 22: Purl to last 6 (6, 8, 10) sts; wrap, turn.

ROW 23: Knit to marker and sl marker, RLI, k14 (15, 16, 17), p4, yo, k2tog, yo, k2, yo, SSK, yo, p4, k14 (15, 16, 17), LLI, sl marker, knit to last 6 (6, 8, 10) sts; wrap, turn—46 (48, 50, 52) sts between markers.

ROW 24: Purl to last 12 (12, 16, 18) sts; wrap, turn.

ROW 25: Knit to marker and sl marker, RLI, k14 (15, 16, 17), p4, k2, yo, k2tog, yo, k2, yo, SSK, yo, k2, p4, k14 (15, 16, 17), LLI, sl marker, knit to last 12 (12, 16, 18) sts; wrap, turn—50 (52, 54, 56) sts between markers.

ROW 26: Purl to last 18 (18, 24, 26) sts; wrap, turn.

ROW 27: Knit to marker and sl marker, RLI, k14 (15, 16, 17), p4, k2tog, k2, yo, k2tog, yo, k2, yo, SSK, yo, k2, SSK, p4, k14 (15, 16, 17), LLI, sl marker, knit to last 18 (18, 24, 26) sts; wrap, turn—52 (54, 56, 58) sts between markers.

ROW 28: Purl to last 22 (22, 30, 32) sts; wrap, turn.

ROW 29: Knit to marker and sl marker, RLI, k14 (15, 16, 17), p4, k2tog, k3, yo, k2tog, yo, k2, yo, SSK, yo, k3, SSK, p4, k14 (15, 16, 17), LLI, sl marker, knit to last 22 (22, 30, 32) sts; wrap, turn—54 (56, 58, 60) sts between markers.

ROW 30: Purl to last 26 (28, 35, 38) sts; wrap, turn.

ROW 31: Knit to marker and sl marker, RLI, k14 (15, 16, 17), p4, k2tog, k4, yo, [sl2-k1-psso, yo] twice, k4, SSK, p4, k14 (15, 16, 17), LLI, sl marker, knit to last 26 (28, 35, 38) sts; wrap, turn—57 sts between markers.

ROW 32: Purl to last 30 (32, 39, 42) sts; wrap, turn.

ROW 33: Knit to marker and sl marker, RLI, k16, p4, k2tog, k5, yo, sl2-k1-psso, yo, k5, SSK, p4, k16, LLI, sl marker, knit to last 30 (32, 39, 42) sts; wrap, turn—53 (55, 57, 59) sts between markers.

ROW 34: Purl to marker and sl marker, p25 (26, 27, 28), yo, p1, yo, p1 (in center st), lift st from decreased st below and p1, yo, p1, yo, purl to last 34 (36, 43, 46) sts; wrap, turn—58 (60, 62, 64) sts between markers.

ROW 35: Knit to marker and sl marker, RLI, k14 (15, 16, 17), p5, k5, SSK, yo, k1, yo, SSK; turn work—89 (95, 102, 108) sts worked. Place rem sts for Right Side on holder.

LEFT CUP

ROW 36: Purl to last 37 (38, 45, 49) sts; wrap, turn.

ROW 37: Knit to marker and sl marker, RLI, k14 (15, 16, 17), p5, k4, [SSK, yo] twice, SSK.

ROW 38: Purl to last 39 (40, 47, 51) sts; wrap, turn.

ROW 39: Knit to marker and sl marker, RLI, k15 (16, 17, 18), p5, k3, [SSK, yo] twice, SSK.

ROW 40: Purl to last 40 (41, 48, 52) sts; wrap, turn.

ROW 41: Knit last 17 sts, p9, k2, [SSK, yo] twice, SSK—88 (94, 101, 107) sts.

ROW 42: Purl to end, lifting each wrap onto needle and purling it tog with the st it wraps.

ROW 43: In k1, p1 rib, bind off 41 (45, 49, 53) sts; knit to last 16 sts, p6, k4, [SSK, yo] twice, SSK—46 (48, 51, 53) sts.

ROW 44 AND ALL WS ROWS: Purl to end.

ROW 45: SSK, knit to 1 st before marker; remove marker and k2tog, PM, k11 (12, 13, 14), p6, k3, [SSK, yo] twice, yo, SSK—43 (45, 48, 50) sts.

ROW 47: SSK, knit to last 15 sts, p7, k2, [SSK, yo] twice, SSK—41 (43, 46, 48) sts.

ROW 49: SSK, knit to 2 sts before marker, k2tog, k9 (10 11, 12), p8, k1, [SSK, yo] twice, SSK—38 (40, 43, 45) sts.

ROW 51: SSK, knit to last 15 sts, p9, [SSK, yo] twice, SSK—36 (38, 41, 43) sts.

ROW 53: SSK, knit to 2 sts before marker, k2tog, k8 (9, 10, 11), p6, k2, [SSK, yo] twice, SSK—33 (35, 38, 40) sts.

ROW 55: SSK, knit to last 13 sts, p6, k1, [SSK, yo] twice, SSK—31 (33, 36, 38) sts.

ROW 57: SSK, knit to 2 sts before marker, k2tog, k5 (6, 7, 8), p9, [SSK, yo] twice, SSK—28 (30, 33, 35) sts.

ROW 59: SSK, k11 (13, 16, 17), p7, k2, [SSK, yo] twice, SSK—26 (28, 31, 33) sts.

ROW 61: SSK, knit to 2 sts before marker, k2tog, k3 (4, 5, 6), p8, k1, [SSK, yo] twice, SSK—23 (25, 28, 30) sts

ROW 63: SSK, k7 (9, 12, 14), p8, [SSK, yo] twice, SSK—21 (23, 26, 28) sts.

ROW 65: SSK, k1 (2, 4, 5), k2tog, k3 (4, 5, 6), p5, k2, [SSK, yo] twice, SSK—18 (20, 23, 25) sts.

ROW 67: SSK, k3 (5, 8, 10), p6, k1, [SSK, yo] twice, SSK—16 (18, 21, 23) sts.

ROW 69: SSK, k0 (0, 1, 2), [k2tog] 0 (0, 1, 1) time, k1 (3, 3, 4), p7, [SSK, yo] twice, SSK—14 (16, 18, 20) sts.

ROW 71: SSK, k0 (1, 3, 5), p4 (5, 5, 5), k2, [SSK, yo] twice, SSK—12 (14, 16, 18) sts.

ROW 73: SSK, k0 (0, 1, 3), p3 (5, 6, 6), k1, [SSK, yo] twice, SSK—10 (12, 14, 16) sts.

SMALL, MEDIUM AND LARGE ONLY

ROW 75: SSK, k(0, 0, 2), p(4, 6, 6), [SSK, yo] twice, SSK—(10, 12, 14) sts.

MEDIUM AND LARGE ONLY

ROW 77: SSK, p(2, 4), k2, [SSK, yo] twice, SSK—(10, 12) sts.

ROW 79: SSK, p(1, 3) k1, [SSK, yo] twice, SSK—(8, 10) sts.

EXTRA SMALL, SMALL AND LARGE ONLY

NEXT ROW (RS): SSK, p2, [SSK, yo] twice, SSK—8 sts.

MEDIUM ONLY

ROW 79: SSK, p1, k1, [SSK, yo] twice, SSK—8 sts.

ALL SIZES

NEXT RS ROW: [SSK] twice, [yo, SSK] twice—6 sts.

NEXT RS ROW: [SSK, yo] twice, SSK—5 sts.

NEXT RS ROW: Change to smaller needles. SSK, yo, k1, yo, SSK—5 sts.

NEXT WS ROW: Purl.

Rep last 2 rows until strap is desired length, then bind off.

RIGHT CUP

Sl sts from holder to needle. With RS facing, join yarn.

ROW 35: k2tog, yo, k1, yo, k2tog, k5, p5, purl to marker, LLI, sl marker, knit to last 34 (36, 43, 46) sts; wrap, turn.

ROWS 36, 38 AND 40: Purl.

ROW 37: [k2tog, yo] twice, k2tog, k4, p5, knit to marker, LLI, sl marker, knit to last 37 (38, 45, 49) sts; wrap, turn.

ROW 39: [k2tog, yo] twice, k2tog, k3, p5, knit to marker, LLI, sl marker, knit to last 39 (40, 47, 51) sts; wrap, turn.

ROW 41: [k2tog, yo] twice, k2tog, k2, p9, knit to end, lifting each wrap onto needle and knitting it tog with the st it wraps—88 (94, 101, 107) sts.

ROW 42: In k1, p1 rib, bind off 40 (44, 48, 52) sts; purl to end—48 (50, 53, 55) sts.

ROW 43: [k2tog, yo] twice, k2tog, k4, p6, knit to last 2 sts, k2tog—46 (48, 51, 53) sts.

ROW 44 AND ALL WS ROWS: Purl.

ROW 45: [k2tog, yo] twice, k2tog, k3, p6, knit to 1 st before marker, move marker 1 st to right, SSK, knit to last 2 sts, k2tog—43 (45, 48, 51) sts.

ROW 47: [k2tog, yo] twice, k2tog, k2, p7, knit to last 2 sts, k2tog—41 (43, 46, 48) sts.

ROW 49: [k2tog, yo] twice, k2tog, k1, p8, knit to marker, SSK, knit to last 2 sts, k2tog—38 (40, 43, 45) sts.

ROW 51: [k2tog, yo] twice, k2tog, p9, knit to last 2 sts, k2tog—36 (38, 41, 43) sts.

ROW 53: [k2tog, yo] twice, k2tog, k2, p6, knit to marker, SSK, knit to last 2 sts, k2tog—33 (35, 38, 40) sts.

ROW 55: [k2tog, yo] twice, k2tog, k1, p6, knit to last 2 sts, k2tog—31 (33, 36, 38) sts.

ROW 57: [k2tog, yo] twice, k2tog, p9, knit to marker, SSK, knit to last 2 sts, k2tog—28 (30, 33, 35) sts.

ROW 59: [k2tog, yo] twice, k2tog, k2, p7, knit to last 2 sts, k2tog—26 (28, 31, 33) sts.

ROW 61: [k2tog, yo] twice, k2tog, k1, p8, knit to marker, SSK, knit to last 2 sts, k2tog—23 (25, 28, 30) sts.

ROW 63: [k2tog, yo] twice, k2tog, p8, knit to last 2 sts, k2tog—21 (23, 26, 28) sts.

ROW 65: [k2tog, yo] twice, k2tog, k2, p5, knit to marker, SSK, knit to last 2 sts, k2tog—18 (20, 23, 25) sts.

ROW 67: [k2tog, yo] twice, k2tog, k1, p6, knit to last 2 sts, k2tog—16 (18, 21, 23) sts.

ROW 69: [k2tog, yo] twice, k2tog, p7, k1 (3, 3, 4), [SSK] 0 (0, 1, 1) times, k0 (0, 1, 2), k2tog—14 (16, 18, 20) sts.

ROW 71: [k2tog, yo] twice, k2tog, k2, p4 (5, 5, 5), k0 (1, 3, 5), k2tog—12 (14, 16, 18) sts.

ROW 73: [k2tog, yo] twice, k2tog, k1, p3 (5, 6, 6), k0 (0, 1, 3), k2tog—10 (12, 14, 16) sts.

SMALL, MEDIUM AND LARGE ONLY

ROW 75: [k2tog, yo] twice, k2tog, p(4, 6, 6), k(0, 0, 2), k2tog—(10, 12, 14) sts.

MEDIUM AND LARGE ONLY

ROW 77: [k2tog, yo] twice, k2tog, k2, p(2, 4), k2tog—(10, 12) sts.

ROW 79: [k2tog, yo] twice, k2tog, k1, p(1, 3), k2tog—(8, 10) sts.

EXTRA SMALL, SMALL AND LARGE ONLY

NEXT ROW (RS): [k2tog, yo] twice, k2tog, p2, k2tog—8 sts.

MEDIUM ONLY

ROW 79: [k2tog, yo] twice, k2tog, k1, p1, k2tog—8 sts.

STRAPS

NEXT RS ROW: [k2tog, yo] twice, [k2tog] twice—6 sts.

NEXT RS ROW: [k2tog, yo] twice, k2tog—5 sts.

NEXT RS ROW: Change to smaller needles. k2tog, yo, k1, yo, k2tog—5 sts.

NEXT WS ROW: Purl.

Rep last 2 rows until strap is same length as left side; bind off.

FINISHING

Using sewing thread, slip the right end of the elastic through the bathing suit closure and sew the elastic closed around the closure. Fold the left end of the elastic onto itself, and pin or baste, leaving a loop for the S-hook to fit into. Try on before sewing, and adjust if necessary. Stretch out the band so these ends slip inside the casing, and sew the fabric around the elastic to hide it. Weave in all ends.

Alternatively, consider knitting the straps shorter and sewing the ends of the straps to the back of the band like a bra. Have an assistant fit carefully with straps well stretched, then graft or sew down the ends to the back of the band.

The lace and the contrast-color facing make this little number look just as good inside-out, so wear it as you like.

sweetheart

THIS SURREALLY INNOCENT PULLOVER HAS A SWEETHEART OF A NECKLINE, bracelet-length sleeves and a pink intarsia bow. I'd been meaning to design a sweater inspired by fashion designer Elsa Schiaparelli's black knit sweaters with white bow tie motifs for years, and I finally got the chance on this one. Instead of the "shocking pink" favored by Elsa, however, I used this gentler shade. If you're after the boy next door, try this one first.

Most of the intarsia charts are made with the same number of stitches so you may easily use the stiletto (page 251), skull (page 177), no hate (page 250) or Bob Dobbs (page 175) on this one. I chose to knit this sample in the demure bow, but you don't have to, kitten!

WHAT YOU WILL LEARN

✘ working in the round (page 52)
✘ intarsia (page 68)
✘ short rows (page 62)
✘ Kitchener grafting (page 80)
✘ mattress stitch (page 78)

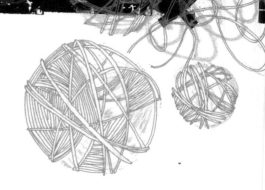

YARN

8 (9, 9, 10, 10) balls (137 yards ea) Filatura di
Crosa Zara 100% merino yarn in color 1469 charcoal gray; 1 ball in color 1510 soft pink

Or substitute any soft yarn that knits to gauge.

NEEDLES

two 32" (81cm) size US 6 (4mm) circular needles

If necessary, change needle size to obtain gauge.

NOTIONS

stitch markers in two colors

darning needle

GAUGE

22 sts and 30 rows = 4" (10cm) in St st

MEASUREMENTS

To fit bust 32 (34, 36, 38, 41)" 81 (86, 91, 97,
104)cm

TERMINOLOGY

RLI (right lifted increase): Lift first leg of st below
next st onto needle and knit this st (see page 56).

LLI (left lifted increase): Lift last leg below last knitted st onto needle and knit this st (see page 56).

PM (place marker): Slide a ring marker onto the
needle whenever the pattern calls for you to place a
marker. When you come to the marker on subsequent rows, simply work the st before it, slip the
marker, and work the subsequent st.

SSP (slip 2, purl 2 together through back loops):
Slip 2 sts one at a time as if to knit, insert left
needle in back of both sts tog, and pass sts tog
back to left needle, then purl 2 tog through the
back loops (see page 60).

psso: Pass slipped st(s) over.

in patt: In pattern. Cont working as est.

Other techniques: SSK and k2tog (see page 58)

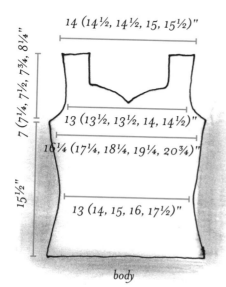

14 (14½, 14½, 15, 15½)"

7 (7¼, 7½, 7¾, 8¼)"

13 (13½, 13½, 14, 14½)"

16¼ (17¼, 18¼, 19¼, 20¾)"

15½"

13 (14, 15, 16, 17½)"

body

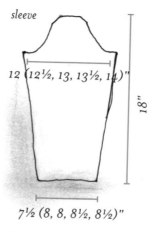

sleeve

12 (12½, 13, 13½, 14)"

18"

7½ (8, 8, 8½, 8½)"

BODY

With a circular needle, cast on 176 (188, 200, 212, 228) sts. Join for working in the rnd, taking care not to twist sts. Work in k1, p1 rib for 8 rnds.

DARTED WAIST DEC: On next rnd, k16 (18, 20, 22, 24), PM, SSK, k52 (54, 56, 58, 62), k2tog, PM, k32 (36, 40, 44, 48), PM, SSK, k52 (54, 56, 58, 62), k2tog, PM, knit to end of rnd—172 (184, 196, 208, 224) sts.

Work 5 rnds even in St st.

NEXT RND: * Knit to marker, sl marker, SSK, knit to 2 sts before marker, k2tog, sl marker; rep from * once more, knit to end—168 (180, 192, 204, 220) sts.

Work waist dec as est on every 6th rnd 6 times more—144 (156, 168, 180, 196) sts.

Work 3 rnds even. Rep decrease rnd once more—140 (152, 164, 176, 192) sts.

DIVIDE FRONT AND BACK: Turn work and p70 (76, 82, 88, 96). Move Front sts to a holder if you wish.

BACK

Work the Back only, back and forth.

NEXT ROW (RS): RLI, work to last st, LLI—72 (78, 84, 90, 98) sts. Purl 1 row.

DARTED WAIST INC (RS): Knit to marker, sl marker, RLI, knit to marker, LLI, sl marker, knit to end—74 (80, 86, 92, 100) sts.

Work waist increases as est on every foll 6th row 8 times more—90 (96, 102, 108, 116) sts.

Work even for 7 rows, ending with a WS row.

ARMHOLE SHAPING

NEXT ROW (RS): Bind off 6 (6, 6, 7, 7) sts.

NEXT ROW: Bind off 6 (6, 6, 7, 7) sts, purl to last st, sl last st—78 (84, 90, 94, 102) sts.

ARMHOLE DEC ROW (RS): Sl first 2 sts, pass first st over second st to bind off 1, knit to last st, sl last st.

ARMHOLE DEC ROW (WS): Sl first 2 sts, pass first st over second st to bind off 1, purl to last st, sl last st.

Rep the last 2 rows 2 (4, 6, 7, 10) times more. Do not slip last st on last row—72 (74, 76, 78, 80 sts).

Work even until armhole measures 4¼ (4½, 4¾, 5, 5½)" (11 [12, 12, 13, 14]cm), ending with a WS row.

ARMHOLE INC ROW (RS): k3, RLI, knit to last 3 sts, LLI, knit to end—72 (76, 78, 80, 82) sts.

Rep Armhole Inc Row every 8th row twice more—76 (80, 82, 84, 86) sts.

Work even until armhole measures 7 (7¼, 7½, 7¾, 8¼)" (18 [19, 19, 20, 21] cm), ending with a WS row.

SHOULDER SHAPING

Knit to last 6 sts, wrap, turn. Purl to last 6 sts, wrap, turn. Knit to last 12 sts, wrap, turn. Purl to last 12 sts, wrap, turn. Knit to last 14 (15, 17, 18, 18) sts, wrap, turn. Purl to last 14 (15, 17, 18, 18) sts, wrap, turn. Knit 1 complete row, picking up and knitting wraps tog with their sts. Purl 1 complete row, picking up and purling wraps tog with their sts. Place all sts on holder.

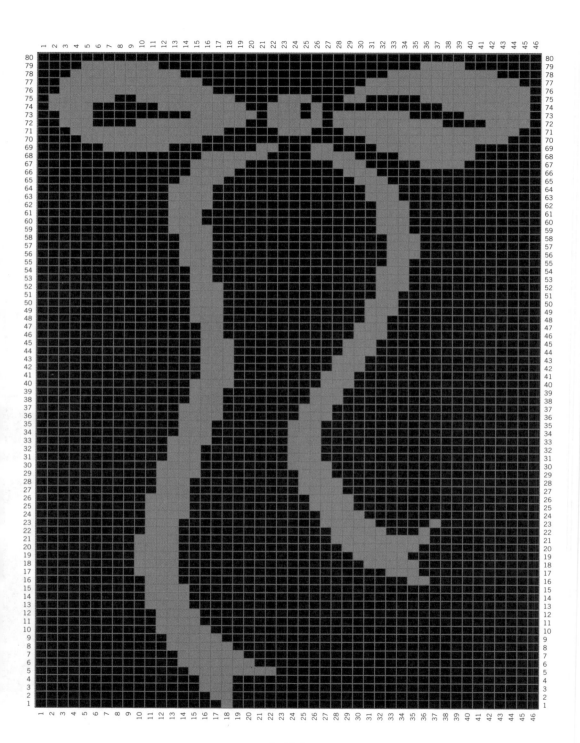

FRONT

With WS facing, join yarn and purl 1 row.

BEGIN INTARSIA BOW

On the next row, you will begin working the chart. Take note that to keep track of the chart, you'll need to count from right to left for the RS rows, and left to right for the WS rows. The next row will direct you to place markers 46 sts apart, the width of the chart. These markers should be a different color than the dart markers, and should remain 46 sts apart for the whole length of the chart. This means that for all but the largest size, you will need to move each marker 1 st inward to the center as the waist inc progress, until the waist inc are being worked outside of the 46-st chart area. Removable markers or loops of scrap yarn make this easy to do. After the first row, these markers will not be mentioned in the instructions.

From here on, row numbers refer to rows marked on the chart. If specific instructions are not given for a particular row, it is to be worked even in patt, without inc or dec.

WORK BOW CHART

ROW 1: k12 (15, 18, 21, 25), place chart marker, work first row of chart, place chart marker, k12 (15, 18, 21, 25).

DARTED WAIST INC: Knit to (dart) marker, sl marker, RLI, knit to (dart) marker, LLI, sl marker, knit to end—72 (78, 84, 90, 98) sts.

Work waist inc as est on every foll 6th row 8 times more—88 (94, 100, 106, 114) sts.

SHORT ROW SHAPING FOR BUST

Be careful to stay on track in the chart as you shape the bust and armholes. Resist the temptation to strand the yarn behind the knitting at the top of the bow to prevent adding another bobbin. This will cause the stranded portions to have tension inconsistent with the rest of your work up to this point. This is the focal point of the sweater, and the place where your bosom will be stretching the fabric and drawing negative attention if it has been stranded.

ROW 57: Knit to last 6 sts, wrap, turn.

ROW 58: Purl to last 6 sts, wrap, turn.

ROW 59: Knit to last 12 sts, wrap, turn.

ROW 60: Purl to last 12 sts, wrap, turn.

ROW 61: Knit to last 16 sts, wrap, turn.

ROW 62: Purl to last 16 sts, wrap, turn.

ROW 63: Knit all sts, picking up and knitting wraps tog with their sts.

ROW 64: Purl all sts, picking up and knitting wraps tog with their sts.

Work even for 4 rows more, ending with chart row 68.

ARMHOLE SHAPING

ROW 69 (RS): Bind off 5 (5, 5, 6, 6) sts.

ROW 70: Bind off 5 (5, 5, 6, 6) sts, purl to last st, sl last st—78 (84, 90, 94, 102) sts.

ROW 71: Sl first 2 sts, pass first st over second st to bind off 1, knit to last st, sl last st.

ROW 72: Sl first 2 sts, pass first st over second st to bind off 1, purl to last st, sl last st.

EXTRA SMALL ONLY

ROWS 73–76: Rep Rows 71–72 twice more. Do not sl last st on row 76—72 sts.

Work 4 rows even.

SMALL ONLY

ROWS 73–80: Rep Rows 71–72 four times more. Do not sl last st on Row 80—74 sts.

MEDIUM, LARGE, EXTRA LARGE ONLY

ROWS 73–80: Rep Rows 71–72 four times more—80 (84, 92) sts.

The chart is now complete.

NECK SHAPING
EXTRA SMALL AND SMALL ONLY

NEXT ROW (RS): k35 (36), bind off center 2 sts, knit to end.

Now work the right side only (right side as worn, left side as looking at it RS up).

NEXT ROW (WS): Purl to last st, sl last st.

NEXT ROW: Sl first 2 sts, pass first st over second st to bind off 1, bind off 2 more, knit to end.

Rep these 2 rows 7 times more—11 (12) sts.

MEDIUM, LARGE AND EXTRA LARGE ONLY

NEXT ROW (RS): Sl first 2 sts, pass first st over second st to bind off 1, knit until there are 38 (40, 44) sts on right-hand needle, bind off center 2 sts, knit to last st, sl last st.

Now work the right side only (right side as worn, left side as looking at it RS up).

NEXT ROW (WS): Sl first 2 sts, pass first st over second st to bind off 1, purl to last st, sl last st—38 (40, 44) sts.

NEXT ROW (RS): Sl first 2 sts, pass first st over second st to bind off 1, bind off 2 more, knit to last st, sl last st.

NEXT ROW: Sl first 2 sts, pass first st over second st to bind off 1, purl to last st, sl last st—34 (36, 40) sts.

Rep the last 2 rows 0 (1, 4) times more—34 (32, 24) sts.

NEXT ROW: Sl first 2 sts, pass first st over second st to bind off 1, bind off 2 more, knit to end.

NEXT ROW: Purl to last st, sl last st.

Rep the last 2 rows 6 (5, 2) times more. Do not slip last st on last row—13 (14, 15) sts.

ARMHOLE SHAPING

Work even until armhole measures 4¼ (4½, 4¾, 5, 5½)" (11 [11½, 12, 13, 14]cm), ending with a WS row.

ARMHOLE INC ROW (RS): Knit to last 3 sts, LLI, knit to end—12 (13, 14, 15, 16) sts.

Repeat Armhole Inc Row every 8th row twice more—14 (15, 17, 18, 18) sts.

Work even until armhole measures 7 (7¼, 7½, 7¾, 8¼)" (18 [19, 19, 20, 21]cm), ending with a WS row.

SHOULDER SHAPING

Knit to last 6 sts, wrap, turn. Purl 1 row. Knit to last 12 sts, wrap, turn. Purl 1 row. Knit 1 complete row, picking up and knitting wraps tog with their sts. Place all sts on holder.

LEFT SIDE NECK SHAPING

Join yarn at neck edge.

EXTRA SMALL AND SMALL ONLY

NEXT ROW (WS): Sl first 2 sts, pass first st over second st to bind off 1, bind off 2 more, purl to end.

NEXT ROW: Knit to last st, sl last st.

Rep these 2 rows 7 times more. Do not sl last st on last row—11 (12) sts.

MEDIUM, LARGE AND EXTRA LARGE ONLY

NEXT ROW (WS): Sl first 2 sts, pass first st over second st to bind off 1, bind off 2 more, purl to last st, sl last st.

NEXT ROW: Sl first 2 sts, pass first st over second st to bind off 1, purl to last st, sl last st—34 (36, 40) sts.

Rep last 2 rows (0, 1, 4) times more—34 (32, 24) sts.

NEXT ROW: Sl first 2 sts, pass first st over second st to bind off 1, bind off 2 more, knit to end.

NEXT ROW: Purl to last st, sl last st.

Rep the last 2 rows 6 (5, 2) times more. Do not slip last st on last row—13 (14, 15) sts.

ARMHOLE SHAPING

Work even until armhole measures 4¼ (4½, 4¾, 5, 5½)" (11 [12, 12, 13, 14]cm), ending with a WS row.

ARMHOLE INC ROW (RS): k3, RLI, knit to end—12 (13, 14, 15, 16) sts.

Rep Armhole Inc Row every 8th row twice more—14 (15, 17, 18, 18) sts.

Work even until armhole measures 7 (7¼, 7½, 7¾, 8¼)" (18 [18.5, 19, 19.5, 21] cm), ending with a RS row.

FINAL SHOULDER SHAPING

Purl to last 6 sts, wrap, turn. Knit 1 row. Purl to last 12 sts, wrap, turn. Knit 1 row. Purl 1 complete row, picking up and purling wraps together with their sts. Place all sts on holder.

SLEEVES

Cast on 41 [43, 43, 47, 47] sts.

ROW 1: * k1, p1; rep from * to last st, k1.

ROW 2: * p1, k1; rep from * to last st, p1.

Rep Rows 1–2 until sleeve measures 3" (8cm) from cast on edge, ending with Row 2.

INC ROW: k2, RLI, knit to last 2 sts, LLI, k2—43 (45, 45, 49, 49) sts.

Work even in St st until sleeve measures 5" (13cm) from cast-on edge, ending with a WS row.

Work Inc Row on next and every foll 6th row 11 (11, 12, 12, 13) times more—67 (69, 71, 75, 77) sts.

Work even until sleeve measures 18" (46cm) or desired length to underarm, ending with a WS row.

SHAPE CAP

Bind off 5 (5, 5, 6, 6) sts at beg of next 2 rows—57 (59, 61, 63, 65) sts.

DEC ROW: k2, SSK, knit to last 4 sts, k2tog, k2.

NEXT ROW: Purl.

Rep these 2 rows 12 (15, 16, 17, 21) times more—31 (27, 27, 27, 21) sts.

EXTRA SMALL, SMALL, MEDIUM AND LARGE ONLY

NEXT ROW (RS): k2, SSK, knit to last 4 sts, k2tog, k2.

NEXT ROW (WS): p2, p2tog, purl to last 4 sts, SSP, p2.

Rep the last 2 rows 2 (1, 1, 1) times more—19 (19, 19, 21) sts.

Bind off all sts (all sizes).

FINISHING

GRAFT SHOULDERS AND SEW SIDE SEAMS

Join the sleeves to the body with Kitchener stitch (see page 80) at the underarm and mattress stitch (see page 78) on the vertical seams. Sew side seams.

NECK EDGING

With RS facing, join yarn at right shoulder. Knit across back sts. Pick up and k3 sts for every 4 rows along left front neck. Place marker. Across the front neck, notice that sts are clustered in groups of 3, with a small gap between them from the sts that smooth the bind off. * Pick up and k3 in the 3 sts below the bind-off row, then pick up and k1 in the gap; rep from * to center front bind off. Pick up and k3 at center front. * Pick up and k1 in the gap and then pick up and k3 below the bind off row; rep from * to corner of right front neck. Place marker. Pick up and k3 sts for every 4 rows along left front neck. Join for working in the rnd.

Count sts. If you do not have a multiple of 2, dec 1 st inconspicuously on next rnd.

RND 1: * k1, p1; rep from * to end.

RND 2: * k1, p1; rep from * to 1 st before first marker, work 2 sts tog in patt (removing marker), cont in ribbing to 1 st before second marker, work 2 sts tog in patt (removing marker), cont in ribbing to end.

RND 3: * k1, p1; rep from * to 3 sts at center front, sl2, k1, psso, cont in ribbing to end.

Bind off in patt. Weave in all ends.

DIVA HALTER

skill level
APPRENTICE

LACE UP OR ZIP DOWN...OR BOTH IF YOU'RE FEELING ADVENTUROUS. You can knit this sexy little top in only a few hours—start it in the morning and then go all night. The contrast color adds a bit of knitting interest, and the ribs hug the body for an alluring look. Add an optional corset lacing in the center back wedge for an extra helping of sexy.

I recommend knitting this design a size smaller than you usually wear, which will make the knit ribs pop and highlight your curves. For a C-cup or larger, wear it with a strapless or halter bra underneath. Did I mention that tight sweaters save yarn?

WHAT YOU WILL LEARN

✘ intarsia (page 68)
✘ short rows (page 62)
✘ mattress stitch (page 78)
✘ Kitchener stitch (page 80)
✘ installing a zipper (page 86)

YARN

6 (7, 8, 10, 11) balls (56 yards ea) Aurora Karabella 100% merino bulky yarn in color 7 mauve
(MC); 3 (4, 4, 5, 6) balls in color 14 plum (CC)

NEEDLES

size US 9 (5.5mm) needles

If necessary, change needle size to obtain gauge.

NOTIONS

12" (30cm) nylon zipper in color to match CC

sewing needle and thread to match zipper

½ yard flat elastic

2 yards (1.8m) satin rattail for corset lacing (optional)

two darning needles

GAUGE

22½ sts and 22 rows = 4" (10cm) in k1, p1 rib

MEASUREMENTS

To fit bust 34 (36, 38, 40, 43)" 86 (91, 97, 102,
109)cm

*See schematic on page 196 for complete measure-
ments.*

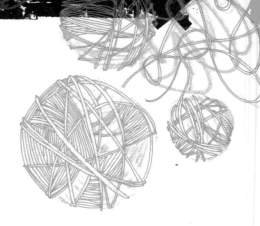

TERMINOLOGY

wrap, turn (short row wrap): Work a partial row and
slip 1 st wyif, turn the piece, then slip the same st
back wyif. Knit the wrap and its st tog on the following row. The wrap prevents a hole in the knitting
and keeps the fabric firm (see page 62).

SSP (slip 2, purl 2 together through back loops):
Slip 2 sts 1 at a time as if to knit, insert left needle
in back of both sts tog, and pass sts tog back to left
needle, then purl 2 tog through the back loops (see
page 60).

RLI (right lifted increase): Lift first leg of st below
next st onto needle and knit this st (see page 56).

LLI (left lifted increase): Lift last leg below last knitted st onto needle and knit this st (see page 56).

PM (place marker): Slide a ring marker onto the
needle whenever the pattern calls for you to place a
marker. When you come to the marker on subsequent rows, simply work the st before it, slip the
marker, and work the subsequent st.

Rev St st (reverse Stockinette st): Purl every RS row,
knit every WS row.

In patt: In pattern. Cont working as est.

Other techniques: p2tog and k2tog (see pages 58
and 60), SSK (see page 58)

notes:

- When switching from one yarn color to the other, drop the old yarn in back for the RS rows, in front for the WS rows. Pick up the new yarn from under the old yarn, interlocking the 2 yarns and preventing a hole in the knitting.
- After the first 2 rows, the first and last 14 (14, 16, 16, 16) sts are worked in CC, and the rest of the sts are worked in MC.
- Work decs for side shaping as follows: Work to first side marker, slip marker and dec as SSP if first st is purl and dec as SSK if first st is knit; work to 2 sts before second side marker and dec as p2tog if first st is purl and dec as k2tog if first st is knit.
- Front and Back insets are worked in Rev St st.

BODY

With CC, cast on 143 (155, 165, 177, 189) sts using long tail style.

ROW 1 (RS): * k1, p1; rep from * to last st, k1.

ROW 2: Knit the knit sts and purl the purl sts.

ROW 3: Cont in rib, work 14 (14, 16, 16, 16) sts, drop CC; join MC, work 22 (25, 25, 28, 31) sts, PM for side marker, work to last 36 (39, 41, 44, 47) sts, PM for side marker, work to last 14 (14, 16, 16, 16) sts, drop MC; join CC and work to end.

Cont working in rib, working first and last 14 (14, 16, 16, 16) sts with CC and rem sts with MC until 15 rows total have been worked.

SIDE SHAPING

See notes for how to dec.

(WS) Work in patt to marker, SSK or SSP, sl marker, work in patt to 2 sts before last marker, k2tog or p2tog, sl marker, work in patt to end. Rep dec row every 2 rows 0 (0, 1, 1, 0) time(s), every 4 rows 0 (2, 7, 8, 6) times, then every 6 rows 4 (3, 0, 0, 2) times, removing markers at last dec. AT THE SAME TIME when piece measures 5¾ (5¾, 4½, 4¼, 4)" 15 (15, 12, 11, 10)cm from beg, ending with a RS row, place markers on last row as foll: Work 26 (26, 28, 30, 30) sts, PM for front inset; work to center back st, PM on each side of st, work to last 26 (26, 28, 30, 30) sts, PM for front inset, work to end.

BACK AND FRONT INSET SHAPING

(WS) While working in patt and cont side shaping, work to front inset marker, LLI, sl marker; work to back inset marker, sl marker, RLI, work to next back inset marker, LLI, sl marker, work to other front inset marker, sl marker, RLI, work to end. Working insets in Rev St st, rep inc for front insets every 4 rows 5 (2, 0, 0, 0) times, every 6 rows 0 (3, 5, 1, 2) times, then every 8 rows 0 (0, 1, 5, 5) times and rep inc for back inset every 4 rows 2 times, then every 6 rows 3 (4, 6, 7, 8) times. Work 2 rows even in patt—157 (169, 179, 191, 209) sts.

CENTER BACK SHAPING

From this point on, shaping occurs on RS rows only to bind off sts to shape center back with a graduated bind off at the beg of each RS row.

ROW 1 (RS): Work in patt for 24 (24, 26, 28, 28) sts, PM, SSK, purl to inset marker and remove, work rib to 2 sts before back inset marker and place all sts just worked on holder; bind off 2 sts in rib, bind off 13 (15, 19, 21, 23) back inset sts in knit, bind off 2 sts in rib, work in rib to inset marker and remove, p6 (6, 7, 7, 8), k2tog, PM, work in rib to end—69 (74, 77, 82, 90) sts each on needle and on hold.

LEFT FRONT

ROW 2 AND ALL WS ROWS: Knit the knit sts and purl the purl sts, sl last st.

ROWS 3 AND 5 (RS): Sl first 2 sts, pass first st over second to bind off 1, bind off 7 more sts, work in patt to 2 sts before marker, k2tog, work in rib to end—51 (56, 59, 64, 72) sts.

ROW 7: Sl first 2 sts, pass first st over second, bind off 5 (7, 7, 7, 7) more sts, work in patt to 2 sts before marker, k2tog, work in rib to end—44 (47, 50, 55, 63) sts.

ROW 9: Sl first 2 sts, pass first st over second, bind off 5 (5, 4, 6, 6) more sts, work in patt to 2 sts before marker, k2tog, work in rib to end—37 (40, 44, 47, 55) sts.

ROW 11: Sl first 2 sts, pass first st over second, bind off 3 (5, 3, 4, 6) more sts, work in patt to 2 sts before marker, k2tog, work in rib to end—32 (33, 39, 41, 47) sts.

ROW 13: Sl first 2 sts, pass first st over second, bind off 1 (2, 1, 1, 4) more st(s), work in patt to 2 sts before marker, k2tog, work in rib to end—29 (29, 36, 38, 41) sts.

MEDIUM, LARGE AND EXTRA LARGE ONLY

ROW 15: Sl first 2 sts, pass first st over second, bind off 1 more st, work in patt to 2 sts before marker, k2tog, work in rib to end—(33, 35, 38) sts.

EXTRA LARGE ONLY

ROW 17: Rep Row 15—35 sts.

ALL SIZES

NEXT ROW (RS): Work 3 (3, 5, 5, 5) sts in rib, p2tog, work in patt to end—28 (28, 32, 34, 34) sts.

NEXT ROW (WS): Knit the knit sts and purl the purl sts, sl last st.

Rep last 2 rows until there are 19 (19, 23, 23, 23) sts. Work even in rib for 3½" (9cm) more, end with a WS row.

*SHORT ROW 1 (RS): Work 12 (12, 14, 14, 14) in rib; wrap and turn; work back.

NEXT ROW (RS): Work 12 (12, 14, 14, 14) in rib, lift wrap and purl it tog with the st it wrapped, work to end.

NEXT ROW (WS): Work in rib.

Rep from * until strap, when slightly stretched, reaches center back neck. Place sts on a holder.

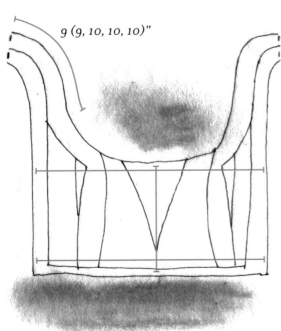

9 (9, 10, 10, 10)"

3½ (3½, 4, 4, 4)"

circumference at underarm:
28 (30, 32, 34, 37)"

height from bottom of halter to
top of back: 11 (12, 13, 14, 15)"

circumference at bottom:
25½ (27½, 29½, 31½, 33½)"

RIGHT FRONT

ROW 1: With WS facing and MC, pick up and k1 in the last bound-off st; p1 and pass the first st over the second, bind off in patt 8 more sts, work in patt to end—61 (66, 69, 74, 82) sts.

ROW 2 AND ALL RS ROWS THROUGH ROW 10 (10, 12, 14, 16): Work in rib to marker, SSK, work in patt to end, sl last st.

ROW 3 (RS): Sl first 2 sts, pass first st over second to bind off 1, bind off 7 more sts, work in patt to end—52 (57, 60, 65, 73) sts.

ROW 5: Sl first 2 sts, pass first st over second, bind off 5 (7, 7, 7, 7) more sts, work in patt to end—45 (48, 51, 56, 64) sts.

ROW 7: Sl first 2 sts, pass first st over second, bind off 5 (5, 4, 6, 6) more sts, work in patt to end—38 (39, 45, 48, 56) sts.

ROW 9: Sl first 2 sts, pass first st over second, bind off 3 (5, 3, 4, 6) more sts, work in patt to end—33 (34, 40, 42, 48) sts.

ROW 11: Sl first 2 sts, pass first st over second, bind off 1 (2, 1, 1, 4) more st(s), work in patt to end—30 (30, 37, 39, 42) sts.

MEDIUM, LARGE AND EXTRA LARGE ONLY

ROW 13: Sl first 2 sts, pass first st over second, bind off 1 more st, work in patt to end—(34, 36, 39) sts.

EXTRA LARGE ONLY

ROW 15: Rep Row 13—65 sts.

ALL SIZES

NEXT ROW (RS): Work in patt to marker and remove, SSP, PM, rib to end—29 (29, 33, 35, 35) sts.

NEXT ROW (WS): Knit the knit sts and purl the purl sts.

NEXT ROW (RS): Work in patt to 2 sts before marker, SSP, rib to end—28 (28, 32, 34, 34) sts.

Rep last 2 rows until there are 19 (19, 23, 23, 23) sts. Work even in rib for 3½" (9cm) more, end with a RS row.

*SHORT ROW 1 (WS): Work 12 (12, 14, 14, 14) in rib; wrap and turn; work back.

NEXT ROW (WS): Work 12 (12, 14, 14, 14) in rib, lift wrap and purl it tog with the st it wrapped, work to end.

NEXT ROW (RS): Work in rib.

Rep from * until strap, when slightly stretched, reaches center back neck. Place sts on a holder.

FINISHING

SEAM CENTER FRONT

Using yarn tail from beg of piece, sew up halter center front with mattress stitch to lowest desired zip point. Double back yarn and weave in end securely.

FIT AND GRAFT HALTER STRAP

Try on the halter. If the halter strap is too short or too long, simply work or rip out an equal number of rows on each side to adjust. Graft or sew tog the active sts at the back of the neck (see page 80). Due to the nature of ribbing, it will not be possible for this graft to be totally invisible, so don't make yourself crazy over it.

INSTALL ZIPPER

Place the zipper stop RS up just below where the mattress stitch seam ends at center front. Sew the zipper tape to each side of halter. Keep the tape hidden by sewing it to the inner knit rib with WS tog. Fold down the corner of the zipper tape toward the inside and stitch down at the top edge. See page 86 for further information on installing a zipper.

CORSET LACING (OPTIONAL)

If you wish to add the ornamental corset lacing at the back, cut a length of satin rattail (or other smooth lace material) to at least 2 yds (1.8m). Thread each end of the cord through a separate darning needle. What comes next is similar to lacing up a shoe, although it's not quite the same. As you lace, be sure to insert the darning needles under all plies of the yarn, since it is possible to snag the yarn while working. Work slowly to be sure you do not snag.

1. Count up about 3 sts from the bottom of the in-set at center back, or wherever you wish to begin the lacing. Pass one darning needle through both legs of the st to the left and to the right of the inset, making sure that these sts are within the same row of knitting.

2. Center the lace so there is an equal length of cord on each side of the inset.

3. With each needle working on the side where it just passed through, and working from outside to inside, insert each needle through both legs of the next st above in the same column of sts and draw the lace through loosely on that side.

4. Now count up 3 sts (or more if you prefer, but do be consistent) and bring the darning needle across the inset to the opposite side and pass the needle through the st 3 rows above where the previous cord was passed, moving from inside to outside.

5. Repeat steps 3 and 4 until you reach the top of the inset.

6. Gently ease the lacing in as consistently as possible.

7. Pass each cord end through the knitting to the back of the piece and sew each end down with a needle and thread.

swizzle vest

skill level

DOMIKNITRIX

THIS TAILORED LITTLE VEST IS EQUALLY
STRIKING ON A GAL dashing off on her Vespa
after tossing back a milkshake or on a vixen at an indie club
throwing back her second Manhattan. It's a great layering
piece for the urban lifestyle. It's just the thing to wear when
there's a nip in the air. Throw it on over a collared shirt or
on top of a plain T-shirt. Either way the effect is tasty all
around.

The pockets are made in the easiest possible way. The
tubular cast on and bind off are the challenges in this project. Sewing tricks make it couture while the tubular cast on
gives this gilet a prêt-à-porter feel.

WHAT YOU WILL LEARN

✘ tubular cast on (page 47)
✘ provisional cast on (page 46)
✘ intarsia (page 68)
✘ pockets (page 88)
✘ tubular bind off (page 77)

YARN

4 balls (60 yards ea) Tahki Stacy Charles Baby 100% merino super bulky yarn in black (MC); 1 ball in red (CC)

NEEDLES

size US 13 (9mm) needles for cast-on row

size US 15 (10mm) needles

NOTIONS

darning needle

crochet hook

20" to 22" (51cm to 56cm) separating zipper in complementary color

sewing needle and thread

GAUGE

9 sts and 13 rows = 4" (10cm) in St st on size US 15 (10mm) needles

MEASUREMENTS

One size fits most, up to 40" (102cm) bust

**This design will be more fitted on a larger size, and will hang more loosely on a smaller frame.

take heed

If you want the zip to go all the way to the top of the collar, you'll need a 22" (56cm) long zipper. If you want it to end below the top of the collar, 20" (51cm) will suffice.

TERMINOLOGY

RLI (right lifted increase): Lift first leg of st below next st onto needle and knit this st (see page 56).

LLI (left lifted increase): Lift last leg below last knitted st onto needle and knit this st (see page 56).

wrap, turn (short row wrap): Work a partial row and pass 1 st wyif, turn the piece, then pass the same st back wyif. Knit the wrap and its st tog on the following row. The wrap prevents a hole in the knitting and keeps the fabric firm (see page 62).

SSP (slip 2, purl 2 together through back loops): Slip 2 sts one at a time as if to knit, insert left needle in back of both sts tog, and pass sts tog back to left needle, then purl 2 tog through the back loops (see page 60).

PM (place marker): Slide a ring marker onto the needle whenever the pattern calls for you to place a marker. When you come to the marker on subsequent rows, simply work the st before it, slip the marker and work the subsequent st.

[ ] (repeat operation): Rep operation in brackets the number of times indicated.

wyif and wyib: With yarn in front or back.

Other techniques: k2tog and SSK (see page 58)

BACK

With size US 13 (9mm) needles, cast on 45 sts tubular style. Switch to size US 15 (10mm) needles to knit first row.

ROW 1 (WS): [p1, k1] across row, end with p1.

ROW 2: [k1, p1] across row, end with k1.

ROWS 3–4: Rep Rows 1–2.

ROWS 5–11: Beg with a purl row, work even in St st.

ROW 12: k12, PM, SSK, k17, k2tog, PM, k12—43 sts.

ROW 13 AND ALL WS ROWS: Purl.

ROW 14 AND RS ROWS THROUGH ROW 20: Knit to marker, SSK, knit to 2 sts before next marker, k2tog, knit to end of row—35 sts at end of Row 20.

ROWS 21–25: Work even in St st.

ROW 26: k12, RLI, k11, LLI, k12—37 sts.

ROWS 27–29: Work even.

ROW 30: Knit to first marker, sl marker, RLI, knit to next marker, LLI, sl marker, knit to end—39 sts.

ROWS 31–33: Work even.

ROW 34: Rep Row 30—41 sts.

ROWS 35–39: Work even.

ROW 40: Rep Row 30—43 sts.

ROWS 41–45: Work even.

ROW 46: Bind off 3 sts, k8, RLI, k19, LLI, k12, removing markers—42 sts.

ROWS 47: Bind off 3 sts and purl to last st, slip last st as if to purl wyif—39 sts.

ROWS 48–49: Sl 2 sts as if to purl, pass first st over second st to bind off 1, bind off 1 more st, knit to last st, and sl st as if to purl wyib—35 sts.

ROW 50: Sl 2 sts as if to purl and pass the first st over second st to bind it off. Knit to last st, and sl st as if to purl wyib—34 sts.

ROW 51: Sl 2 sts as if to purl, pass first st over second st to bind off 1, purl to end of row—33 sts.

ROW 52: SSK, k4, RLI, k21, LLI, k4, k2tog—33 sts.

ROW 53 AND ALL WS ROWS THROUGH ROW 71: Purl.

ROW 54: k2, SSK, k25, k2tog, k2—31 sts.

ROW 56: K2, SSK, RLI, k23, LLI, k2tog, k2—31 sts.

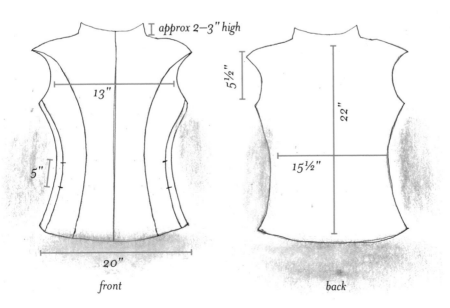

I approx 2–3" high

5½"

13"

22"

5"

15½"

20"

front

back

ROW 58: k2, k2tog, k23, SSK, k2—29 sts.

ROW 60: k2, PM, RLI, k25, LLI, PM, k2—31 sts.

ROW 62 AND ALL RS ROWS THROUGH ROW 66: Knit to marker, sl marker, RLI, knit to next marker, LLI, sl marker, knit to end—37 sts at end of Row 66.

ROWS 67–69: Work even.

ROW 70: Rep Row 62—39 sts.

ROW 71: Purl.

Place sts on a holder to be grafted later for shoulders and to be picked up for back neck of Collar. Leave at least a 16" (41cm) yarn tail for grafting shoulder seam.

RIGHT FRONT

notes:

Tubular cast on is not used here because it would show every other st in MC for CC section. Instead, provisional cast on is removed and sts are bound off tubular style.

Each front is worked in intarsia. Leave a long yarn tail of at least 12" (30cm) from each ball of yarn for the tubular bind off.

Cast on 25 sts using provisional cast on.

ROW 1: With MC, [k1, p1] 5 times; leaving yarn tail from CC ball and using CC, [k1, p1] 4 times, k1; with new ball of MC, leave yarn tail and [p1, k1] 3 times.

After completing ribbing, move sts to holder, remove the cast-on row, then bind off sts tubular style to create a CC border that goes all the way to the cast-on edge. As you complete each section of color with tubular bind off, interlock MC and CC and cont with next color. If you struggle with the challenging tubular bind off, you only have a bit of work to rip out before starting over to get it right, or to substitute a traditional or tubular cast on.

ROWS 2–4: Work in St st intarsia as est.

ROW 5: With MC, k1, p1, k8; with CC, k9; with MC, k6.

ROW 6: Purl in intarsia as est.

ROWS 7–10: Rep Rows 5–6 twice more.

ROW 11: With MC, k1, p1, k6, k2tog; with CC, k9. Do not work final 6 MC sts and do not twist yarns. Place 6 MC sts on a holder.

WORK RIGHT POCKET OPENING

Work pocket opening in 2 pieces, only knitting the sts on your right. Foll st counts reflect only active sts.

ROW 12 AND ALL WS ROWS: Purl as est.

ROW 13: With MC, k1, p1, k7; with CC, k5, k2tog, k2—17 sts.

ROW 15: With MC, k1, p1, k5, k2tog; with CC, k8—16 sts.

ROW 17: With MC, k1, p1, k6; with CC, k4, k2tog, k2—15 sts.

ROW 19: With MC, k1, p1, k6; with CC, k7.

ROW 21: With MC, k1, p1, k6; with CC, k3, k2tog, k2—14 sts.

ROW 35: With MC, k1, p1, k9; with CC, k5, LLI, k2; with MC, k5—24 sts.

ROW 37: Knit in intarsia as est.

ROW 39: With MC, k1, p1, k9; with CC, k6, LLI, k2; with MC, k5—25 sts.

ROW 41: With MC, k1, p1, k9; with CC, k7, LLI, k2; with MC, k5—26 sts.

ROW 43: With MC, k1, p1, k6, k2tog, k1; with CC, k10; with MC, k5—25 sts.

ROW 44: With MC, bind off 3 sts, p1; with CC, p10; with MC, p8, k1, p1—22 sts.

ROW 45: With MC, k1, p1, k8; with CC, k1, SSK, k6, SSK (second st will be MC); with MC, k1—20 sts.

Cut MC, leaving a tail for weaving in.

ROW 46: With CC, SSP, p8; with MC, p8, k1, p1—19 sts.

ROW 47: With MC, k1, p1, k8; with CC, k1, SSK, knit to last st, and sl st as if to purl wyib—18 sts.

ROW 48: With CC, sl 2 sts as if to purl and pass the first st over second to bind off 1, p6; with MC, p8, k1, p1—17 sts.

ROW 49: Rep Row 47—16 sts.

ROW 50: With CC, sl 2 sts as if to purl and pass the first st over second to bind off 1, p4; with MC, p8, k1, p1—15 sts.

ROW 51: With MC, k1, p1, k7, LLI, k1; with CC, k1, SSK, k2—15 sts.

ROW 52 AND ALL WS ROWS THROUGH ROW 60: Purl in intarsia as est.

ROW 53: With MC, k1, p1, k8, LLI, k1; with CC, k1, SSK, k1—15 sts.

ROW 55: With MC, k1, p1, RLI, k9, LLI, k1; with CC, k1, SSK—16 sts.

ROW 57: With MC, k1, p1, k11, LLI, k1; with CC, k2—17 sts.

ROW 59: With MC, k1, p1, RLI, k12, LLI, SSK (second st will be CC); with CC, k1—18 sts.

ROW 61: With MC, k1, p1, k14, LLI, SSK (second st will be CC)—18 sts.

Cut CC yarn, leaving a tail for weaving in.

ROW 23: With MC, k1, p1, k5, LLI, k1; with CC, k6—15 sts.

ROWS 25 AND 27: With MC, k1, p1, k7; with CC, k6.

RESUME RIGHT FRONT

Work from 6 sts on holder and sts, allowing sts on right to rest. Resume with inactive MC yarn end waiting beside the CC section and pocket opening.

ROWS 11–14: Work sts on holder even in St st.

ROW 15: k2, k2tog, k2—5 sts.

ROWS 16–26: Work even, ending with a WS row. Yarn will be next to pocket opening and left piece will be 1 row shorter than right.

COMPLETE POCKET

ROW 27: Working across ALL sts, twist the yarns tog and with MC on the left, k5 to complete Row 27 and close pocket at top—20 sts.

ROW 28 AND ALL WS ROWS THROUGH ROW 42: Purl in intarsia as est.

ROW 29: With MC, k1, p1, k6, LLI, k1; with CC, k6; with MC, k5—21 sts.

ROW 31: With MC, k1, p1, k8; with CC, k4, LLI, k2; with MC, k5—22 sts.

ROW 33: With MC, k1, p1, k7, LLI, k1; with CC, k7; with MC, k5—23 sts.

NECK EDGE AND SHOULDER SHAPING

ROW 62: p15, wrap, turn.

ROW 63: k14, LLI, k1.

ROW 64: p14, wrap, turn.

ROW 65: k13, LLI, k1.

ROW 66: p13, wrap turn.

ROW 67: k12, LLI, k1.

ROW 68: p13, wrap, turn.

ROW 69: k12, LLI, k1.

ROW 70: p14.

Graft shoulder sts to Back using yarn tail left from Back and working from shoulder edge to neck edge with Kitchener stitch (see page 80). Place all waiting sts from front edge on a holder for collar.

note:

If you prefer, you may wait until you have knit both pieces and graft both at the same time. I recommend leaving the ball attached to the front piece so you can use this yarn to knit the collar later and save yourself from weaving in extra ends with such bulky yarn.

LEFT FRONT

Cast on 25 sts with provisional cast on.

ROW 1 (RS): With MC, [k1, p1] 3 times; leaving yarn tail from CC ball and using CC, [k1, p1] 4 times, k1; with new ball of MC leave yarn tail and [p1, k1] 5 times.

ROWS 2–4: Work intarsia in St st as est.

ROW 5: With MC, k6; with CC, k9; with MC; k8, p1, k1.

ROW 6: Purl in intarsia as est.

ROWS 7–10: Rep Rows 5–6 twice more.

ROW 11: With MC, k6; (do not twist these yarns— this will be the pocket opening); with CC, k9; with MC, SSK, k6, p1, k1—24 sts. Place 6 MC sts on a holder.

WORK RIGHT POCKET OPENING

Work pocket opening in 2 pieces, only knitting the sts on your left. Foll st counts reflect only active sts.

ROW 12: With MC, p1, k1, p7; with CC, p9—18 sts.

ROW 13: With CC, k2, SSK, k5; with MC, k7, p1, k1—17 sts.

ROW 14 AND ALL WS ROWS: Purl as est.

ROW 15: With CC, k8; with MC, SSK, k5, p1, k1—16 sts.

ROW 17: With CC, k2, SSK, k4; with MC, k6, p1, k1—15 sts.

ROW 19: With CC, k7; with MC, k6, p1, k1.

ROW 21: With CC, k2, SSK, k3; with MC, k6, p1, k1—14 sts.

ROW 23: With CC, k6; with MC, k1, RLI, k5, p1, k1—15 sts.

ROW 25: With CC, k6; with MC, k7, p1, k1.

RESUME RIGHT FRONT

Work from 6 sts on holder, allowing sts on left to rest. Resume with MC yarn end waiting beside the CC section and pocket opening. Knit as for Left Front through Row 27—20 sts.

ROW 28 AND ALL WS ROWS THROUGH ROW 44: Purl in inatrsia as est.

ROW 29: With MC, k5; with CC, k6; with MC, k1, RLI, k6, p1, k1—21 sts.

ROW 31: With MC, k5; with CC, k2, RLI, k4; with MC, k8, p1, k1—22 sts.

ROW 35: With MC, k5; with CC, k2, RLI, k5; with MC, k9, p1, k1—24 sts.

ROW 37: With MC, k5; with CC, k8; with MC, k9,p1, k1—24 sts.

ROW 39: With MC, k5; with CC, k2, RLI, k6; with MC, k9, p1, k1—25 sts.

ROW 41: With MC, k5; with CC, k2, RLI, k7; with MC k9, p1, k1—26 sts.

ROW 43: With MC, k5; with CC, k10; with MC, k1, k2tog, k6, p1, k1—25 sts.

ROW 45: With MC, bind off 3; with CC, k2tog (second st will be CC), k6, k2tog, k1; with MC, k8, p1, k1—20 sts.

ROW 46: With MC, p1, k1, p8; with CC, p8, p2tog (second st will be MC)—19 sts.

ROW 47: With CC, SSK, k4, k2tog, k1; with MC, k8, p1, k1—17 sts.

ROW 48: With MC, p1, k1, p8; with CC, p6, slip last st as if to purl wyif.

ROW 49: With CC, slip 2 sts as if to purl and pass the first st over second st to bind it off, k2, k2tog, k1; with MC, k8, p1, k1—15 sts.

NECK EDGE AND SHOULDER SHAPING

ROW 62 AND ALL WS ROWS THROUGH ROW 70: Purl.

ROW 63: k1, RLI, k12, wrap, turn.

ROW 65: k1, RLI, k11, wrap, turn.

ROW 67: k1, RLI, k11, wrap, turn.

ROW 69: k1, RLI, k11, wrap, turn.

Graft shoulder sts to Back using yarn tail left from Back and working from shoulder edge to neck edge with Kitchener stitch (see page 80). Place all waiting sts from front edge on a holder for Collar.

COLLAR

Pass all waiting sts for collar onto a size US 15 (10mm) circular needle: 8 sts from Right Front, 9 sts from Left Front, and 11 back neck.

PICK UP STITCHES

Beg at right side of neck where yarn ball is rem from Right Front. With RS facing, pick up and k4 along right side neck. Knit back neck sts on needle, pick up and k3 at left side neck, [k1, p1] 4 times, end k1—35 sts. Cont in k1, p1 rib for 6 rows.

NEXT ROW: Sl first st as if to purl, bind off this st and 25 sts more. Finish row in rib pattern.

NEXT ROW: Slip first st as if to purl, bind off this st and remainder of row.

You may also choose to bind off tubular style for collar sts.

Weave in ends, sewing the first st into the bind-off row to conceal mismatch in row count.

FINISHING

Sew side seams with mattress stitch (see page 78). Weave in all ends.

Install zipper (see page 86).

Add grosgrain ribbon backing to back side of CC pocket welt to flatten out Stockinette curl.

Make and sew in pocket backs using stretchy fabric or knit piece to match MC, approximately 7" (18cm) tall by 8½" (22cm) wide. While sewing the pocket bags in place, flatten out the curl of the MC pocket welt. See the City Coat pattern on page 230 for more detailed instructions on sewing in pocket bags. See page 88 in Tying Up for additional methods of creating pockets.

ROW 50: With MC, p1, k1, p8; with CC, p4, slip last st as if to purl wyif.

ROW 51: With CC, k2, k2tog, k1; with MC, k1, RLI, k7, p1, k1—15 sts.

ROW 52 AND ALL WS ROWS THROUGH 60: Work in intarsia as est.

ROW 53: With CC, k1, k2tog, k1; with MC, k1, RLI, k8, p1, k1—15 sts.

ROW 55: With CC, k2tog, k1; with MC, k1, RLI, k9, LLI, p1, k1—16 sts.

ROW 57: With CC, k2; with MC, k1, RLI, k11, p1, k1—17 sts.

ROW 59: With CC, k1; with MC, k2tog, RLI, k12, LLI, p1, k1—18 sts.

ROW 61: With MC, k2tog (bottom st will be CC), RLI, k13, wrap, turn.

Cut CC yarn, leaving a tail for weaving in.

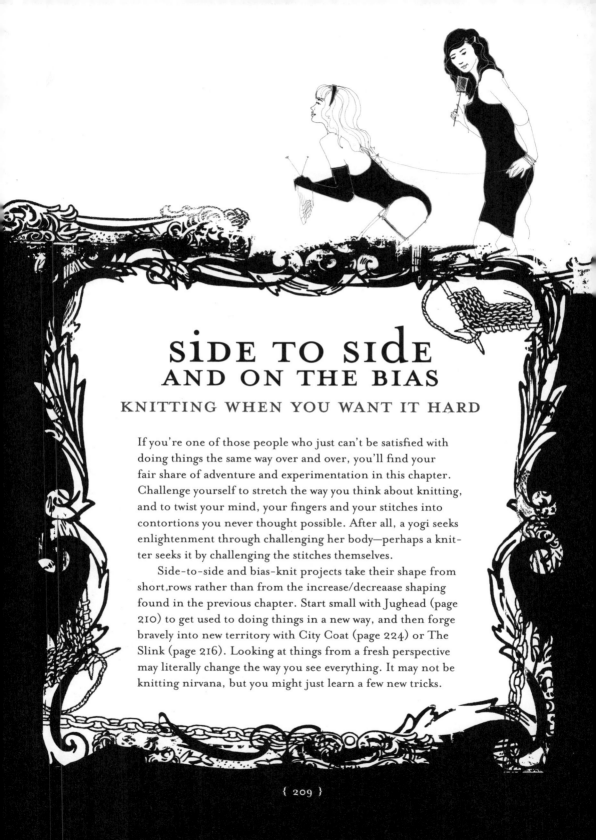

SiDE TO SiDE
AND ON THE BIAS
KNITTING WHEN YOU WANT IT HARD

If you're one of those people who just can't be satisfied with
doing things the same way over and over, you'll find your
fair share of adventure and experimentation in this chapter.
Challenge yourself to stretch the way you think about knitting,
and to twist your mind, your fingers and your stitches into
contortions you never thought possible. After all, a yogi seeks
enlightenment through challenging her body—perhaps a knitter seeks it by challenging the stitches themselves.

Side-to-side and bias-knit projects take their shape from
short rows rather than from the increase/decreaase shaping
found in the previous chapter. Start small with Jughead (page
210) to get used to doing things in a new way, and then forge
bravely into new territory with City Coat (page 224) or The
Slink (page 216). Looking at things from a fresh perspective
may literally change the way you see everything. It may not be
knitting nirvana, but you might just learn a few new tricks.

JUGHEAD HAT

skill level
APPRENTICE

I HAVE A THEORY THAT JUGHEAD IS THE ARCHETYPE UPON WHICH Shaggy from Scooby-Doo was based, along with every slacker character who has come after who eats too much but never gains an ounce. This hat would be just as at home on a Bowery Boy as on Bart Simpson. There's just something about this hat that makes your boy look, well…bad. Ladies, I caution you this is not a girl hat. Sure, you can wear it, but it just looks better on boys.

Bring out the naughty boy in your favorite guy with this mischievous hat. If he's already a prankster, you might want to think twice. Unless you like your fellas extra-bad, that is.

WHAT YOU WILL LEARN
✗ provisional cast on (page 46)
✗ removing cast-on edge (page 65)
✗ short rows (page 62)
✗ grafting garter (page 82)

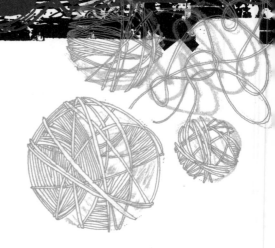

YARN

1ball (123 yards) Rowan Harris DK 100% new wool yarn in color 4 Gray Tweed or 1 skein (200 yards) Plymouth Encore worsted in color 0217 Black

Substitute any DK weight yarn.

NEEDLES

size US 8 (5mm) needles

size US 8 (5mm) DPNs

NOTIONS

stitch markers in two colors

darning needle or crochet hook

GAUGE

17 sts and 32 rows = 4" (10cm) in garter st

Gauge should match both vertically and horizontally to avoid fit problems.

MEASUREMENTS

one size fits most: 21" to 23" (54cm to 58cm)

✗ *read this first* ✗

Jughead is knit sideways in garter stitch. It is made up of six sections. Each wedge is knit with short rows to create the unique shape.

A note about staying oriented: The closer together the markers are, the nearer you are to the top of the hat (and the top of head when worn). Knowing the orientation of the hat helps you anticipate what comes next in the pattern. After a section or two, let mindless knitting ensue.

TERMINOLOGY

wrap, turn (short row wrap): Work a partial row and slip 1 st wyif, turn the piece, then slip the same st back wyif. Knit the wrap and its st tog on the following row. The wrap prevents a hole in the knitting and keeps the fabric firm.

PM (place marker): Slide a ring marker onto the needle whenever the pattern calls for you to place a marker. When you come to the marker on subsequent rows, simply work the st before it, slip the marker, and work the subsequent st.

KFB (knit 1 front and back): Work 2 sts in 1 st without sliding the st from the needle after making the first st (see page 57).

[ ] (repeat operation): Rep operation in brackets the number of times indicated.

Other techniques: k2tog and p2tog (see pages 58 and 60), SSK (see page 58)

HAT

Cast on 42 sts using provisional cast on (see page 46). The cast-on row will be removed later so you can graft the seam invisibly since both the inside and outside show when the hat is worn.

ROW 1: Knit.

ROW 2: Knit, placing markers as follows: [k2, PM] twice, k3, PM, k4, PM, k5, PM, k7, PM, k11, PM with different color for bottom of hat, k8.

ROW 3: Knit to last marker, wrap, turn.

ROW 4 AND ALL EVEN ROWS THROUGH 16: Knit to last 2 sts, SSK.

ROW 5: Knit to next to last marker, wrap, turn.

ROW 7: Knit to 5th marker, wrap, turn.

ROW 9: Knit to 4th marker, wrap, turn.

ROW 11: Knit to 3rd marker, wrap, turn.

ROW 13: Knit to 2nd marker, wrap, turn.

ROW 15: k36 (knit to end).

ROW 17: Knit to 2nd marker, wrap, turn.

ROW 18 AND REM EVEN ROWS: Knit to last st, KFB.

ROW 19: Knit to 3rd marker, wrap, turn.

ROW 21: Knit to 4th marker, wrap, turn.

ROW 23: Knit to 5th marker, wrap, turn.

ROW 25: Knit to next to last marker, wrap, turn.

ROW 27: Knit to last marker, wrap, turn.

ROW 29: k41 (knit to end).

ROW 30: k40, KFB.

Rep Rows 3–30 five times more. When you are finished knitting, there will be 6 peaks at the top of the hat and 6 valleys at the base.

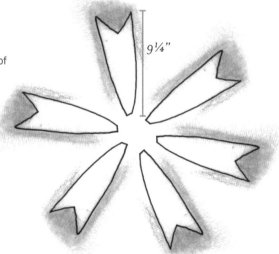

Jughead is constructed of six sections knitted together in one piece

FINISHING
REMOVE CAST-ON ROW
Remove the cast-on row by slowly unraveling the crocheted yarn and placing the sts on a waiting needle (see page 65 in Knitting Directions). There are 41 sts on the cast-on side and 42 sts on the side you were knitting. One yarn end will be at the top of the hat and one at the bottom.

GRAFT EDGES TOGETHER
With RS facing, match up the edges of the hat with active sts. Graft the pieces together with Kitchener stitch (see page 82 in Tying Up). It is important when grafting in garter stitch that there is a purl row on one side and a knit row on the other. Otherwise your grafting will show as a knit or purl row rather than disappearing into the garter st. For this hat, it's best to start at the bottom of the hat and work toward the top so the yarn ends are in the right place to close the hole in the top of the hat.

Once you have grafted the row, tie the 2 yarn ends together securely. Turn the hat RS out (whichever side looks better to you) and pull the longer yarn end through to the RS and shorter end to the WS.

PICK UP STITCHES FOR TOP OF HAT
With DPNs, pick up and k13 sts around the top of the hat, 6 on the first needle and 7 on the second. Work in rnds as follows:

RND 1: [p2, p2tog] 3 times, p1—10 sts.

RND 2: [k2tog] 5 times—5 sts.

FINISH HAT
Draw yarn end through rem sts with a yarn needle or crochet hook and pull closed. Pull yarn end to inside of hat and tie a knot with the other yarn end already there.

THE slINK

SLINK INTO A BLACK LEATHER SKIRT,
AND THEN SLINK ON DOWN to your favorite
night spot to dance the night away. This versatile top will
bring a sexy little sparkle into your life. Alter this design
to be as bad as you want to be...you can make the V-neck as
deep as you like, for minimal or maximal attention to your
décolleté.

I designed this slinky tee in two lengths because not everyone wants a T-shirt to graze her midriff. Today's fashion
is all about daytime sparkle, and this is an easy way to whip
some up for yourself. Both lengths are perfect for a sparkly
day at the boardwalk or a night out on the town.

WHAT YOU WILL LEARN
✖ provisional cast on (page 46)
✖ lifted (raised) increases (page 56)
✖ removing cast on edge (page 65)
✖ grafting ribbing (page 83)
✖ short rows (page 62)
✖ Kitchener stitch (page 80)

YARN

8 (8, 8, 9, 9) balls (90 yds ea) of Crystal Palace Shimmer acrylic/nylon blend yarn for short version

9 (9, 10, 10, 10) balls of Shimmer for long version

Or substitute a similar yarn with a heavy, drape-y feel to it. Light frothy yarns are not recommended.

NEEDLES

size US 9 (5mm) circular needle

size US 11 (8mm) circular needle

If necessary, change needles to obtain gauge.

NOTIONS

four stitch markers

stitch holders

darning needle

GAUGE

20 sts and 28 rows = 4" (10cm) in St st

20 sts and 33 rows = 4" (10cm) in stitch pattern

**Gauge is intentionally tight. Recommended gauge on ball band is 14 sts and 16 rows = 4" (10cm) on size US 10–11 (6–8mm) needles.

MEASUREMENTS

See schematics on page 220 for measurements for both short and long version of Slink. **Keep in mind that with the sideways knit, stretching to fit is more flattering than in the traditional bottom-to-top construction.

take heed

Circular needles are recommended for this project, as straight needles place extra strain on neckline and underarm stitches during knitting.

TERMINOLOGY

RLI (right lifted increase): Lift first leg of st below next st onto needle and knit this st (see page 56).

LLI (left lifted increase): Lift last leg below last knitted st onto needle and knit this st (see page 56).

PM (place marker): Slide a ring marker onto the needle whenever the pattern calls for you to place a marker. When you come to the marker on subsequent rows, simply work the st before it, slip the marker, and work the subsequent st.

psso: Pass slipped st(s) over.

Other techniques: SSK and k2tog (see page 58)

✖ *read this first* ✖

This piece is cast on at the right underarm seam and worked sideways. The underarm is shaped before more stitches are cast on for the upper back. Then it is easily knit with no shaping across the back until armhole stitches are moved to holder or bound off; then the underarm is shaped and stitches cast on again for the front. Stitches are bound off and cast on again for the neckline, and then the opposite armhole is bound off and underarm shaped. Stitches for cap sleeves are picked up around the shoulders and knit, finishing with a stitched-down rolled edge at sleeves and V-neck.

What makes this such a fun piece to knit is that once you have set up the rows with markers, you will be doing exactly the same thing for all rows in the lower portion of the Slink. You need to pay attention only to what's going on above the shoulders and bust line. There is no shaping across the entire lower ¾ of the back. Get ready for mindless knitting!

The shorter version is the first set of numbers, and the longer version is in brackets in gray. If there is only one set of numbers, it applies to all sizes or both versions. For ease in working, consider circling the numbers for your size.

STITCH PATTERN

ROW 1 (RS): Knit to marker, purl to marker, knit to marker, [p1, k2] to end.

ROW 2: [p2, k1] to marker, purl to end.

ROW 3: Rep Row 1.

ROW 4: [p2, k1] to marker, purl to marker, knit to marker, purl to end.

ROW 5: Knit to last marker, [p1, k2] to end.

ROW 6: Rep Row 4.

Rep Rows 1–6 for Stitch Pattern.

BACK
RIGHT SIDE

Cast on 66 (67, 67, 68, 70) [81, 82, 82, 83, 85] sts using provisional or loop method. You will be ripping out the cast-on row later and picking up the sts, so do not use long tail cast on.

ROW 1 (RS): k11 (12, 12, 13, 15), PM, p35 [40], PM, k11 [15], PM, * p1, k2; rep from * 3 [5] times.

ROWS 2–13: Beg with Row 2, rep Rows 1–6 of Stitch Pattern twice, then Row 1 once more, and AT THE SAME TIME, inc at beg of Rows 9, 11 and 13 with k1, RL1—69 (70, 70, 71, 73) [84, 85, 85, 86, 88] sts.

ROW 14: Work Stitch Pattern Row 2 to last 2 sts, k1-p1 in next st, k1, cast on 26 (28, 28, 28, 30) sts at end of row—96 (99, 99, 100, 104) [111, 114, 114, 115, 119] sts.

ROWS 15–18: Work Stitch Pattern Rows 3–6.

CENTER
note:

Mark next row to make it easier to keep track of your progress. Each repeat creates 2 purl ridges at the waist when viewed from the RS.

Rep Stitch Pattern Rows 1–6 14 (15, 16, 17, 19) more times, then Rows 1–4 once more. Piece will measure 13½ (14¼, 15¼, 16, 17¾)" 35 (36, 39, 41, 45)cm from shoulder to shoulder.

(+/-) If you wish to adjust this top for larger or smaller sizes, you may knit more or fewer repeats here. It is important that you work the whole 6-row repeat, or your modification will leave a trace in the purl ribs defining the waist.

LEFT SIDE

NEXT ROW: Work Stitch Pattern Row 5.

NEXT ROW: Work Stitch Pattern Row 6 to last 26 (28, 28, 28, 30) sts, turn and PM, leaving rem sts unworked—70 (71, 71, 72, 74) [85, 86, 86, 87, 89] working sts.

ROW 1: Work Stitch Pattern Row 1.

ROW 2: Work Stitch Pattern Row 2 to 2 sts before last marker, turn leaving rem 28 (30, 30, 30, 32) sts unworked—68 (69, 69, 70, 72) [83, 84, 84, 85, 87] working sts.

ROW 3: Work Stitch Pattern Row 3.

ROW 4: Work Stitch Pattern Row 4 to 3 sts before marker, turn leaving rem 29 (31, 31, 31, 33) sts unworked—67 (68, 68, 69, 71) [82, 83, 83, 84, 86] working sts.

ROW 5: Work Stitch Pattern Row 5.

ROW 6: Work Stitch Pattern Row 6 to 4 sts before marker, turn leaving rem 30 (32, 32, 32, 34) sts on holder—66 (67, 67, 68, 70) [81, 82, 82, 83, 85] working sts.

ROWS 7–12: Work Stitch Pattern Rows 1–6 once more.

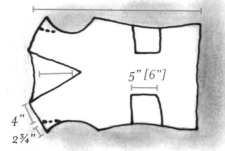

front

19¼ (19¾, 19¾, 20, 20¾)"
[22¼, 22¾, 22¾, 23, 23¾]"

5" [6"]

4"

2¾"

V-neck depth: 8 (8¼, 8¼, 8½, 9)"

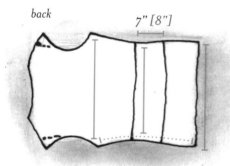

back

7" [8"]

seam along dotted line

circumference at underarm:
34 (35¾, 38, 39¼, 37¾)"

circumference at waist:
29½ (31¼, 33¼, 34¼, 37¾)"

circumference at bottom:
34 (35¾, 38, 39¼, 42¾)"

FRONT

LEFT SIDE

ROWS 1–2: Work Stitch Pattern Rows 1–2, removing last marker on Row 2. **Note:** Marker between Stockinette and purl ribs moves down 10 sts from the back to form the defining line under the bust.

ROW 3: k1, RLI, k20 (21, 21, 22, 24), PM, cont as for Stitch Pattern Row 1—67 (68, 68, 69, 71) [82, 83, 83, 84, 86] sts.

ROWS 4–18: Work Stitch Pattern Rows 4–6 once, then Stitch Pattern Rows 1–6 twice more. AT THE SAME TIME, inc at beg of rows 7, 11, 13, 15 and 17 with k1, RLI—72 (73, 73, 74, 76) [87, 88, 88, 89, 91] sts.

ROW 19: Work Stitch Pattern Row 1, inc at beg of row with k1, RLI—73 (74, 74, 75, 77) [88, 89, 89, 90, 92] sts.

ROW 20: Work Stitch Pattern Row 2.

LEFT ARMHOLE SHAPING

ROW 21: Cast on 5 sts at beg of row, then work Stitch Pattern Row 3—78 (79, 79, 80, 82) [93, 94, 94, 95, 97] sts.

ROW 22: Work Stitch Pattern Row 4.

ROW 23: Cast on 5 sts at beg of row, k5, lift st below onto needle and k2tog (to smooth the edge), cont in Stitch Pattern Row 5—83 (84, 84, 85, 87) [98, 99, 99, 100, 102] sts.

ROW 24: Work Stitch Pattern Row 6.

ROW 25: Cast on 5 sts at beg of row, k5, lift st below onto needle and k2tog, cont in Stitch Pattern Row 1—88 (89, 89, 90, 92) [103, 104, 104, 105, 107] sts.

ROW 26: Work Stitch Pattern Row 2.

ROW 27: Cast on 5 sts at beg of row, k5, lift st below onto needle and k2tog, cont in Stich Pattern Row 3—93 (94, 94, 95, 97) [108, 109, 109, 110, 112] sts.

ROW 28: Work Stitch Pattern Row 4.

ROW 29: Rep Row 23—98 (99, 99, 100, 102) [113, 114, 114, 115, 117] sts.

LEFT FRONT

ROW 30: Work Stitch Pattern Row 6.

ROWS 31–43: Rep Stitch Pattern Rows 1–6 twice, then work Stitch Pattern Row 1 once more. AT THE SAME TIME, inc at beg of Rows 33 and 39 with k1, RLI—100 (101, 101, 102, 104) [115, 116, 116, 117, 119] sts.

LEFT V-NECK EDGE

(+/-) If you wish to have a deeper neckline, on the next row purl fewer sts up to the V, and move more sts to the holder. If you want a higher neckline, purl more sts up to the V, and move fewer sts to the holder. Just remember, you still need enough ease to get your head through this neck. If you are not sure how deep you wish the neckline to be, move more sts to the holder now and plan to sew up the neckline at the base of the V if it is too deep for your taste.

NEXT ROW: [p2, k1] to marker, p51 [60] (or desired number), place rem sts on holder for neck edge, turn work—60 [75] sts unless neckline was changed. Sts on holder will be worked after seaming the shoulders.

CENTER FRONT

NEXT ROW: Knit to last marker, [p1, k2] to end.

RIGHT V-NECK EDGE

NEXT ROW: [p2, k1] to marker, purl to end, firmly cast on the same number of sts placed on holder for neck edge—103 (104, 104, 105, 107) [118, 119, 119, 120, 122] sts.

Cont working even as est for 0 (4, 8, 10, 16) more rows.

RIGHT SIDE

ROWS 1–14: Cont as est and AT THE SAME TIME, dec at beg of Rows 1, 7 and 13 wtih k1, SSK—100 (101, 101, 102, 104) [115, 116, 116, 117, 119] sts.

ROWS 15–32: Work Stitch Pattern Rows 1–6 three times. AT THE SAME TIME, dec at beg of Rows 19, 25 and 31 with k1, SSK—97 (98, 98, 99, 101) [112, 113, 113, 114, 116] sts.

RIGHT ARMHOLE SHAPING

ɴoᴛe:
All slipped sts are slipped as if to purl; do not twist sts.

ROW 33: Bind off 4 sts at beg of row, cont in Stitch Pattern Row 1—93 (94, 94, 95, 97) [108, 109, 109, 110, 112] sts.

ROW 34: Work Stitch Pattern Row 2, sl last st as if to purl.

ROW 35: Sl first 2 sts and pass first st over second st (to smooth edge), then bind off 4, cont in Stitch Pattern Row 3—88 (89, 89, 90, 92) [103, 104, 104, 105, 107] sts.

STOCKINETTE CENTER FRONT BEGINS

ROW 44: [p2, k1] to marker, purl to end.

ROW 45: k1, RLI, knit to last marker, [p1, k2] to end—101 (102, 102, 103, 105) [116, 117, 117, 118, 120] sts.

ROW 46: [p2, k1] to marker, purl to end.

ROW 47: Knit to last marker, [p1, k2] to end.

ROWS 48–57: Rep Rows 46–47, and AT THE SAME TIME, inc at beg of Rows 51 and 57 with k1, RLI—103 (104, 104, 105, 107) [118, 119, 119, 120, 122] sts.

Cont working even as est for 0 (4, 8, 10, 16) more rows.

ROWS 36–41: Work Stitch Pattern Rows 4–6, then Rows 1–3. AT THE SAME TIME, sl last st as if to purl on all WS rows and sl2, psso, bind off 4 sts on all RS rows—73 (74, 74, 75, 77) [88, 89, 89, 90, 92] sts.

ROW 42: Work Stitch Pattern Row 4.

RIGHT UNDERARM SHAPING

ROWS 43–57: Work Stitch Pattern Rows 5–6, then rep Stitch Pattern Rows 1–6 twice, then Row 1 once more, and AT THE SAME TIME, dec at beg of Rows 43, 45, 47, 49, 53 and 57 with k1, SSK—67 (68, 68, 69, 71) [82, 83, 83, 84, 86] sts.

ASSEMBLY
SEAM SHOULDERS AND SIDE

Sew both shoulder seams with mattress stitch. Remove cast-on row, placing each loop on needle with right leg to front of needle (see Knitting Directions, page 65). Graft side seam using Kitchener stitch (see Knitting Directions, page 80). Pay special attention to grafting the ribbing at the midsection (see Tying Up, page 83). I've set up the pattern so you'll be grafting in knit only at the waist and underarm, though you'll see purl sts on either side.

SLEEVES
LEFT SLEEVE

Be aware that sleeve does not go all the way around armhole. Do not pick up sts at underarm, or sleeve will be too tight.

With top RS facing, sl30 (32, 32, 32, 34) left arm-

hole sts to circular needle. With left needle point at bottom armhole edge, tie on yarn (directly across from the first cast-on st from the opposite shoulder edge). Starting in the first cast-on st, pick up and k27 (29, 29, 29, 31) sts, 1 per st, to the shoulder seam—57 (61, 61, 61, 65) sts. Wrap the next st but do not turn work. As you knit the foll rows, each time you come to a short row wrap, lift it onto your needle and knit (or purl) it tog with the st above it.

ROW 1: k9, wrap, turn.

ROW 2: p11, wrap, turn.

ROW 3: k18, wrap, turn.

ROW 4: p22, wrap, turn.

ROW 5: k5, k2tog, k18, wrap, turn.

ROW 6: p28 (29, 29, 29, 30), wrap, turn.

ROW 7: k30 (31, 31, 31, 32), wrap, turn.

ROW 8: p32 (33, 33, 33, 34), wrap, turn.

ROW 9: k10 (11, 11, 11, 12), k2tog, k22 (23, 23, 23, 24), wrap, turn.

ROW 10: p35 (37, 37, 37, 39), wrap, turn.

ROW 11: k37 (38, 38, 38, 39), wrap, turn.

ROW 12: p39 (40, 40, 40, 41), wrap, turn.

ROW 13: k13 (14, 14, 14, 15), k2tog, k26 (27, 27, 27, 28), wrap, turn.

ROW 14: p42 (43, 43, 43, 45), wrap, turn.

ROW 15: k44 (45, 45, 45, 47), wrap, turn.

ROW 16: p47 (49, 49, 49, 51), wrap, turn.

ROW 17: k17 (19, 19, 19, 21), k2tog, k29 (31, 31, 31, 33).

ROW 18: Knit—53 (57, 57, 57, 61) sts. This row begins the rolled sleeve edge.

ROW 19: Purl.

ROW 20: Knit.

ROW 21: Purl.

ROW 22: Lift purl bump 4 rows below onto needle and k2tog, * lift purl bump 4 rows below onto needle and k2tog, pass first st over second st; rep from * to end of row to join the rolled edge to finish cap sleeve.

RIGHT SLEEVE

With RS facing, starting at back bottom armhole edge, approx 1" (3cm) past seam, pick up and k4 sts along bottom of armhole, then 26 (28, 28, 28, 30) sts along armhole edge ending at last bound-off st—57 (61, 61, 61, 65) sts. Break yarn. Sl first 30 (32, 32, 32, 34) sts to right end of needle, ending at shoulder seam. Join yarn. Turn WS out and work as foll:

ROW 1: p9, wrap, turn.

ROW 2: k11, wrap, turn.

ROW 3: p18, wrap, turn.

ROW 4: k22, wrap, turn.

ROW 5: p5, p2tog, p18, wrap, turn.

ROW 6: k28 (29, 29, 29, 30), wrap, turn.

ROW 7: p30 (31, 31, 31, 32), wrap, turn.

ROW 8: k32 (33, 33, 33, 34), wrap, turn.

ROW 9: p10 (11, 11, 11, 12), p2tog, p22 (23, 23, 23, 24), wrap, turn.

ROW 10: k35 (37, 37, 37, 39), wrap, turn.

ROW 11: p37 (38, 38, 38, 39), wrap, turn.

ROW 12: k39 (40, 40, 40, 41), wrap, turn.

ROW 13: p13 (14, 14, 14, 15), p2tog, p26 (27, 27, 27, 28), wrap, turn.

ROW 14: k42 (43, 43, 43, 45), wrap, turn.

ROW 15: p44 (45, 45, 45, 47), wrap, turn.

ROW 16: k47 (49, 49, 49, 51), wrap, turn.

ROW 17: p17 (19, 19, 19, 21), p2tog, p29 (31, 31, 31, 33).

ROW 18: Knit—53 (57, 57, 57, 61) sts.

ROW 19: Knit. This row begins the rolled sleeve edge.

ROWS 20–23: Rep Rows 19–22 of Left Sleeve.

ROLLED V-NECK

ROW 1: Sl neck sts from holder to needle, pick up and k24 sts across back neck, then along right front neck, pick up and knit the same number of sts that were on holder for left front neck, ending at V-neck, turn. Turn the work at the V-neck each time you reach it, or you will get a U-neck.

ROW 2: Knit.

ROWS 3–6: Beg with a knit row, work 4 rows in Stockinette.

ROW 7: Switch to needles 2 sizes larger. Lift purl bump 4 rows below onto needle and k2tog, * lift purl bump 4 rows below onto needle and k2tog, pass first st over second st; rep from * to end of row to join the rolled edge to finish cap sleeve.

FINAL SEAMING

Sew the V-neck rolled edges vertically across the bottom of the V and anchor the yarn securely. The 2 sides should meet flat against each other, like 2 sides of a scroll, not rounded at the bottom. If you wish to sew the bottom of the V higher for modesty, you should do so now, and check the fit before weaving in ends.

CiTY COaT

skill level

APPRENTICE

THIS FLUFFY AND WARM BLEND OF
MERINO WOOL AND MICROFIBER knits up
quickly and has a lively spring to it. I thought I'd emphasize
the latter by knitting garter stitch sideways so the coat would
bounce when I walked. And boy does it! This coat demands
to be worn with a high-heeled shoe or, better yet, a tall
boot—and most importantly—a supermodel strut.

Zips at both ends leave room for your stride. The sleeve
is flared and overly long. A simple purled welt conceals a
fabric pocket and maintains the clean line. Try the Mod
Coat for a swinging 60s variation (á la Austin Powers, not
summer of love), or get military by adding brass buttons.

WHAT YOU WILL LEARN
✘ short rows (page 62)
✘ welt pockets (page 88)
✘ slip stitch edge (page 66)
✘ grafting garter (page 82)
✘ installing a zipper (page 86)

YARN

CITY COAT

29 (29, 30, 31, 33) skeins (57m ea), of GGH Muench Aspen merino/microfiber blend yarn

MOD COAT

31 (31, 32, 33, 35) skeins (57m ea), of GGH Muench Aspen merino/microfiber blend yarn

Substitute one strand each KnitPicks Sierra and KnitPicks Andean Treasure held together, or any bulky-weight yarn.

NEEDLES

size US 8 (5mm) needles

If necessary, change needles to obtain gauge.

NOTIONS

stitch markers

darning needle

30" (76cm) minimum separating plastic sport zipper with a pull at both ends

¼ yard flannel fabric for pocket lining

one yard stay tape, substantial ribbon or flannel remnants from pockets to stabilize shoulders and collar

sewing needle and thread

MOD COAT

twelve 7/8" (2cm) shank buttons

one plastic button

take heed

Matching small needles with bulky yarn creates a dense fabric, and it also means tight knitting. To test your gauge over a larger swatch, consider knitting up an entire ball to demonstrate the hand of the coat fabric. Because this is a sideways knit, gauge should match both vertically and horizontally to avoid fit problems.

GAUGE

15 sts and 33 rows = 4" (10cm) in garter st

**Gauge is intentionally tight. Recommended gauge on ball band is 10 sts and 14 rows = 4" (10cm) on US 11–13 (8–9mm) needles.

MEASUREMENTS

To fit sizes XS (S, M, L, XL). Coat is 40" (102cm) long.

See schematics on page 227 for exact measurements.

TERMINOLOGY

wrap, turn (short row wrap): Work a partial row and slip 1 st wyif, turn the piece, then slip the same st back wyif. Knit the wrap and its st tog on the following row. The wrap prevents a hole in the knitting and keeps the fabric firm (see page 62).

PM (place marker): Slide a ring marker onto the needle whenever the pattern calls for you to place a marker. When you come to the marker on subsequent rows, simply work the st before it, slip the marker, and work the subsequent st.

wyif or wyib: with yarn in front or in back.

Other technique: k2tog (see page 58)

notes:

If portability is paramount, or if you are knitting during warm summer months, consider knitting the coat in separate pieces (left center back, left front, right center back, right front and sleeves) and grafting them together when finished. If you prefer to avoid seaming, work it all in one piece, and pick up the sts for right center back along the left center back after making the vent, instead of casting them on. However, the project will be large, warm and not very portable if you choose the latter.

POCKET WELT (MAKE 2)

Cast on 23 sts using long tail style. Purl 6 rows, marking first row as RS. (Purl garter st presents a nicer edge to the pocket opening than knit garter st.) Put sts on holder and set aside.

LEFT CENTER BACK

Loosely cast on 144 sts.

ROW 1 (RS): Mark beg of this row at RS and shoulder. Purl.

Knit 16 rows, ending with a RS row at hem. Knit 5 more rows, inc in last shoulder st on every WS row 3 times—147 sts.

BEGIN NECK SHAPING

ROW 1 (RS): Inc in first st, knit to hem—148 sts.

NEXT ROW: Knit to shoulder, inc in last st, cast on 0 (0, 1, 1, 2) st(s)—149 (149, 150, 150, 151) sts.

Knit 0 (0, 2, 2, 2) more rows even.

BEGIN SHOULDER AND WAIST SHAPING
note:

For the left side of the coat, work all short row wraps wyif. For the right side, work all short row wraps wyib. This will keep the symmetry correct on the finished coat. If you know techniques to hide the short row wraps, DO NOT use them in this pattern. The wraps blend in nicely with garter st and subtly define the tailoring of the coat.

Knit 2 rows even, then beg short row shaping as foll:

SHORT ROW 1 (RS): k2tog, k45, wrap and turn, PM for top of waist shaping.

SHORT ROW 2 (WS): k36, wrap and turn for shoulder dart; knit to hem—148 (148, 149, 149, 150) sts.

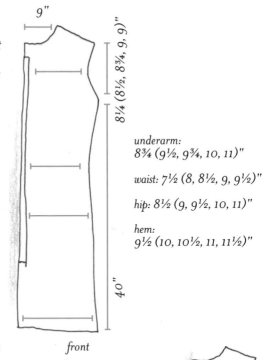

9"

8¼ (8½, 8¾, 9, 9)"

40"

front

underarm:
8¾ (9½, 9¾, 10, 11)"

waist: 7½ (8, 8½, 9, 9½)"

hip: 8½ (9, 9½, 10, 11)"

hem:
9½ (10, 10½, 11, 11½)"

underarm:
9 (9½, 9¾, 10¼, 10¾)"

waist: 7¾ (8¼, 8¾, 9¼, 9½)"

hip: 8½ 8¾, 9¼, 9¾, 10¼)"

hem: 9½ (10, 10½, 11, 11½)"

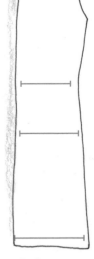

back

SHORT ROW 3 (WS): k72, wrap and turn, PM for bottom of waist shaping; knit to hem.

Knit 7 rows, working k2tog at beg of 4th row—147 (147, 148, 148, 149) sts.

*SHORT ROW 4 (RS): k2tog, knit to first marker, wrap and turn; knit to shoulder—146 (146, 147, 147, 148) sts.

NEXT ROW (RS): Knit to hem.

SHORT ROW 5 (WS): Knit to first marker, wrap and turn; knit to hem.

Knit 5 rows, ending at shoulder *. [k2tog, knit to end. Knit 5 rows even] twice—144 (144, 145, 145, 146) sts. Rep from * before Short Row 4 to * after knitting 5 rows, ending at shoulder—143 (143, 144, 144, 145) sts.

NEXT ROW: k2tog, knit to end. Knit 1 (3, 5, 7, 9) row(s) even—142 (142, 143, 143, 144) sts.

SHORT ROW 6 (RS): k2tog, k50, wrap and turn.

SHORT ROW 7 (WS): k30 (29, 28, 27, 27) sts, PM for top of underarm curve, wrap and turn; knit to hem—141 (141, 142, 142, 143) sts.

SHORT ROW 8: Rep Short Row 5.

SHORT ROW 9: Knit to 3 sts before underarm marker, wrap and turn; knit back to hem.

SHORT ROW 10: Knit to 6 sts before underarm marker, wrap and turn; knit back.

SHORT ROW 11: Knit to 8 sts before underarm marker, wrap and turn; knit back.

SHORT ROW 12: Knit to 9 sts before underarm marker, wrap and turn; knit back.

SHORT ROW 13: Knit to 10 sts before underarm marker (bottom of armhole). Slip rem sts on your left needle to a holder. They will be grafted to the sleeve later. Turn, knit to hem—110 (109, 109, 108, 109) working sts; 31 (32, 33, 34, 34) sts on holder.

SHORT ROW 14: k62, wrap and turn; knit back to hem.

SHORT ROW 15: k52, wrap and turn; knit back.

SHORT ROW 16: k42, wrap and turn; knit back.

SHORT ROW 17: k32, wrap and turn; knit back.

Knit 3 rows even.

NEXT ROW (RS): Purl to form faux side seam.

LEFT SIDE FRONT

Knit 2 rows even.

SHORT ROW 1 (WS): k27, wrap and turn; knit to hem.

SHORT ROWS 2–5: Cont in this manner, working 4 more sets of short rows (1 set = a WS row and a RS row), knitting 10 more sts with each set—67 sts worked on last short row.

NEXT ROW (WS): Knit to underarm.

SHORT ROW 6 (RS): k27, wrap and turn; knit back to underarm.

SHORT ROW 7: k2, inc 1, k13, wrap and turn; knit back—111 (110, 110, 109, 110) sts.

Knit 2 (4, 6, 8, 10) rows, inc at beg of first row as k2, inc 1; and inc in the last st of the last row at underarm.

Knit 6 rows, inc at beg of first row and end of last row as before—115 (114, 114, 113, 114) sts.

NEXT ROW (RS): Inc 1, k4, inc 1, knit to hem—117 (116, 116, 115, 116) sts.

NEXT ROW: Knit to underarm, inc 1 in last st—118 (117, 117, 116, 117) sts.

NEXT ROW: Inc 1, knit to hem—119 (118, 118, 117, 118) sts.

NEXT ROW: Knit to underarm, inc 0 (1, 1, 1, 1) in last st—119 (119, 119, 118, 119) sts.

NEXT ROW: Inc 0 (0, 1, 1, 1), knit to hem—119 (119, 120, 119, 120) sts.

NEXT ROW: Knit to underarm, inc 0 (0, 0, 1, 1) in last st; cast on 20 sts—139 (139, 140, 140, 141) sts.

Knit 4 rows, inc in last st of last row at shoulder—140 (140, 141, 141, 142) sts.

BUST SHAPING

SHORT ROW 8 (RS): k47, wrap and turn.

SHORT ROW 9 (WS): k36, PM for shoulder dart, wrap and turn.

SHORT ROW 10 (RS): k30, PM for bust (this hits under the bust, at the bra band line), wrap and turn.

SHORT ROW 11 (WS): k19, wrap and turn.

SHORT ROW 12 (RS): k13, wrap and turn; k5, inc 1, knit to shoulder—141 (141, 142, 142, 143) sts.

(RS) Knit 2 (2, 4, 6, 6) rows ending last row at last marker (shoulder dart).

SHORT ROW 13 (RS): k42, wrap and turn.

SHORT ROW 14 (WS): k37, wrap and turn.

SHORT ROW 15 (RS): k26, wrap and turn.

SHORT ROW 16 (WS): k20, wrap and turn; knit back to hem.

SHORT ROW 17: Knit to first marker (bottom of waist), wrap and turn; knit back.

SHORT ROW 18: k48, wrap and turn; knit back.

NEXT ROW (WS): k48, loosely bind off 23 sts for pocket opening, knit to shoulder—70 (70, 71, 71, 72) sts above pocket opening.

JOIN POCKET WELT

NEXT ROW (RS): Knit to one st before pocket opening, M1. With RS facing, place pocket welt on top of pocket opening, knit last st before pocket opening tog with first st of welt, k22 rem welt sts, knit to hem—141 (141, 142, 142, 143) sts.

LEFT FRONT

SHORT ROW 19 (WS): k78, wrap and turn; knit to hem.

Knit 5 rows, inc in last st of last row, ending at shoulder—142 (142, 143, 143, 144) sts.

SHORT ROW 20 (RS): Knit to 2nd marker (bust), wrap and turn.

SHORT ROW 21 (WS): Knit to shoulder marker, wrap and turn; knit back to hem.

SHORT ROW 22: Knit to first marker (bottom waist), wrap and turn; knit back.

Knit 12 rows, inc in last st of 7th row at shoulder—143 (143, 144, 144, 145) sts.

SHORT ROW 23 (WS): Knit to first marker, wrap and turn; knit to hem.

SHORT ROW 24 (WS): Knit to last marker (shoulder dart), wrap and turn.

SHORT ROW 25 (RS): Knit to marker (bust), wrap and turn; knit to end.

Knit 4 rows, ending at shoulder.

FRONT NECK SHAPING

NEXT 4 ROWS (RS): At front neck, bind off at beg of RS rows 3 (3, 4, 4, 5) sts once, 3 sts once, 2 sts once, then 1 st once, ending with a WS row—134 sts.

SHORT ROW 26 (RS): Knit to 2nd marker (bust), wrap and turn; knit to neck.

NEXT ROW: Knit to hem.

SHORT ROW 27: Knit to marker (bottom waist), wrap and turn; knit to hem.

Knit 6 rows even, then bind off loosely. Hang the piece to see if the bind-off row is too tight; this would negatively affect the drape of the coat.

RIGHT CENTER BACK

Cast on 32 sts for the back vent using long tail style. (If you prefer a longer walking vent, cast on more sts, but then subtract the extra sts from the number to be cast on in the next step.)

ROW 1 (RS): Purling every row and marking first row as RS, inc in last st (this will be the top) on this row and every other row 4 times more, ending with a WS row—37 sts.

NEXT ROW (RS): Knit, inc in last st, cast on 106 sts—144 sts.

Cont as for Left Back after Row 1, reversing all shaping: work shoulder incs at end of RS rows and beg of WS rows and work decs as SSK instead of k2tog. **Note:** Wrap the short rows wyib.

Work through last short row before faux side seam, ending at hem. Knit 2 rows even.

NEXT ROW (RS): Purl to form faux side seam.

NEXT ROW: Knit.

RIGHT FRONT

Cont as for Left Front through end of center front, reversing shaping as est.

ASSEMBLY

Seam the shoulder seams tog with mattress stitch (see page 79 for instruction on seaming garter). Once you reach the end, turn and sew it once again from the back for extra strength, since the weight of the whole coat will be hanging from this seam.

SEW IN POCKETS

Sew down the corners of the pocket welts. Place your hand on a piece of paper with wrist at top and fingertips at bottom. Trace around your hand, leaving 2" (5cm) of extra space all around. Cut out the template. Now place the template against the inside of the coat, between the pocket opening and the edge. Trim the template so it overlaps the pocket opening by ¾" (2cm) and the front of the coat by ¾" (2cm). Place it on top of the a doubled layer of fabric and cut out 4 pocket pieces.

Mark 2 of the pocket pieces with a notch two-thirds down the pocket for the opening. (Do not sew the pocket pieces together yet.) This notch should be at least 6" (15cm) below top of pocket for hand to fit. Cut in ¾" (2cm) and fold down the piece from cut to top of pocket ¾" (2cm) from edge and press with iron. Sew this piece to the inside of the coat along pocket welt with WS facing.

Sew the pocket piece without the notch to the inner pocket edge where sts were bound off. Insert your hand into pocket opening to check your work. If it doesn't fit, make necessary adjustments. Sew 2 layers of pocket together all around the edge to close the pocket bag. Serge or zig-zag stitch the edges of

pocket bag to finish the raw edges. Sew the pocket down loosely from the bound-off front edge where zipper will be sewn.

SEW BACK SEAM

Graft in garter the center back seam of coat and secure angled top of back vent with a few extra sts, since this is a stress point when walking.

SLEEVES (MAKE 2)

notes:

On every RS row, slip the last st at the cuff edge wyib. Both sleeves are worked the same. One sleeve will be turned "inside out" so the WS becomes the RS.

Leaving a yarn tail for sewing up, cast on 68 (68, 68, 68, 69) sts. Knit 3 (5, 7, 9, 11) rows, marking beg of first row as RS and underarm, ending at cuff.

SHORT ROW 1 (WS): k16, wrap and turn; knit to cuff.

Knit 5 rows, inc in last st at underarm on last row—69 (69, 69, 69, 70) sts.

Knit 2 rows, inc in last st at underarm on last row —70 (70, 70, 70, 71) sts.

[Knit 4 rows, inc in last st at underarm on last row] twice—72 (72, 72, 72, 73) sts.

Knit 2 rows, inc in last st at underarm on last row —73 (73, 73, 73, 74) sts.

Cont working in garter st, and at underarm cast on at end of WS rows 2 sts once, 1 st once, 2 sts twice, then 3 sts once, ending with a RS row—83 (83, 83, 83, 84) sts.

SHORT ROW 2 (WS): Rep Short Row 1.

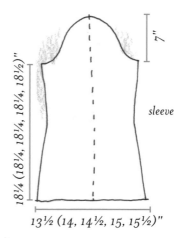

7"

18¼ (18¼, 18¼, 18¼, 18½)"

sleeve

13½ (14, 14½, 15, 15½)"

At underarm, cast on at end of WS rows 3 sts once, 2 sts twice, then inc 1 st in last st 4 times—94 (94, 94, 94, 95) sts.

Knit 13 rows even, ending at cuff.

SHORT ROW 3: Rep Short Row 1.

Knit 4 rows even.

SHORT ROW 4 (WS): k93 (93, 93, 93, 94), wrap and turn; knit to cuff.

SHORT ROWS 5–11: Work 7 more short row sets, working 1 less st each time before wrap and turn—86 (86, 86, 86, 87) sts worked on last row.

SHORT ROW 12 (WS): k84 (84, 84, 84, 85), wrap and turn.

SHORT ROW 13 (RS): k31, wrap and turn; knit to shoulder.

NEXT ROW (RS): Knit to cuff.

SHORT ROW 14 (WS): k82 (82, 82, 82, 83), wrap and turn; knit back to cuff.

SHORT ROW 15: k16, wrap and turn; knit back.

SHORT ROW 16: k80 (80, 80, 80, 82), wrap and turn; knit back.

SHORT ROW 17: k78 (78, 78, 78, 79), wrap and turn; knit back.

SHORT ROW 18: k77 (77, 77, 77, 78), wrap and turn; knit back.

SHORT ROW 19: k75 (75, 75, 75, 76), wrap and turn; knit back.

SHORT ROW 20: k74 (74, 74, 74, 75), wrap and turn; knit back.

SHORT ROW 21: k72 (72, 72, 72, 73), wrap and turn; knit back.

SHORT ROW 22: k71 (71, 71, 71, 72), wrap and turn; knit back.

SHORT ROW 23: k70 (70, 70, 70, 71), wrap and turn.

SHORT ROW 24 (RS): k24, wrap and turn; knit to underarm.

NEXT ROW (RS): Knit to cuff.

SHORT ROW 25: k69 (69, 69, 69, 70), wrap and turn; knit back to cuff.

SHORT ROW 26: k68 (68, 68, 68, 69), wrap and turn; knit back.

SHORT ROW 27: k16, wrap and turn; knit back.

Working on the first 68 (68, 68, 68, 69) sts only, leaving the rem 26 sts unworked, knit 2 (4, 6, 8 10) rows. Bind off 68 (68, 68, 68, 69) sts. Put the rem 26 sts on holder to be grafted to the back of the coat.

GRAFT SLEEVE

Flip one sleeve over so WS becomes RS. Before grafting on the sleeve, pin it to the coat and try it on if possible to be sure it hangs properly. I find it easier to set in the sleeve before sewing up the underarm, because the grafting is tricky! But if you prefer, sew up the sleeve first, which makes it easier to try on. Either graft the sleeve closed at the underarm seam, or bind off on the last row (above) and then sew it shut.

Graft in purl the 26 sts from the sleeve cap to the sts on hold at the back of the coat. The rem body sts on hold will be eased in and grafted at the top of the sleeve cap, ending with the center row of the sleeve (see page 79 in Tying Up). Then grafting of the bound-off to cast-on sts begins. Grafting garter stitch is a challenge, and requires a knit row at one edge and a purl row at the other. I find it easier to

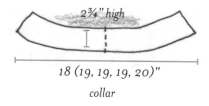

2¾" high

18 (19, 19, 19, 20)"

collar

graft this sleeve on with a purl, which looks more like the faux seams on the coat. If you graft the sts one row away from the cast-on row, it hides the cast on (see page 82 in Tying Up).

COLLAR

notes:

On every WS row, slip the last st wyif, except the cast-on row. Do NOT slip the st at other edge also, or it will bind and prevent you from sewing the seam invisibly. Wrap all sts wyif.

Leaving a yarn tail of at least 30" (76cm), cast on 9 sts long tail style. The tail marks the bottom of the collar and will be used to sew the collar on later. When looking at the collar piece, RS is up when yarn end is to the left.

ROW 1 (WS): Knit (do not sl last st).

ROWS 2–10: Knit 9 rows, sl last st of WS rows wyif, and inc 1 st in last st of last row—10 sts.

* SHORT ROW 1 (WS): k4, wrap and turn; knit back.

Knit 12 rows even *. Rep from * to * 4 (5, 5, 5, 5) times more. Piece measures approx 9 (9½, 9½, 9½, 10)" 23 (24, 24, 24, 26)cm long when measured along bottom curve. Mark this row for center back.

Knit 10 (2, 2, 2, 6) rows, ending with a RS row.

Rep from * to * 4 (5, 5, 5, 5) times, then rep Short Row 1 once more.

Knit 9 rows, working k2tog at end of 2nd row; bind off.

Collar measures approx 18 (19, 19, 19, 20)" 46 (48, 48, 48, 51)cm long when measured along the curve at the bottom of the collar. It should be symmetrical when folded at the centerline.

SEW ON COLLAR

Orient collar so the slip stitch edge is at the top. Butt the collar piece against the top edge of the neck so the bound-off edge on front of coat appears continuous with collar. Sew on collar using garter seaming technique (see page 82). After you've stitched the seam once, pass the needle through to back side and sew it again to add stability.

ZIPPER

When installing the zipper, it's critical to try on the coat and have an assistant pin it down on each side of the zipper, then zip it up to be sure the fabric matches up correctly. If you do not have the aid of an assistant, it is possible the portion you pin while bent from the waist will not be correct. The weight of the coat will cause the zipper to draw in if you sew it on without pinning while fitting first. Stitch down the zipper either by hand or with a sewing machine, whichever is more comfortable for you. If using a sewing machine, I recommend decreasing the presser foot pressure before stitching. See Tying Up for more in-depth information on installing a zipper (page 86).

MOD COAT

THE DARK GREEN COAT FEATURED IN
SOME OF THESE PHOTOGRAPHS is the Mod
Coat, a variation of the City Coat. It's essentially the same
coat, but with a few additions, including button tabs, a
double-breasted collar, sleeve bands and a button tab at the
back of the waist.

MOD COAT

Knit the body and sleeves for
Mod Coat exactly as for City Coat.

COLLAR

notes:
*Slip all sts wyif. The slipped st
will make a twist-like chain to
bind the buttonhole and trim
the edge of the collar.*

Cast on 3 sts.

ROWS 1–5: Sl 1 wyif, inc 1, knit
to end—8 sts at end of Row 5.

ROW 6: Sl 1, k3, place rem 4 sts
on holder.

Rep Row 6 on 4 sts until this
side of buttonhole is 1" (3cm)
long, 8 rows, or desired length to
fit button. Cut yarn.

Join yarn at buttonhole edge,
and work on 4 sts from hold as
follows:

ROW 1: Sl 1 wyif, k3.

Rep Row 1 until same length as
other side, ending at outer edge.

Work in garter st across all 8 sts
for 14 rows. Piece measures 2½"
(6cm) from point. Decide which
side looks neater and mark as
RS. If necessary, knit 1 row to be
ready for a RS row. Do not sl first
st; only sl last st on WS rows.

Beg with Row 2, work as for City
Coat collar to center back—9 sts.

Piece measures approx 11½ (12, 12, 12, 12½)" 29 (31, 31, 31, 32)cm long when measured along bottom curve to point. Mark this row for center back. Cont as for City Coat collar, but do not bind off—8 sts.

Sl first st of every row, knit 13 rows.

Cont as for beg of Mod Collar, from Row 6 until buttonhole is made and 14 rows worked in garter st.

DEC ROWS 1–5: Sl 1, k2tog, knit to end—3 sts at end of Row 5.

Bind off as foll: Pass the first st over the second st, and then pass the third st over the second st. Pass the yarn end through the rem st and sew it to the back of the button tab. Collar should be 23 (24, 24, 24, 25)" 59 (61, 61, 61, 64)cm long when measured along the curve at the bottom of the collar. It should be symmetrical when folded at the centerline.

BUTTON TABS (MAKE 3)

Work as for Mod Coat Collar through buttonhole and 14 rows garter st. Cont in garter st until piece measures 4¾" (12cm) from point. Work Dec Rows 1–5 and bind off as for Mod Coat Collar.

23 (24, 24, 24, 25)"

collar

2½" high

button tab

center back tab

sleeve bands

Mod Coat accessories (all accessories same height)

button tab: 4¾"

center back tab: 6"

sleeve bands: 15"

SLEEVE BANDS (MAKE 2)

Work as for Mod Coat Collar through buttonhole and 14 rows garter st. Cont in garter st until piece measures 15" (38cm) from point. Bind off and sew together the end of the band so it meets just before the buttonhole. Sew to each sleeve 14 sts from the edge of the sleeve with the band point at top side and sew on button. Stitch band to sleeve at seam also.

CENTER BACK TAB

Work as for Mod Coat Collar, omitting buttonhole. Cont in garter st until piece measures 6" (15cm) from point, then work Dec Rows 1–5 and bind off as for Mod Coat Collar.

ASSEMBLY
INSTALL ZIPPER

Install the zipper as for the City Coat.

SEW ON COLLAR

With slip stitch edge at top and plain edge at bottom, leave 2½" (6cm) of collar protruding at each side. Pin on collar at fronts, center back and shoulder seams. Seam in garter st (see page 82). As for City Coat, once you sew seam on RS, pass needle through fabric and stitch on WS to reinforce.

SEW ON BUTTONS AND BUTTON TABS

Working with RS up, place first button tab at waist with side without hole toward right (as worn) side of coat. Sew around the edge of the tab from behind to secure tab to right side of coat only. Space remaining tabs equally between collar and bottom tab and sew to secure.

SEW ON CENTER BACK TAB

Be sure to pin on the center back tab while fitting, as coat will stretch and cause tab to swag otherwise. Sew only the ends of tab, leaving the center free.

SEW ON BUTTONS

Zip coat shut and mark button placement, one at the outer edge of each buttonhole, and one to match it on the opposite end of each tab. Overlap the collar in the same manner as the button tabs, so the right end is on top. Sew the button to the spot on left collar underlapping the right buttonhole. Stitch down all buttons as marked, finishing with the for-show-only button on the right collar. On the inside of this collar button, sew one more button. Sew a final button at each end of center back tab.

ELFiN BRiDe + GOTHLeT

skill level

DOMIKNITRIX

THESE ARE MY FINEST EXAMPLES OF
SWEATERS knitted organically from start to finish. I
think of these pieces as testaments to my knitting insanity.
When I created these pieces, I was trying to bend my knitting
and see just how far I could take it...how weird could I make
it? How challenging? So it's intentionally difficult and not
for the faint-hearted or for a beginner. If you complete one
of these sweaters, you've demonstrated mastery of this craft.

Because of space and time constraints, the patterns for
these two complex pieces are not printed in this book. If
you are an absolute glutton for punishment, go to my Web
site (www.domiknitrix.com) and click on the link for the
Gothlet pattern. Follow the directions and you'll be granted
access to the inner lair of patterns. Otherwise, just enjoy the
delicious eye candy on the following pages, you voyeur.

WHAT YOU WILL LEARN
✘ lace knitting (page 63)
✘ bias knitting
✘ short rows (page 62)
✘ symmetrical increases and
decreases (pages 58–60)
✘ picking up stitches (page 64)

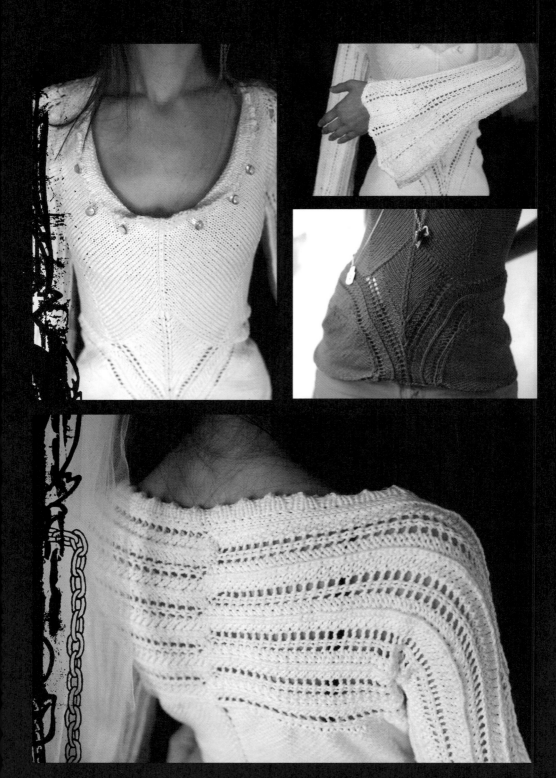

NITTY GRITTY

ABBREVIATIONS

ALT	ALTERNATE
BEG	BEGINNING
BO	BIND OFF
CC	CONTRAST COLOR
CO	CAST ON
DEC	DECREASE
DPN(S)	DOUBLE POINTED NEEDLE(S)
EST	ESTABLISHED
FOLL	FOLLOWING
IN PATT	IN PATTERN
INC	INCREASE
K	KNIT
K2TOG	KNIT 2 TOGETHER
LLI	LEFT LIFTED INCREASE
M1	MAKE ONE INCREASE
MC	MAIN COLOR
P	PURL
P2TOG	PURL 2 TOGETHER
PM	PLACE MARKER
PSSO	PASS SLIPPED STITCH OVER
REM	REMAINING
RS	RIGHT SIDE
REP	REPEAT
RLI	RIGHT LIFTED INCREASE
SL	SLIP
SSK	SLIP, SLIP, KNIT
SSP	SLIP, SLIP, PURL 2 TOGETHER THROUGH BACK LOOP
ST(S)	STITCH(ES)
ST ST	STOCKINETTE STITCH
TBL	THROUGH BACK LOOP
WRAP, TURN	SHORT ROW WRAP
WS	WRONG SIDE
WYIB	WITH YARN IN BACK
WYIF	WITH YARN IN FRONT
YO	YARN OVER
YOYO	DOUBLE YARN OVER

knitting needle conversions

2mm	US 0
2.25mm	US 1
2.75mm	US 2
3.25mm	US 3
3.5mm	US 4
3.75mm	US 5
4mm	US 6
4.5mm	US 7
5mm	US 8
5.5mm	US 9
6mm	US 10
6.5mm	US 10½
8mm	US 11
9mm	US 13
10mm	US 15
12.75mm	US 17
15mm	US 19
	US 36

GENERAL GUIDELINES FOR YARN WEIGHTS

Since the names given to different weights of yarn can vary widely depending on the country of origin or the yarn manufacturer's preference, The Craft Yarn Council of America has put together a standard yarn weight system to impose a bit of order on the sometimes unruly yarn labels. Look for a picture of a skein of yarn with a number 1–6 on most kinds of yarn to figure out its "official" weight. Gauge is given over Stockinette stitch. The information in the chart below is taken from www.yarnstandards.com.

	SUPER BULKY (6)	BULKY (5)	MEDIUM (4)	LIGHT (3)	FINE (2)	SUPERFINE (1)
ALSO INCLUDES	bulky, roving	chunky, craft, rug	worsted, afghan, aran	dk, light, worsted	sport, baby	sock, fingering, baby
GAUGE OVER 4" (10CM)	6–11 sts	12–15 sts	16–20 sts	21–24 sts	23–26 sts	27–32 sts
RECOM-MENDED NEEDLE SIZE (US)	11 and larger	9 to 11	7 to 9	5 to 7	3 to 5	1 to 3

SUBSTITUTING YARNS

If you substitute yarn, be sure to select a yarn of the same weight as the yarn recommended for the project. Take special note of any project that indicates an intentionally tight gauge for yarn. In these cases, you must substitute a yarn that knits to the same gauge as the recommended yarn, not the gauge you find in the pattern. Be sure to compare the ball band gauge of the recommended yarn to the ball band on the yarn you wish to substitute. The recommended gauge indicated on the ball band is given for all projects where the gauge is intentionally tight. Even after checking that the recommended gauge on the yarn you plan to substitute is the same as for the yarn listed in the pattern, make sure to swatch and see. For more information on substituting yarn, see You Must Knit a Gauge Swatch in the Eight Rules to Knit By chapter (page 22) and Pick Your Poison in the Getting Equipped chapter (beginning on page 34).

{ 241 }

GLOSSARY
knitting terms and techniques

BINDING OFF

Binding off is taking all the stitches off your needles by knitting then passing stitches over each other until the tail can be pulled through the final loop. See page 76.

ELASTIC BIND OFF

This method of binding off produces an edge that looks just like a garter row and is more elastic than traditional bind off. See page 77.

TUBULAR BIND OFF

Tubular bind off is another technique that will give your piece couture flair. It is worked with a darning needle instead of with knitting needles. See page 77.

CASTING ON

Casting on is simply creating the number of new stitches needed for the first row of any project. Sometimes you'll need to cast on new stitches at the beginning or end of a row for an armhole or pocket opening. Pick the cast-on method that's best for your project. See page 44.

LONG TAIL CAST ON

When done correctly, this is a stable cast-on method good for most projects. It's stretchy but not loose. See page 45.

LOOP CAST ON

This is the simplest of cast-on methods. Although it is quick and easy, it is just a row of loops, not stitches as with the long tail method. Start with this one, but once you've mastered it, move on to a more stable method. See page 44.

PROVISIONAL CAST ON

Use this temporary cast on when you plan to do something with the live stitches later. This method involves making a crochet chain with scrap yarn and picking up stitches in the loops on the back of the chain. See page 46.

CASTING ON WITH CIRCULAR NEEDLE

Long tail cast on works best when working with circular needles. Make sure your cast-on row stretches easily all the way from one end of the circular needle to the other. If the stitches don't stretch, switch to a smaller needle. See page 52.

CASTING ON WITH DPNS

Cast-on stitches are simply divided evenly between three or four DPNs. The remaining DPN is for knitting. See page 54.

COLOR WORK
DUPLICATE STITCH

If you want to work with only one yarn at a time, this is the color work method for you. The color is added after the piece is finished using a darning needle and yarn. See page 69.

FAIR ISLE OR STRANDED KNITTING

This kind of color work uses the most yarn, and it's best for patterns that repeat across the entire row. Yarns of different colors are swagged or stranded behind the knitting. See page 70.

INTARSIA

At each color change, yarns are wrapped around each other at the back of the work to prevent holes in the fabric. This method works best when a color needs to be carried along for more than five stitches. See page 68.

MOSAIC KNITTING

Also known as slip-stitch color work, this method calls for you to work only certain color stitches in each row. Some stitches will not be worked, but rather slipped and worked on the following row(s). See page 70.

CONTINENTAL KNITTING

In this style of knitting, working yarn is held in the left hand and stitches are picked with the right hand. See page 48.

DECREASES

Decreases reduce the number of stitches on your needles and make the knitted fabric smaller. Each method of decreasing has a unique look, so it's important to choose the best method to acheive the look you want. See page 58.

KNIT {OR PURL} TWO TOGETHER {K2TOG OR P2TOG}

Simply knit (or purl) two stitches together just as you would knit (or purl) a single stitch. Some patterns also call for k3tog or k4tog. Simply knit the indicated number of stitches together as one stitch, just as for k2tog. See pages 58 and 60.

MIRRORED DECREASES

When decreases are a part of the design, they should lean toward each other to create a pleasing effect. The most common way to work mirrored decreases is to knit two together (k2tog) on one side (usually the right side), and to work slip-slip-knit (SSK) decreases on the other side (usually the left side). See page 58.

SLIP, SLIP, KNIT {SSK}

The SSK is the left-leaning symmetrical sister of k2tog worked on the right side. Slip two stitches individually from the left needle to the right needle as if to knit, then insert the left needle into the fronts of both stitches and knit them together as one. Some patterns also call for SSSK, which is done in the same way as SSK with three stitches instead of just two. See page 58.

SLIP, SLIP, PURL TWO TOGETHER THROUGH BACK LOOPS {SSP}

This is a very seamless decrease, the wrong side cousin of the SSK. Slip two stitches knitwise one at a time. Pass them both back together to the left needle, then purl them together through their back loops. See page 60.

SLIP, SLIP, KNIT ONE, PASS SLIPPED STITCH OVER {SL2-K1-PSSO}

This type of decrease is often used when knitting lace. Slip two stitches knitwise together, knit one, then pass the two slipped stitches over the knitted stitch. This double decrease shows the center stitch on top. See page 63.

ENGLISH KNITTING

In this style of knitting, working yarn is held in the right hand and stitches are picked with that hand as well. See page 50.

GAUGE SWATCH

A gauge swatch is generally a 4" (10cm) square knitted before beginning a project to measure how many stitches and rows make up 4" (10cm). See page 22.

I-CORD

This is an easy way to make a tiny knitted tube perfect for a cord. It's basically knitting without ever turning your work, which links the edge stitches together. See page 72.

INCREASES

Increases create stitches, making the knitted fabric larger. Each method of increasing has a unique look, so it's important to choose the best method to achieve the look you want. If the pattern simply says inc 1, use the method of your choice. See page 56.

KNIT ONE IN FRONT AND BACK {KFB}

Simply work two stiches in one loop without sliding the stitch from the needle after making the first stitch. This increase is easy, but it will show up as a small bar in your knitting. See page 57.

LIFTED INCREASES

Lifted increases create the most defined line, and are often used to create "darts." There is a left and a right version, so together they work great as mirrored increases. To make a right lifted increase (RLI), lift first leg of stitch below next stitch onto needle and knit this stitch. To make a left lifted increase (LLI), lift last leg below last knitted stitch onto needle and knit this stitch. See page 56.

JOINING NEW YARN

Splitting the yarn tails and twisting them together creates a seamless join. See page 61.

PLACE MARKER {PM}

Slide a marker (or markers) onto your needle as indicated in the pattern. Move the marker from one needle to the other when you come to it.

PICKING UP STITCHES

Stitches may be picked up along a top, bottom or side edge of a knitted piece. Make sure to always pick up and knit. If you neglect to knit each picked-up stitch, you'll end up with hole-ridden fabric. See page 64.

PLACING STITCHES ON A HOLDER

Many patterns require you to place some stitches onto a holder to be worked later. (These are called live, or active, stitches.) You may buy a stitch holder and slide the stitches onto it, or just use a piece of scrap yarn in a contrasting color.

SEAMING

Knitted pieces are generally seamed together from the right side. One method of seaming is used for cast-on or bound-off stitches, and another version for active stitches.

KITCHENER STITCH

Use this method to seamlessly connect the active stitches on two separate pieces of knitting. Use a piece of yarn and a darning needle to effectively knit the two pieces together. See page 80.

MATTRESS STITCH

Use this method to create a vertical seam along the sides of two knitted pieces. Use a piece of yarn and a darning needle to replicate the stitches on either side of the seam. See page 78.

SHORT ROWS

Short rows are worked over only a portion of the stitches in a row, hence the row is "short." They are usually used to add curves like bust shaping and sock heels. See page 62.

SHORT ROW WRAP {WRAP, TURN}

Abbreviated as "wrap, turn" this action always appears at the turning edge of a short row. Short row wraps are worked a bit differently on knit and purl rows, but both require you to always slip the last stitch purlwise.

When knitting, hold the yarn in back and slip one stitch, then bring yarn to front and slip same stitch back to left needle and turn the work. When you come to the wrapped stitch on the following purl row, hide it by inserting the right needle (purlwise) under the wrap and purling it together with the stitch it wrapped.

When purling, hold the yarn in front and slip one stitch, then bring yarn to back and slip same stitch back to left needle and turn the work. When you come to the wrapped stitch on the following knit row, hide it by using the right needle to lift the wrap onto the left needle and knitting it together with the stitch it wrapped.

STITCHES

GARTER STITCH

Knit every row to make garter stitch. A garter ridge is two knit rows. Garter stitch fabric lays flat and does not curl at the edges.

RIBBING

Simply alternate between knitting and purling to create ribbing. Use a one-by-one rib, a two-by-two rib, a one-by-three rib, etc. Ribbing is often used for sweater waistbands, cuffs and neckbands, and also for hat brims, because it does not curl up at the edge.

ROLLED SLIP STITCH EDGE

Stockinette is notorious for curling at the edges. Simply slip the first and last stitch on every right side row to create a beautiful chained edge that curls less than Stockinette. Ideally, this edge will add stability, though it also makes the edge less elastic. See page 66.

STOCKINETTE STITCH

Knit on the right side and purl on the wrong side to work in Stockinette. If you're knitting in the round, knitting every row produces effortless Stockinette with no purling.

TWISTED KNITTING

To make tighter and irregular-looking stitches, knit into the backs of the stitches on the right side rows and purl into the backs of the stitches on the wrong side rows. See page 67.

YARN OVER {YO}

A yarn over makes a hole in your knitting and is usually used in knitting lace. Wrap the working yarn around the right-hand needle and continue knitting as usual. On the following row, knit or purl the wrapped yarn. A row with yarn overs is often combined with decreases.

WORKING IN THE ROUND

Make any kind of circular or dimensional object with circular needles. They're also good for working with large projects worked straight. Cast on as usual and make sure the row is not twisted. Spread out the stitches and make sure they stretch all the way from one end of the needle to the other without pulling. Hold the needle with the working yarn in your right hand, and insert it into the first stitch on the left needle to connect the stitches. Knit every row to produce Stockinette stitch. See page 52.

USING TWO CIRCULAR NEEDLES TO MAKE A TUBE

Working on the same principle as for knitting an I-cord, you can create a double-thick fabric or any other kind of tube. Divide stitches in half between two circular needles, then turn the work when you get to the end of either half so you're working in one flattened circle. See page 73.

reference library

RESOURCES AND HISTORY

At any given point in your knitting life, there will always be questions in need of answers. A good reference book (or two or three or ten) is invaluable. Call me old-school, but I turn to the classics when I need knitting help. While you're at it, you might just become fascinated with the craft of knitting. There's plenty of reading to do there as well.

Barbara G. Walker's *Treasuries* series and *Charted Knitting Designs,* and *The Harmony Guides Volumes 1—4,* published by Collins & Brown, Ltd. These collections of knit texture patterns include stitches, ranging from simple knit and purl textures to the most fabulous cables and lace. These are the books I turn to when dreaming up new designs.

Confessions of a Knitting Heretic
BY ANNIE MODESITT

This book is a godsend to knitters who are constantly told they are twisting stitches or doing something wrong. It's not wrong, it's just different, and this book will help you adapt any pattern to your unique style of knitting.

Hand Knitting New Directions
BY ALISON ELLEN

This book inspired me to try diagonal knitting!

Knitting from the Top
BY BARBARA G. WALKER

Knitting from the top will help you examine your knitting from a different direction—upside down.

Knitting Without Tears
BY ELIZABETH ZIMMERMANN

This classic knitting book tells you pretty much everything you need to know to be a good knitter. Plus Elizabeth Zimmermann is witty and wise—a joy to read.

Mary Thomas's Knitting Book and Mary Thomas's Book of Knitting Patterns
BY MARY THOMAS

These charming books from the 30s provide a history of knitting and a thorough understanding of how knit fabric is formed.

Reader's Digest Knitter's Handbook
BY MONTSE STANLEY

This comprehensive guide to knitting is an excellent resource for a new knitter. When I taught my dad to knit, I gave this book as a reference.

PATTERN AND DESIGN

What's knitting with no pattern? Just yarn and sticks, that's what. Compile some favorites you can turn to again and again. Here are some of mine.

Jean Frost Jackets: Fabric, Fit, and Finish for Today's Knits
BY JEAN FROST
These tailored jackets are incredibly wearable and well designed.

The Knitter's Handy Book of Sweater Patterns
BY ANN BUDD
This book's "open source" approach encourages you to customize each design for any gauge and for any size, from kids to grown-ups!

Loop-d-Loop
BY TEVA DURHAM
Durham's creative designs are inspiring for knitters at all levels.

Norsk Strikkedesign: A Collection from Norway's Foremost Knitting Designers
EDITED BY MARGARETHA FINSETH
This book is packed with inspirational and challenging projects for those who live in colder climes.

Sculptured Knits
BY JEAN MOSS
These tailored and textured projects appeal to the romantic knitter.

AlterKnits
BY LEIGH RADFORD
This lovely book encourages you to break out and explore knitting in new ways. And it has a cute little pull-out book to help you document your creative explorations.

GeT YOUR yARn Fix

ARTFIBERS
www.artfibers.com
415.956.6319
Zodiac yarn (Winged Heart Bralet, page 178)

BROWN SHEEP COMPANY, INC.
www.brownsheep.com
800.826.9136
*Lamb's Pride Superwash Bulky and Lamb's Pride
Bulky yarn (Mohawk Hat, page 120)
Bulky yarn (Big Bad Wolf Pullover, page 162)*

CLASSIC ELITE YARNS
www.classiceliteyarns.com
978.453.2837
Provence yarn (Elfin Bride, page 236)

CRYSTAL PALACE YARNS
www.crystalpalaceyarns.com
510.237.9988
*Shimmer yarn (Strings of Purls, page 126; The
Slink, page 216; Snood, page 116; Spiral Mesh
Cap, page 116)*

DALE OF NORWAY {DALEGARN}
www.dale.no
+47 56 59 54 00
Baby Ull yarn (Valentine Candy Pillows, page 104)

FILATURA DI CROSA
www.filaturadicrosa.com
00 39 015 8442600
Zara yarn (Sweetheart, page 184)

MUENCH YARNS
www.muenchyarns.com
800.733.9276
Aspen yarn (City Coat, page 224)
*Goa yarn (Devil Hat, page 138; Valentine Candy
Pillows, page 104)*

**HARRIS YARNS
{DISTRIBUTED BY ROWAN}**
www.harris-tweed.co.uk/knitting.htm
+44 (0)1851 643 300
DK yarn (Jughead Hat, page 210)

KARABELLA YARNS
www.karabellayarns.com
800.550.0898 (for orders)
*Aurora bulky yarn (Diva Halter, page 192; L'il Red
Riding Hoodie, page 152)*

KNIT PICKS
www.knitpicks.com
1.800.574.1323 (for orders)
*Sierra and Andean Treasure yarn (Mod Coat, page
234)
Merino Style yarn (green in Thin Mint, page 100)*

LANAKNITS
www.lanaknits.com
888.301.0011
All Hemp 6 yarn (Homegrown, page 132)

NORO
Japanese manufacturer with Japanese-language
Web site. Visit almost any online yarn supplier to
find Noro yarns.
Kureyon yarn (Flower Pins, page 110)

TAHKI STACY CHARLES, INC.
www.tahkistacycharles.com
800.338.YARN
*Cotton Classic yarn (Elfin Goth, page 236)
Baby yarn (Star Pillow, page 146)*

ALPACANATION
www.alpacanation.com
678.546.6989
*Alpaca Dream yarn (brown in Thin Mint Scarf, page
100)*

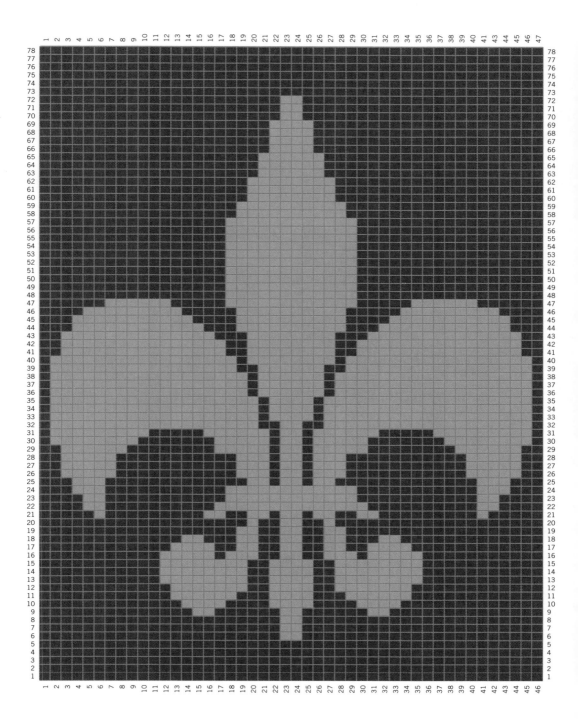

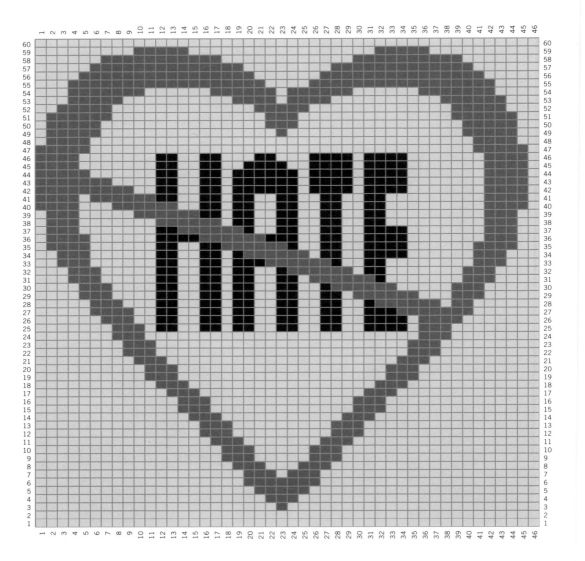

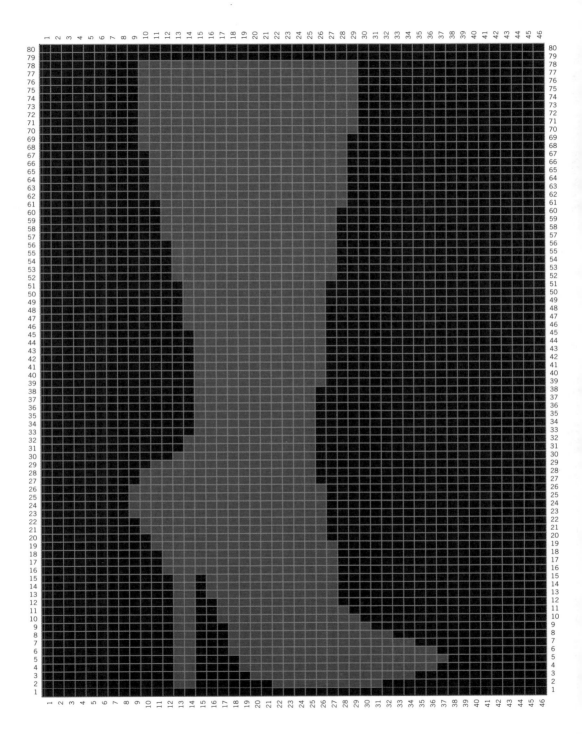

acknowledgments

Wow, this is like accepting an Academy Award. Where do I begin?! My dear friend Leslie Dotson is the person who influenced this manuscript most. I can't imagine how this book would have taken shape without her constant encouragement and guidance. Her warm spirit and clever wit have enriched my life. I dream of finding time to knit with her one day, cocktails at our elbows.

Thank you next to those who did the knitting for this book. It was not humanly possible to do this without you all. Miriam Tegels, my pinch knitter, helped complete the most projects on deadline. I hope she'll hold the speed-knitting world record by the time this book hits the stands. Miriam made the Mod Coat, L'il Red Riding Hoodie and Bob Dobbs vest from start to flawless finish, knit more than half of the Elfin Bride, and completed the Sweetheart sleeves. The joy she took in knitting my projects was an inspiration in itself.

My crew of wonderful, patient and kind knitters is listed here in alphabetical order. They graciously gave their time making samples for the book: Jennifer Borrell, Michelle Bruso, Tish DeForest, Caia Grisar, Arquay Harris, Morgan Hawkins, Saloni Howard-Sarin, Anne Keen, Cassandra Lawson, Cathy Madsen, Sudha Sarin, Jess Saven, Sarah Signiski, Brooke Sinnes, Lisa Ziegler. These knitters really tested my mettle. If not for their helpful suggestions, I never could have gotten this done. Thanks to pattern editor Traci Bunkers for translating my patterns into proper form.

Don McGill and Avni Yagnik are my teammates in the office and are like family. They not only picked up my slack without complaint while I was working on this project, but were incredibly supportive throughout.

Tricia Waddell, formerly of F+W Publications, now at Interweave, "discovered" me while seeking knitting help herself and approached me about writing this book. Jessica Gordon is the editor at F+W who shepherded this book to completion and was a pleasure to work with throughout. Other F+W staff who provided great support for the book include: Greg Hatfield, Steve Koenig, Mike Amann, Shawn Metts, Scott Francis. A special nod to photographer Christine Polomsky, Suzanne Lucas, Christine Doyle, book division president Sara Domville, and CEO David Steward.

Attorney Teresa Derichsweiler's guidance helped me nail the book deal. Her thoughtful advice to "just one more" legal question has been precious. Danielle Maze, PhD, Paul Porter and Stephanie Van Bebber gave helpful feedback and emotional support.

Thank you to Teva Durham and Leslie Barbazette for helping me at the outset. Saloni and Stephen Howard-Sarin and Sudha Sarin proved to be invaluable allies. Saloni and Sudha both offered to knit samples. Saloni's wonderful husband, Stephen, provided valuable support.

Denise Pieracci was my Satin Shadow, the seamstress who helped me to reverse engineer my own designs by making flat patterns from my finished samples. She helped to establish the DomiKNITrix fit.

Vichelle Mixon at Atelier Yarns helped salvage the Valentine Candy Hearts project. Missa at Kpixie sweetly donated the yarns used in developing The Slink design. Karen Johnson and Bridget Suma at KnitPicks gave yarns for the Mod Coat and most of the yarn used in the how-to-knit photos. Peggy Jo at Lamb's Pride generously donated bulky for the Wolf Pullover. Rachel at Karabella contributed yarns for the Bob Dobbs Vest, the Diva Halter, and the L'il Red Riding Hoodie. Nicole at Tahki Stacy Charles donated the yarn for the Gothlet, Swizzle Vest and Star Pillow. Cathy and Susan at Crystal Palace provided Shimmer for the Slinks, Mesh Cap and Snood. Cristina at Muench contributed Aspen for the City Coat, and Goa for the Valentines and Devil Hat. Judy at Classic Elite gave Provence. Special thanks to Stormy Leather for giving me the "entertainer discount" on all that leather!

These friends were lovely and willing models for DomiKNITrix designs on my Web site: Erika Bellas, Cathy Blyther, Stellah De Ville, Sal Gurnani, Justine Nguyen, Stephanie Weaver and Samara Zibitt. Lisa Galli shot The Slink. Ethan O'Brien beautifully shot remaining photography on the site.

Aeronautical engineer Lance Birtcil provided the Mercator equation and drawing used in designing the Jughead Hat. Matt Siegel cleverly suggested the Stiletto chart.

Ron Skilandat is the hair guru who has kept my hair fabulous since 1998, and who trimmed the Mohawk Hat into shape while reminiscing about cutting real Mohawks back in the day when he sported the genuine punk look too. Noel Cragg introduced me to FranklinCovey, the time management system that allowed me to prioritize the most important things in my life, and get this project done. The Honorable Rev. Ivan Stang of Church of the Subgenius generously permitted use of the trademarked image of Bob Dobbs. I look forward to soon taking back the slack.

The photo shoot crew in Cincinnati made me feel like an absolute superstar. Cass Smith transformed my face and hair into total glamour. Stylist Monica Skrzelowski selected the perfect complements to my leather and indoctrinated me into the world of couture by selecting my press outfit. Photographer Brian Steege captured the look they created in glorious living color and delivered the most beautiful photos ever taken of me. Book designer Karla Baker created the look and feel of the book. A million of Karla's decisions add up to something more special than I could have imagined, including inviting artist Rachell Sumpter to add a hearty dose of sass with her charming illustrations.

Eleanor Gomez, most wonderful massage healer, and Allen Wood, powerful chiropractor and physical therapist, helped me to return to health once I had wrecked my body with this project. Gloria Fraser, LCSW, helped repair my soul.

And last, but far from least, I thank my mother, Karen, and grandmothers, Donagene and Jane, who taught me to sew, knit, crochet and embroider. This book would not be in your hands if not for their loving tutelage.

index

check out another fabulous knitting title from
F+W PUBLICATIONS, INC.

YARNPLAY
BY LISA SHOBHANA MASON

YarnPlay shows you how to fearlessly mix yarns, colors and textures to create bold and graphic handknits. You'll learn how to draw from your yarn stash to create stylish, colorful knits, including sweaters, tanks, hats, scarves, blankets, washcloths and more for women, men and children. Best of all, you'll learn knitting independence—author Lisa Shobhana Mason believes in learning the rules so you can break them. She teaches you how to take a pattern and make it your own.

ISBN-13: 978-1-58180-841-4
ISBN-10: 1-58180-841-0
PAPERBACK WITH FLAPS, 128 PAGES, Z0010